## Praise for A WHOLE OTHER BALL GAME

*A Whole Other Ball Game* shares wonderful stories that reveal the "inherent truths" of women's sport from the 1890s to the present—strength, courage, commitment, and passion. As women's sports grow, we will continue to enjoy and appreciate what these truths bring to our daughters and society as a whole.

> —Donna Lopiano
> Executive Director, Women's Sport Foundation

A ground-breaking anthology, full of surprises. Joli Sandoz adds writers of the stature of Adrienne Rich, Toni Cade Bambara, and Ellen Gilchrist to the canon of sports literature, while also bringing talented unknowns before a wider public for the first time.

> —Michael Oriard
> Former Center for the Kansas City Chiefs
> Author of *Dreaming of Heroes: American Sports Fiction, 1968–1980*

Energetic, thoughtful explorations of the liberating possibilities of sport for women. Many of the pieces here deal with the struggles of women—especially adolescents—trying to accept that competition is good, that winning is even better, and that it's possible to be both a woman and an athlete without slighting either.

> —*Kirkus Reviews*

The public simply has little knowledge of the inner life of women engaged in sport. Even legendary athletes like Babe Zaharias were presented in caricature, conforming to social stereotypes. This book offers insight into the meaning of the sport experience through the voices of women. A "women's way of sport" emerges here.

> —Carole A. Oglesby, Ph.D.
> Department of Physical Education, Temple University

the   noonday   press   |   a   division   of
farrar,   straus   and   giroux   |   new   york

# A WHOLE OTHER BALL GAME

## women's literature on
## women's sport

edited and with an introduction by joli sandoz

The Noonday Press
A division of Farrar, Straus and Giroux
19 Union Square West, New York 10003

Introduction and compilation copyright © 1997 by Joli Sandoz
Distributed in Canada by Douglas & McIntyre Ltd.
Printed in the United States of America
Designed by Debbie Glasserman
First edition, 1997

Library of Congress Cataloging-in-Publication Data
A whole other ball game : women's literature on women's sport / edited
and with an introduction by Joli Sandoz.
     p.    cm.
   ISBN 0-374-52521-8 (pbk. : alk. paper)
    1. Women athletes—United States—Literary collections.   2. Sports
for women—Literary collections.   3. American literature—Women
authors.   4. American literature—20th century.   I. Sandoz, Joli,
1952–   .
PS509.W63W49   1997
810.8'0355—dc21                                        97-19260

See page 319 for permissions.

Title page photographs used courtesy of Jim Cummins/FPG International
Corp.

For Ann Strother Sandoz and Ali J. Sandoz
*who put me in the game*
coaches John Starr, Marnie Piper, and Nena Rey Hawkes
*who taught me to play it*
and Joby Winans
*who makes the game worthwhile*

# CONTENTS

# THE SPRINGBOARD

1951

adrienne rich

Like divers, we ourselves must make the jump
That sets the taut board bounding underfoot
Clean as an axe blade driven in a stump;
But afterward what makes the body shoot
Into its pure and irresistible curve
Is of a force beyond all bodily powers.
So action takes velocity with a verve
Swifter, more sure than any will of ours.

# A WHOLE OTHER BALL GAME

women's literature on

women's sport

# INTRODUCTION

April 4, 1896. San Francisco's Armory Hall. Two teams of nine women—one team from Stanford, the other from the University of California at Berkeley—face each other, competing to score the single point awarded for regular baskets and free throws alike. The *San Francisco Examiner*'s report of the game would read in part: "The fighting was hard and the playing good . . . The girls jumped, scrambled and fell over one another on the floor, but they didn't mind it. They were up quick as a flash, chasing after the ball again."

Fans echoed the players' enthusiasm. The *Examiner* described the game's five hundred vocal spectators as

> old women, and young women, and short-haired women, and long-haired women, and pretty women, and plain women, and new women, and—well, there may have been middle-aged women. But the really remarkable thing about them was the immense volume of noise they managed to create.

Women undeniably loved basketball a century ago. And loved it fiercely. When a man looked in at one of the windows of the playing hall, the female spectators met him, the reporter duly noted, with "hisses so loud and vehement that he fled in terror."

Women's fierce love of sport created an athletic tradition in the United States well before this, the first intercollegiate women's basketball game. Just after the end of the Civil War, in 1866, Vassar College already fielded two women's baseball "clubs." The first women's boxing bout took place in 1876. Women competed in six-day "walking matches" for cash prizes as early as 1879. National championships in archery (first held in 1879), tennis (1887), and golf (1895) gave at least some female athletes a focus for sporting discipline and ambition.

But relatively few women actually had opportunities and the social support necessary to play competitively. Many observers considered public spectacles such as boxing matches and pedestrian races to be in poor taste, something in which only women of questionable femininity and background participated. Middle-class female athletes, controversial in the light of contemporary thinking about their proper social roles and physical capabilities, generally played on the sequestered grounds of college campuses and private athletic clubs. Even students attending all-women's schools sometimes found it necessary to write letters home assuring worried parents that physical activity had not damaged their health or personalities.

Then came basketball. Invented in 1891, basketball quickly became the first women's competitive team sport to catch on in a big way. Within the year the new game traveled to California, where the November 19, 1892, issue of the *Berkeley Daily Advocate* called it "football." "Of course it is not regular football," the writer noted, "but it is football modified to suit feminine capabilities."

Sportswomen's enthusiasm forced cultural tensions about women's roles and prevailing definitions of "feminine" into the open. Basketball's very popularity made it a threat to the status quo, fanning the sparks of conflict over suitability of competition for middle-class women, a conflict that still shapes the experiences of American women athletes. Writers of newspaper reports and magazine articles noted the vigor and vehemence of women's play, often in appalled and righteous tones. The issue seemed to be both the game itself and the inappropriateness of women displaying physical competence and emotional intensity. Critics' reactions took on an edge of worry, too, about connections between enthusiastic athleticism and excessive sexual desires. If a woman athlete lost control in one part of her physicality, mightn't she lose control in another? And if she was "mannish" enough to play sport aggressively, then couldn't she be mannish in other things as well, "oversexed" for a female and perhaps even, as some physicians speculated, sexually attracted (like men) to women?

Athletes' love of basketball also threatened the physical education establishment. College students often organized their own athletic associations and teams, playing with little regard to their instructors' requests for a seemly moderation. Women P.E. teachers, themselves members of a new profession only partially accepted, responded by designing rule changes intended to limit movement and physical contact. The changes, meant to preserve both their own professional control and the genteel reputations of their largely white middle-class students, became codified before the game was a decade old.

The tangle of traditional restrictive attitudes and athletes' new enthusiasm for competition and physical activity had complex effects on women. At that first intercollegiate game, the Berkeley captain refused to play before a mixed crowd. A letter published in the school's newspaper praised the decision, noting that the spectacle of women playing before men would not be "conducive to ladylike manners and refinement" and would result in "lowering a certain standard of womanhood."

But in her analysis of the game for the *Examiner*, the captain of another local basketball team (who, we read, "would sooner play ball than eat") referred to the players as "men." The paper followed her lead, noting that "when lovely woman lines up for the strain and stress of a basket ball game she prefers not to be reminded that she is a woman, and so she elects to call herself a man." Even in the eyes of committed sportswomen, apparently, "woman" athletes could not at the same time sweat in public and maintain their own identity as women. At least not yet.

As basketball—and other highly physical competitive sports such as field hockey, track and field, and swimming—caught on into the 1920s and early '30s, two groups rose into leadership. Their differing approaches and goals further fanned the flames of controversy about and within girls' and women's athletics. Middle-class white physical educators continued to follow a philosophy of moderation, changing the rules of some sports to make them less strenuous, and gradually, as the thirties became the forties, gaining ground in their efforts to turn interscholastic competitions into intramurals or loosely competitive "field days" at which fair play, cooperation, and self-control counted for more than athletic excellence. By walking a path apart from that of men's athletics, a separation clearly marked by different rules, clothing, equipment, and attitudes toward competition, women P.E. teachers hoped to shield their charges from exploitation and maintain conventional ideas about women's capabilities and character.

Promoters of women's sport, on the other hand, worked to provide competitive opportunities outside of educational institutions through such organizations as the Amateur Athletic Union and industrial and municipal sport leagues. The success of these ventures frequently depended on box-office draw; promoters' efforts to convince the public that female athletes were worth watching led them to emphasize the ways in which physical fitness made sportswomen more attractive to men. Reporters picked up on this, often judging individual sportswomen not in terms of their athletic competence but against a limited standard of sexual charm. Stereotypical femininity became a selling point, exploited in attempts to increase the popularity—and hence profitability—of sportswomen. To give one well-publicized example, the women who played pro baseball in the All-American Girls Baseball League, a professional venture in the 1940s and '50s, wore uniforms complete with skirts and makeup, and attended mandatory charm school sessions during spring training.

But public ideas about what was "feminine"—and hence seen as normal and healthy for females—proved remarkably resistant to change. By the 1940s, sportswomen's "masculine" affinity for physical strength, speed, and power and displays of physical and emotional competence in pressure-filled competitive situations linked them in some observers' minds to allegations of deviance and even lesbianism, popularly understood as an abnormal "mannishness." Many adult women, even those who as girls played in school environments, no doubt rejected athletics altogether rather than question themselves or their social environment.

Others chose to define "feminine"—and "athlete"—differently. Thousands cheered the feats of sportswomen in the 1920s, when history's largest ticker tape parade to date down New York streets greeted Gertrude Ederle after her swim across the English Channel—some two hours faster than the best previous crosser, a man. Ederle's fame, which also rested on three Olympic medals and eighteen world records at age seventeen, briefly matched that of tennis player Helen Wills Moody, an eight-time Wimbledon champion. The success of U.S. women at the 1932 Los Angeles Olympics created excitement across the country.

The thirty-seven female U.S. Olympians in 1932 won every gold medal but two in track and field and swimming and diving. Texas star Mildred "Babe" Didrikson set world records in the hurdles and javelin throw and took the silver in the high jump. Seattle swimmer Helene Madison won three golds with three Olympic records. As a group, the women represented a cross section of athletic backgrounds, from private sports facilities to city pools and schools.

Then, as now, social class and race often influenced women's sports opportunities. During this period middle-class and wealthy white women continued to train at clubs and schools and, as youths, in some municipal programs. City and industrial leagues provided working-class athletes with chances to play. The latter, backed by business owners and sometimes made up of workers in a single office or factory, flourished in geographical pockets around the United States in the 1930s and '40s. In 1938, close to one thousand women's softball teams, most with commercial sponsors, competed in Southern California alone. Didrikson is one example of an athlete whose early connection to the facilities and coaching provided by a business-backed team catapulted her into national prominence.

Access was far more restricted for African American sportswomen. Although many African American educators and promoters encouraged black girls and women to take part in competitive sport, in early years those opportunities opened within black schools and leagues only. By the early 1930s, African American organizers had established flourishing women's basketball leagues in the mid-Atlantic states and elsewhere, an annual national tennis tournament with regular women's events, and the beginnings of what would be nationally dominant collegiate track programs. But two black women picked for the 1932 Olympic 4 × 100 relay team, Tidye Pickett and Louise Stokes, were replaced at the last minute by white runners. It would be another twenty years before black women regularly competed on integrated international teams representing the United States, and even longer before segregated events became unusual at the local level.

Those in favor of women's participation in serious athletic competition and those against were at a standoff by the 1950s. Basketball, once thought to be suited for women, had long since become known as a men's game; even in the AAU national championship, women—who did still play, and at this high level—had to use six-player rules, which slowed play by limiting dribbling and confining most players to just half the court. Even so, public attitudes toward sportswomen were such that organizers also staged an annual beauty contest among team members as part of the tournament.

Perhaps the double meaning of the phrase "you throw like a boy" best sums up attitudes toward women's athletics on the eve of the turbulent sixties and feminism's second wave. Sportswomen knew they could interpret the words as praise—since males, to most people's minds, set the standards of excellence—or as insult, meant to awaken echoes of "ugly" and "deviant." They took part in charm school sessions and beauty contests, hoping, perhaps, to quiet both critics and personal fears. To love sport, and to be punished for it; to run free until stopped by the center line—American women had known competitive sport's joy, and its price, for nearly one hundred years.

My own delight in sport awakened during the early 1960s. At age nine I swam my first race, a 25-yard leg of a regional championship freestyle relay. I'd been with the team for just a few weeks; my muscles still clench with memories of fighting the water as I struggled against letting my teammates down.

My education in discipline and mental toughness began that day. But I remember being handed my first award, a white third-place ribbon. It still resides in my collection, gold lettering cracking as it ages at the bottom of a shoebox filled with similar gratification.

I was lucky. In their youth, my parents had both been athletes. During the freer thirties my mother starred as the pitcher of a coed softball team representing her two-room grammar school. My father made an all-state team, the first basketball player from his small high school to be so named. And miraculously, the YMCA in our small town sponsored a volunteer age-group swim coach smart enough to know that points scored by girls counted just as much as those scored by boys. My parents let me compete. Through elementary school and junior high, we all wore the soft royal blue team jackets to meets, and we all worked equally hard. Though I wondered at times why I couldn't play Little League baseball when I struck out all of the boys I pitched to in practice, there was always swimming, and shooting baskets with Dad in our driveway, and pro baseball—the Yankees—on TV. I loved sport for its clarity, for the hope it embodied, and because it made me feel powerful and at home.

High school shook me out of my dreams. For the first time, the cultural messages about athletic girls and women, about our "ugliness"—that is, supposed unattractiveness to boys and men—and our questionable sexuality, got through my love of competition. I started asking questions. First, why did the guys in high school get road trips, fans, and newspaper ink while we girls played intramurals (when enough of us made it to the gym), wore pinnies (little top-only aprons dyed red or green, which fit over gym clothes as "uniforms"), and led cheers? And then, since these seemed beyond change, which of my own personas should I be—the "tomboy" who threw a hardball against our brick chimney for hours, climbed the tallest fir trees she could find, and dreamed of changing the world? Or the demure young lady who waited (in vain) to be asked to the prom? I read and reread *My Sister Mike*, a novel featuring a female basketball player, trying to discover why the book focused on succeeding on dates instead of on court. Did the author know something I didn't?

In 1969—my senior season, and year of the Earth-to-moon "giant step for mankind"—our high school yearbook photographer caught me standing with my eyes shut and side turned to the camera. In the picture I wear a white T-shirt, dark shorts embroidered with SANDOZ in block letters, and braces wrapped around each knee. At five foot ten and 120 pounds I look like an awkwardly bent tree trunk, feet planted firmly on the floor, shoulders slumped, one arm waving ineffectually at a second young woman, whose leap is about three inches off the ground. The caption reads "Competing for jump ball."

Under our "girls" basketball rules—direct descendants of those made before 1900—we bounced the ball three times only before passing it to a teammate. Forwards and guards stayed in zones marked on the floor and couldn't cross the center line. Young women in our part of Washington State didn't play team sports against other schools. My awkwardness and lack of opportunity in high school illustrated the end result of unyielding definitions of women's "proper" role coupled with the conservative women's sport tradition which downplayed competition: poor skills, lack of confidence, and an immensely self-conscious confusion.

In the end, though, the commitment behind that confusion saved me.

For, in that *other* hundred-year tradition in women's athletics, the one we made for ourselves, I loved sport. Fiercely. When the first college I attended proved less than serious about women's teams, I transferred to another. There—in the midst of dress and behavior codes meant to regulate our appearance and sexuality, and budgets so minuscule we once got one dollar meal money for an entire season—I met other women who shared that love. The pain of being dismissed as "abnormal" didn't diminish; men's teams still got all the ink and most of the money. But I now knew people, women, who competed in national championships and who made sport the center of their lives. For the first time, my dreams had focus. I ran, threw, hit, shot, and jumped until the sweat ran dry, and when the time came, coached younger women to national competition. Some of them now coach others.

Last fall I attended the first women's pro basketball game played in Seattle. The mayor appeared, along with the American Basketball League president, news reporters, and TV camera crews. Workers stood ready to change numbers on a banner, totalling $100 donations to local girls' and boys' clubs for each three-point shot—a new way to score since my own playing days—sunk by a Seattle player. Vendors did a brisk business in women's basketball gear. The near-sellout crowd, both women and men, reserved its biggest cheers for Venus Lacey, who won a gold medal with the U.S. basketball team at the Atlanta Olympics. This was a women's arena. It said so in big letters painted in gold on the floor: Seattle Reign.

As the game began, I saw it all—fans, refs, coaches, and the marvelous athletes before me—through the lens of pinnies and six-player ball. I admit I wept. Under the next morning's headline, "A Great Day for Reign," Lacey and teammates signaled victory from the *Seattle Post-Intelligencer*. Above the fold. Page one.

Women's competitive sport—and the stories we tell ourselves about sportswomen's abilities and dreams—have been through some changes in the past hundred years.

. . .

The important things, however, remain the same. The earliest piece of women's sport fiction I've discovered, published in 1895, tells it like it was—and is. Witness the response of Miss Katharine Atterbury, college crew captain and tennis standout, to a newspaper article questioning women's suitability for sport.

> "To read this article one would imagine that we were imbecile babies. One would think that a girl was as weak as a kitten, and didn't know a boat from an elevator . . . or a golf club from a sewing-machine . . . he [the reporter] isn't even aware of his unutterable, his colossal ignorance! . . . It is time the public was learning the true state of things—that girls can and do swim, and row and play golf and tennis, and run and walk about, just as their brothers do, and that we have courage and muscle enough to go in for football even, except that we have some *little* regard for our personal appearance!"

Miss Atterbury's outrage—and her revenge, told in gleeful detail later in this collection—ring true today. Her audacity, called "pluck" in her time and "anger" or "aggressiveness" in our own, has kept women's sport alive. Pluck, and the sheer joy of feeling sport free one's authentic self. Of knowing this game is the right one.

Writers of U.S. women's sport literature relish both pluck and joy. Feisty elementary school sprinter Hazel Elizabeth Deborah Parker will happily tell you—via Toni Cade Bambara in our opening story, "Raymond's Run"—"I'm the fastest thing on two feet. There is no track meet that I don't win the first-place medal." Ms. Parker, whose story appeared in 1971, also rejects utterly the mistake she made in nursery school of dancing the part of a strawberry in a pageant. She much prefers sport, where, when she looks at her chief rival after a race, they can begin smiling at each other until

> We stand there with this big smile of respect between us. It's about as real a smile as girls can do for each other, considering we don't practice smiling every day, you know, cause maybe we're too busy being flowers or fairies or strawberries instead of something honest and worthy of respect . . . you know . . . like being people.

Sportswomen "being people"—real individuals in our own right apart from the "flowers" and "fairies" of society's expectations—focuses the selections in *A Whole Other Ball Game*. The stories and poems here tell of something new to most readers, though older than the twentieth century: *women's* experiences and dreams related to organized competitive athletics. Besides focusing on women, a woman author, and strong, vivid writing, selection criteria included previous publication or distribution of the piece in the United States, and focus on competitive sport. As the book came together, though, this last seemed less important, so that several pieces tell of women's experiences in fitness activities, pickup games, and coed sport. Not all of us throughout the last century, after all, have had the chance to play competitively, or in women-only settings.

If pluck and joy were all of women's experience of sport, our literature about it would be straightforward tales of victory. But as we've seen, for sportswomen "being people" involves more than reaching for goals. Poet Barbara Lamblin speaks eloquently in "First Peace" about the personal cost of "stares past my tank suit" and the "nameless fears / about my undiscovered womanhood." Cynthia Macdonald writes of the price a pitcher pays to remain at once herself and a World Series victor. Lucy Jane Bledsoe chills us with the damage fear of lesbians can cause, and the hostility the fear gives rise to. Ellen Gilchrist's Rhoda shows what it felt like in the 1940s to be young, Southern, shut out of sport . . . and in need of putting it right.

Caught between liberating experiences in sport and cultural messages about "proper" behavior, girls and women who love to play can be cumbered by confusion. Jessie Rehder explores this inner weightedness. In Rehder's 1939 story, "Atalanta in Cape Fair," Joanna Prokosch repeatedly brings the hometown fans to their feet during the state basketball championship, playing the game of a lifetime—which, of course, is exactly what this is. The rest of her life will begin on her date with the football star at the country club dance that night.

One result of internal disjunction can be a deepening of perception, as one is forced to consider the truths of sport against its pain. In an excerpt from *Water Dancer*, novelist Jenifer Levin shows us the necessity of redefining our concepts of competition. Adrienne Rich and Tess Gallagher write of momentum, and the inexorableness of commitment. Poems by Carolyn Kremers and Eloise Klein Healy voice sport's role in helping them move beyond youth, while Australian poet Judith Wright sets sport squarely in the frame of human mortality.

Women's struggle in sport has led us to draw together. Mariah Burton Nelson and Carol Anshaw remind us of the kinship in competition. Ellen Cooney, Sara Vogan, and Sara Maitland tell of athletes and their families. In Pat Griffin's humorous story "Diamonds, Dykes and Double Plays," a feminist softball team circles-up after games to process the experience.

Finally, as athletes and writers, women celebrate their love for the game. Susan Firer commemorates Oshkosh women's softball, where the Sunlight Dairy Team hitters "pump energy into / them bats" and the softballs fly in the night "like an-gelfood cake batter folded through devilsfood." Even straw-berry ice cream fails to tempt Bette Bao Lord's Shirley, newly emigrated from China, away from baseball broadcasts on the radio. And Joan Benoit wins the 1984 Olympic Marathon, Rina Ferrarelli reminds us,

> . . . not even out of breath
> and standing.

There is, in Healy's words, "the spill of one white star / out of a hand."

A century after the first intercollegiate women's basketball game—and publication of the first fiction about women's com-petitive sport written by women—this truth remains: finding oneself through sport is a radical, difficult, and joyous step for a woman.

As the first comprehensive anthology of women's literature about women's competitive sport, *A Whole Other Ball Game* signals a subtle and genuine cultural shift. Despite lingering conservative definitions of "feminine," everywhere we look— in print, on TV; at gyms, pools, courts, weight rooms, clubs and playing fields—American girls and women are choosing to be themselves through sport. And loving it.

Not that it's easy. For both women and men, "being people" will never be free from effort and pain. Sport itself sees to that. In Jenifer Levin's story "Her Marathon," an office worker named Celía glimpses Alberto Salazar leading the New York City Marathon. The sight inspires her to give up booze for running. During her first race, Celía says,

. . . blind with pain, sweating and gasping and almost dead, I stared down and saw that there was a little hole in the tip of my right tennis shoe, near the little toe; it had rubbed the toe raw and, around the little hole, the dirty white fabric was soaking through with blood. Then I felt all the dried-up pieces of me come to life and, suffering, I ran on the breath of the wind. Until, after a while, the wind deserted me. Just before six miles. Left me, one faulty woman, in a mob of suffering moving flesh, to finish the last few hundred yards alone . . .

Girlfriend, I said, get some pride.

I did.

Since the late 1800s, women have repeatedly proven their fitness for competitive sports . . . by simply playing the game. Any game. Off court and on; despite all opposition. Instead of listening to the more popular stories told through the years about sportswomen's proper place in and out of the gym, some of us have simply written our own. Here we speak *our* experience: the ecstasy of scoring from center court, the tension of teammate rivalries, and the agony of losing before hometown fans. Here we voice the deep and abiding satisfactions of competitive sport: the bonds between sportswomen, and disciplined pursuit of goals at once meaningful and fleet. Here, at last, we can tell the truth: women play, we play hard and well, and we love it—the struggle, the skill and the game.

—Joli Sandoz

# RAYMOND'S RUN

1971

toni cade bambara

I don't have much work to do around the house like some girls. My mother does that. And I don't have to earn my pocket money by hustling; George runs errands for the big boys and sells Christmas cards. And anything else that's got to get done, my father does. All I have to do in life is mind my brother Raymond, which is enough.

Sometimes I slip and say my little brother Raymond. But as any fool can see he's much bigger and he's older too. But a lot of people call him my little brother cause he needs looking after cause he's not quite right. And a lot of smart mouths got lots to say about that too, especially when George was minding him. But now, if anybody has anything to say to Raymond, anything to say about his big head, they have to come by me. And I don't play the dozens or believe in standing around with somebody in my face doing a lot of talking. I much rather just knock you down and take my chances even if I am a little girl with skinny arms and a squeaky voice, which is how I got the name Squeaky. And if things get too rough, I run. And as anybody can tell you, I'm the fastest thing on two feet.

There is no track meet that I don't win the first-place medal. I used to win the twenty-yard dash when I was a little kid in kindergarten. Nowadays, it's the fifty-yard dash. And tomorrow I'm subject to run the quarter-meter relay all by myself and come in first, second and third. The big kids call me Mercury cause I'm the swiftest thing in the neighborhood. Everybody knows that—except two people who know better, my father and me. He can beat me to Amsterdam Avenue with me having a two fire-hydrant head start and him running with his hands in his pockets and whistling. But that's private information. Cause can you imagine some thirty-five-year-old man stuffing himself into PAL shorts to race little kids? So as far as everyone's concerned, I'm the fastest and that goes for Gretchen, too, who has put out the tale that she is going to win the first-place medal this year. Ridiculous. In the second place, she's got short legs. In the third place, she's got freckles. In the first place, no one can beat me and that's all there is to it.

I'm standing on the corner admiring the weather and about to take a stroll down Broadway so I can practice my breathing exercises, and I've got Raymond walking on the inside close to the buildings cause he's subject to fits of fantasy and starts thinking he's a circus performer and that the curb is a tightrope strung high in the air. And sometimes after a rain he likes to step down off his tightrope right into the gutter and slosh around getting his shoes and cuffs wet. Then I get hit when I get home. Or sometimes if you don't watch him he'll dash across traffic to the island in the middle of Broadway and give the pigeons a fit. Then I have to go behind him apologizing to all the old people sitting around trying to get some sun and getting all upset with all the pigeons fluttering around them, scattering their newspapers and upsetting the waxpaper lunches in their laps. So I keep Raymond on the inside of me, and he plays like he's driving a stage coach, which is O.K. by me so long as he doesn't run me over or interrupt my breathing exercises, which I have to do on account of I'm serious about my running, and I don't care who knows it.

Now some people like to act like things come easy to them, won't let on that they practice. Not me. I'll high-prance down 34th Street like a rodeo pony to keep my knees strong even if it does get my mother uptight so that she walks ahead like she's not with me, don't know me, is all by herself on a shopping trip and I am somebody else's crazy child. Now you take Cynthia Procter for instance. She's just the opposite. If there's a test tomorrow, she'll say something like, "Oh, I guess I'll play handball this afternoon and watch television tonight," just to let you know she ain't thinking about the test. Or like last week when she won the spelling bee for the millionth time, "A good thing you got 'receive,' Squeaky, cause I would have got it wrong. I completely forgot about the spelling bee." And she'll clutch the lace on her blouse like it was a narrow escape. Oh, brother. But of course when I pass her house on my early morning trots around the block, she is practicing the scales on the piano over and over and over and over. Then in music class she always lets herself get bumped around so she falls accidentally on purpose onto the piano stool and is so surprised to find herself sitting there that she decides just for fun to try out the ole keys. And what do you know—Chopin's waltzes just spring out of her fingertips and she's the most surprised thing in the world. A regular prodigy. I could kill people like that. I stay up all night studying the words for the spelling bee. And you can see me any time of day practicing running. I never walk if I can trot, and shame on Raymond if he can't keep up. But of course he does, cause if he doesn't someone's liable to walk up to him and get smart, or take his allowance from him, or ask him where he got that great big pumpkin head. People are so stupid sometimes.

So I'm strolling down Broadway breathing out and

breathing in on counts of seven, which is my lucky number, and here comes Gretchen and her sidekicks: Mary Louise, who used to be a friend of mine when she first moved to Harlem from Baltimore and got beat up by everybody till I took up for her on account of her mother and my mother used to sing in the same choir when they were young girls, but people ain't grateful, so now she hangs out with the new girl Gretchen and talks about me like a dog; and Rosie, who is as fat as I am skinny and has a big mouth where Raymond is concerned and is too stupid to know that there is not a big deal of difference between herself and Raymond and that she can't afford to throw stones. So they are steady coming up Broadway and I see right away that it's going to be one of those Dodge City scenes cause the street ain't that big and they're close to the buildings just as we are. First I think I'll step into the candy store and look over the new comics and let them pass. But that's chicken and I've got a reputation to consider. So then I think I'll just walk straight on through them or even over them if necessary. But as they get to me, they slow down. I'm ready to fight, cause like I said I don't feature a whole lot of chit-chat. I much prefer to just knock you down right from the jump and save everybody a lotta precious time.

"You signing up for the May Day races?" smiles Mary Louise, only it's not a smile at all. A dumb question like that doesn't deserve an answer. Beside's there's just me and Gretchen standing there really, so no use wasting my breath talking to shadows.

"I don't think you're going to win this time," says Rosie, trying to signify with her hands on her hips all salty, completely forgetting that I have whupped her behind many times for less salt than that.

"I always win cause I'm the best," I say straight at Gretchen who is, as far as I'm concerned, the only one in this ventriloquist-dummy routine. Gretchen smiles, but it's not a smile, and I'm thinking that girls never really smile at each other because they don't know how and don't want to know how and there's probably no one to teach us how, cause grown-up girls don't know either. Then they all look at Raymond who has just brought his mule team to a standstill. And they're about to see what trouble they can get into through him.

"What grade you in now, Raymond?"

"You got anything to say to my brother, you say it to me, Mary Louise Williams of Raggedy Town, Baltimore."

"What are you, his mother?" sasses Rosie.

"That's right, Fatso. And the next word out of anybody and I'll be *their* mother too." So they just stand there and Gretchen shifts from one leg to the other and so do they. Then Gretchen puts her hands on her hips and is about to say something with her freckle-face self but doesn't. Then she walks around me looking me up and down but keeps walking up Broadway, and her sidekicks follow her. So me and Raymond smile at each other and he says, "Gidyap" to his team and I continue with my breathing exercises, strolling down Broadway toward the ice man on 145th with not a care in the world cause I am Miss Quicksilver herself.

I take my time getting to the park on May Day because the track meet is the last thing on the program. The biggest thing on the program is the May Pole dancing, which I can do without, thank you, even if my mother thinks it's a shame I don't take part and act like a girl for a change. You'd think my mother'd be grateful not to have to make me a white organdy dress with a big satin sash and buy me new white babydoll shoes that can't be taken out of the box till the big day. You'd think she'd be glad her daughter ain't out there prancing around a May Pole getting the new clothes all dirty and sweaty and trying to act like a fairy or a flower or whatever you're supposed to be when you should be trying to be yourself, whatever that is, which is, as far as I am concerned, a poor Black girl who really can't afford to buy shoes and a new dress you only wear once a lifetime cause it won't fit next year.

I was once a strawberry in a Hansel and Gretel pageant when I was in nursery school and didn't have no better sense than to dance on tiptoe with my arms in a circle over my head doing umbrella steps and being a perfect fool just so my mother and father could come dressed up and clap. You'd think they'd know better than to encourage that sort of nonsense. I am not a strawberry. I do not dance on my toes. I run. That is what I am all about. So I always come late to the May Day program, just in time to get my number pinned on and lay in the grass till they announce the fifty-yard dash.

I put Raymond in the little swings, which is a tight squeeze this year and will be impossible next year. Then I look around for Mr. Pearson, who pins the numbers on. I'm really looking for Gretchen if you want to know the truth, but she's not around. The park is jam-packed. Parents in hats and corsages and breast-pocket handkerchiefs peeking up. Kids in white dresses and light-blue suits. The parkees unfolding chairs and chasing the rowdy kids from Lenox as if they had no right to be there. The big guys with their caps on backwards leaning against the fence swirling the basketballs on the tips of their fingers, waiting for all these crazy people to clear out the park so they can play. Most of the kids in my class are carrying bass drums and glockenspiels and flutes. You'd think they'd put in a few bongos or something for real like that.

Then here comes Mr. Pearson with his clipboard and his cards and pencils and whistles and safety pins and fifty million other things he's always dropping all over the place with his clumsy self. He sticks out in a crowd because he's on stilts. We used to call him Jack and the Beanstalk to get him mad. But

I'm the only one that can outrun him and get away, and I'm too grown for that silliness now.

"Well, Squeaky," he says, checking my name off the list and handing me number seven and two pins. And I'm thinking he's got no right to call me Squeaky, if I can't call him Beanstalk.

"Hazel Elizabeth Deborah Parker," I correct him and tell him to write it down on his board.

"Well, Hazel Elizabeth Deborah Parker, going to give someone else a break this year?" I squint at him real hard to see if he is seriously thinking I should lose the race on purpose just to give someone else a break. "Only six girls running this time," he continues, his head shaking sadly like it's my fault all of New York didn't turn out in sneakers. "That new girl should give you a run for your money." He looks around the park for Gretchen like a periscope in a submarine movie. "Wouldn't it be a nice gesture if you were . . . to ahhh . . ."

I give him such a look he couldn't finish putting that idea into words. Grownups got a lot of nerve sometimes. I pin number seven to myself and stomp away, I'm so burnt. And I go straight for the track and stretch out on the grass while the band winds up with "Oh, the Monkey Wrapped His Tail Around the Flag Pole," which my teacher calls by some other name. The man on the loudspeaker is calling everyone over to the track and I'm on my back looking at the sky, trying to pretend I'm in the country, but I can't, because even grass in the city feels hard as sidewalk, and there's just no pretending you are anywhere but in a "concrete jungle" as my grandfather says.

The twenty-yard dash takes all of two minutes cause most of the little kids don't know no better than to run off the track or run the wrong way or run smack into the fence and fall down and cry. One little kid, though, has got the good sense to run straight for the white ribbon up ahead so he wins. Then the second-graders line up for the thirty-yard dash and I don't even bother to turn my head to watch cause Raphael Perez always wins. He wins before he even begins by psyching the runners, telling them they're going to trip on their shoelaces and fall on their faces or lose their shorts or something, which he doesn't really have to do since he is very fast, almost as fast as I am. After that is the forty-yard dash which I used to run when I was in first grade. Raymond is hollering to me from the swings cause he knows I'm about to do my thing cause the man on the loudspeaker has just announced the fifty-yard dash, although he might just as well be giving a recipe for angel food cake cause you can hardly make out what he's saying for the static. I get up and slip off my sweat pants and then I see Gretchen standing at the starting line, kicking her legs out like a pro. Then as I get into place I see that ole Raymond is on line on the other side of the fence, bending down with his fingers on the ground just like he knew what he was doing. I was going to yell at him but then I didn't. It burns up your energy to holler.

Every time, just before I take off in a race, I always feel like I'm in a dream, the kind of dream you have when you're sick with fever and feel all hot and weightless. I dream I'm flying over a sandy beach in the early morning sun, kissing the leaves of the trees as I fly by. And there's always the smell of apples, just like in the country when I was little and used to think I was a choo-choo train, running through the fields of corn and chugging up the hill to the orchard. And all the time I'm dreaming this, I get lighter and lighter until I'm flying over the beach again, getting blown through the sky like a feather that weighs nothing at all. But once I spread my fingers in the dirt and crouch over the Get on Your Mark, the dream goes and I am solid again and am telling myself, Squeaky, you must win, you must win, you are the fastest thing in the world, you can even beat your father up Amsterdam if you really try. And then I feel my weight coming back just behind my knees then down to my feet then into the earth and the pistol shot explodes in my blood and I am off and weightless again, flying past the other runners, my arms up and down and the whole world is quiet except for the crunch as I zoom over the gravel in the track. I glance to my left and there is no one. To the right, a blurred Gretchen, who's got her chin jutting out as if it would win the race all by itself. And on the other side of the fence is Raymond with his arms down to his side and the palms tucked up behind him, running in his very own style, and it's the first time I ever saw that and I almost stop to watch my brother Raymond on his first run. But the white ribbon is bouncing toward me and I tear past it, racing into the distance till my feet with a mind of their own start digging up footfulls of dirt and brake me short. Then all the kids standing on the side pile on me, banging me on the back and slapping my head with their May Day programs, for I have won again and everybody on 151st Street can walk tall for another year.

"In first place . . ." the man on the loudspeaker is clear as a bell now. But then he pauses and the loudspeaker starts to whine. Then static. And I lean down to catch my breath and here comes Gretchen walking back, for she's overshot the finish line too, huffing and puffing with her hands on her hips, taking it slow, breathing in steady time like a real pro and I sort of like her a little for the first time. In first place . . . and then three or four voices get all mixed up on the loudspeaker and I dig my sneaker into the grass and stare at Gretchen who's staring back, we both wondering just who did win. I can hear old Beanstalk arguing with the man on the loudspeaker and then a few others running their mouths about what the stopwatches say. Then I hear Raymond yanking at the fence to call me and I wave to shush him, but he keeps rattling the fence like a gorilla in a cage like in them gorilla movies, but then like a dancer or something he starts climbing up nice and easy but very fast. And it occurs to me, watching how smoothly he climbs hand over hand and remembering how he looked running with his arms down to his side and with the wind pulling his mouth back and his teeth showing and all, it occurred to me that Raymond would make a very fine runner. Doesn't he always keep up with me on my trots? And he surely knows how to breathe in counts of seven cause he's always doing it at the dinner table, which drives my brother George up the wall. And I'm smiling to beat the band cause if I've lost this race, or if me and Gretchen tied, or even if I've won, I can always retire as a runner and begin a whole new career as a coach with Raymond as my champion. After all, with a little more study, I can beat Cynthia and her phony self at the spelling bee. And if I bugged my mother, I could get piano lessons and become a star. And I have a big rep as the baddest thing around. And I've got a roomful of ribbons and medals and awards. But what has Raymond got to call his own?

So I stand there with my new plans, laughing out loud by this time as Raymond jumps down from the fence and runs over with his teeth showing and his arms down to the side, which no one before him has quite mastered as a running style. And by the time he comes over I'm jumping up and down so glad to see him my brother Raymond, a great runner in the family tradition. But of course everyone thinks I'm jumping up and down because the men on the loudspeaker have finally gotten themselves together and compared notes and are announcing. In first place Miss Hazel Elizabeth Deborah Parker. (Dig that.) In second place Miss Gretchen P. Lewis. And I look over at Gretchen wondering what the "P" stands for. And I smile. Cause she's good, no doubt about it. Maybe she'd like to help me coach Raymond; she obviously is serious about running, as any fool can see. And she nods to congratulate me and then she smiles. We stand there with this big smile of respect between us. It's about as real a smile as girls can do for each other, considering we don't practice smiling every day, you know, cause maybe we're too busy being flowers or fairies or strawberries instead of something honest and worthy of respect . . . you know . . . like being people.

# 74TH STREET

1972

myra cohn livingston

Hey, this little kid gets roller skates.
She puts them on.
She stands up and almost
flops over backwards.
She sticks out a foot like
she's going somewhere and
falls down and
smacks her hand. She
grabs hold of a step to get up and
sticks out the other foot and
slides about six inches and
falls and
skins her knee.

And then, you know what?

She brushes off the dirt and the
blood and puts some
spit on it and then
sticks out the other foot

*again.*

# POSTING-UP

1990

stephanie grant

**M**y senior year fourteen girls showed up to our first practice. The year before, the team had been only half as strong: not enough bodies to scrimmage even. Which didn't bother our coach, Sr. Agnes, who had spent thirty of her seventy-odd years as a cloistered nun and who confused basketball with dodge-ball. Sr. Agnes had retired at the end of last season. My dad said it was A Blessing In Disguise. Rumor was that our new coach, Sr. Bernadette, had gone to college on basketball scholarship. She was late getting to the first practice, though, so we all stood around shooting baskets and checking each other out. I counted four, maybe five, point guards.

Every player in the city knew Kate Malone, if not by sight —she was six feet tall, with a mass of bright red hair—then by reputation. She led the Catholic league in total points scored for both boys and girls, and she had been kicked out of five Catholic schools in three years. Whatever school she ended up with, she took to the Catholic League Tourney; I'd watched her win with a different team all three years. Kate was the only new student at Immaculata in 1973 who wasn't fleeing a court order: Immaculata was her last hope for a parochial school education. The school before us—Sacred Heart—was in Dorchester, but not the Irish part. Kate had been the only white starter for Sacred Heart, which seemed more incomprehensible than her eighteen or nineteen points per game.

She stood at one end of the gym, shooting. Two other new girls waited beneath the basket for her to miss. Basketball etiquette required them to pass back the ball whenever she sank it. They looked pretty bored.

At the opposite hoop, Irene Fahey was practicing lay-ups. The rest of us stood in a rough semicircle around the basket, taking turns with the remaining ball. Irene wove in and out of us, charging from the left, then right, retrieving her own rebounds—whether or not she scored—dribbling out and flying back in, all the while asking questions about Immaculata and the team.

"What was your record last year? I mean are you guys the losingest team in history? Who's your new coach? Is she a million and one years old like your last coach? I can't imagine losing all the time. I mean did you guys like to lose, or what?"

Irene was the second best basketball player and biggest mouth in the Catholic league. The year before, she took Perpetual Faith to the playoffs with a 13-and-2 record. They lost to Kate's team in the next-to-last round by three points.

"You got a team this year, that's for sure. I've never seen so many freaking guards in one place before. I wonder who she's gonna start?"

Irene left Perpetual Faith, she confided in us at the top of her lungs, because her mother felt "the quality of education was deteriorating." Eventually I learned what that meant: Irene left because Perpetual Faith was one of the few Catholic schools in Boston that had black students, and it had accepted more blacks since the busing crisis began. Not only white parents took their children out of public school after the court order became final. Most of the black families removed their kids because they were concerned for their safety, which was exactly what the white parents said. Even I knew that the black people had real reason to worry. The first day of school a busload of black second-graders got stoned by white parents in Southie. We watched it on the news. My mom and dad were so disturbed they shut off the TV.

"Couldn't wait to get outta Perpetual Faith, that's for sure. Goin' downhill, you know what I'm saying?" Irene stomped on my toes on her way to the hoop.

Her lay-ups became so disruptive to our shooting that we were forced to join her. The girls who had been shooting with Kate (or hoping to shoot with Kate) left her to practice with us. Kate didn't budge, and Irene didn't ask.

Irene made me anxious. She sighed loudly at each of our mistakes, like somehow we were personally disappointing her. I missed every lay-up because I knew she was watching. We kept quiet during the drill and grew bored, but we were afraid to say anything. A tiny, dark-haired girl suggested we scrimmage. She was very serious-looking. I had never seen her before, which was weird because I went to all the league games, Catholic and city, and I knew all the ball players. Irene was irritated.

"Ya, and who are you? Where'd you play? Not in this league, I don't think. Not too many guineas in this league. Not that I have anything against Italians. Don't get me wrong. Just never seen them play any kinda b-ball."

"Assumption," the girl replied, unflinching. I stared at the gym floor, nauseated; we didn't use words like *guinea* in my house.

"Assumption?" Irene looked puzzled. "Never heard of it. Where's Assumption?"

"Springfield," she responded, still indifferent. Her voice was low and steady.

"Ya, then how come I never heard of it? I got relatives in

Springfield, and I've never heard of Assumption. You wouldn't be lying to me, would you? I hope not, lying is a cardinal sin, you know; it'll put a black mark on your soul, and guineas start out with half-black souls because of the Mafia. You can't afford too many cardinal sins."

"No, I wouldn't lie to you. You haven't heard of Assumption because it's not a high school. Assumption College." Ice edged the dark girl's words.

"I don't get it. What's your name?" Irene lost some of the color in her face.

"Bernadette. Sr. Bernadette. And you're Irene Fahey. That right?"

Irene nodded, ash-grey. All of us looked a little ill, except Kate, who was still shooting baskets. The bounce bounce of her ball kept time.

"Why didn't you tell us who you were?" Irene choked. "And how the hell old are you, anyway?"

Sr. Bernadette shrugged. "I just wanted to see you play relaxed, without knowing the coach was watching. And it's none of your business how old I am. Just graduated from Assumption last spring and took my vows at the same time. Any more questions?"

Silence. Then Irene: "Don't they have a height requirement for nuns, for Christ's sake?"

There was a collective gasp. Everything I'd ever heard about Irene Fahey was true.

"No, but there are requirements for being on this team." Sr. Bernadette took a step toward Irene. "One of them is respect. If I get any more lip from you, your behind is going to be warming the bench all season. I don't care who you are or how good you play. Got that?"

"Got it," Irene smiled a big, fake smile. "Got it, got it. I mean you're the boss, right? You're about as big as my kid sister, but you're the coach and whatever the coach says, goes."

I was sweating. Irene lived by the axiom that the best defense is a good offense.

Sr. Bernadette fixed Irene with a glare so cold that every girl within ten feet hugged her arms to her body. I remembered what I had heard in school about Italians and the evil eye and was instantly ashamed.

"Kate, come down here, will you? We're gonna scrimmage. I'd like everyone to introduce herself first. Tell us your name, what school you played for last year, and what position."

There did seem to be something sort of otherworldly about Sr. Bernadette, I had to admit. Like how come she already knew our names?

Everyone shifted her weight from leg to leg as we went around the circle. There were six new girls.

"Maura Duggan, Dorchester High, point guard."

"Frances Fitzgerald, Southie, point guard."

"Peggy Gallagher, Charlestown High, forward."

"Pat Gallagher, Charlestown High, forward."

"Irene Fahey, Perpetual Faith, point guard."

"Kate Malone, Sacred Heart, point guard."

Point guard is like quarterback, only for basketball. She's your best player. She controls the ball. My dad says point guards are born, not made, that it's their disposition more than their skill that a coach looks for. I had never seen so many in one room.

Sr. Bernadette bounced up and down on the balls of her feet. All the guards stared at their hightops: only one of them would get to play point. Kate and Irene never looked at each other.

I started playing basketball because my dad wanted me to. He used to coach boys basketball at Most Precious Blood and coached my brother Tim when he went there. It was sort of like a dynasty, Dad and Tim together for four years. *The Meagher Dynasty* people called it. Dad insisted I play because of my height: I'm 5 foot, 11½ inches tall, and have been since eighth grade. My brother is 5 foot 7. Tim played guard at Most Precious Blood, but was too short for college ball. I think it made him crazy that I got the right body for basketball but didn't know how to use it. Of course, if Dad had given me one-fifth the attention he gave Tim growing up, I'm sure I'd have been a lot better. For a while I was hoping Tim and I were going to be the dynasty— *The Tim and Theresa Meagher Dynasty.* But it never worked out.

When I enrolled at Immaculata in 1969, it was a small, eggheady parochial school for girls who would rather read than do just about anything else. Our basketball team had had thirty-seven consecutive losing seasons. My senior year, everything changed. Busing doubled the enrollments of Boston's Catholic schools. Even though we were technically outside the neighborhoods designated for desegregation, we were close enough to absorb the shock of white students leaving the public schools. Not counting the incoming class, seventy-one new students matriculated in 1973. Six of them were basketball stars. The Sisters said it was God's will.

The whole first week of practice was like tryouts. Sr. Bernadette tried every possible combination of players. She ran very serious practices. The first hour we did drills: ball handling, lay-ups, shooting, and passing. The second hour we broke into teams and scrimmaged ourselves. When boys did this the two teams were called shirts and skins, because one team played barechested. When we scrimmaged, one team had to put on these horrible green smocks called pinneys. Everyone complained when they had to wear them. Irene said they looked queer. Sr.

Bernadette called the team wearing pinneys "green" and the team without "white." Kate was always on the white team.

Tall people like Kate usually don't play point guard because more often than not they're lousy dribblers. The ball has so far to travel to get to the ground that it's easy to steal from them. Taller girls like me play underneath the basket, as forwards or centers. We spend most of our time fighting for good position and pulling down rebounds, so we don't get a lot of experience dribbling, faking people out, or setting up plays, which is what guards do. We mostly get a lot of experience hitting people. The few tall players who dribble are often so awkward that you don't have to guard against them very closely. Their Own Worst Enemy, as my dad would say. But Kate was not like that. She had a very low dribble for someone her height, and it was almost impossible to steal from her. She never seemed to crouch or bend over when dribbling, which left me with the impression that her arms were abnormally long. In fact, I would have sworn that her hands hung down past her knees. Though, when I saw her off the basketball court, her arms were normal: long, but in proportion with the rest of her.

Irene was built a lot more like your average high school point guard than Kate: short and skinny. Really skinny. No hips and breasts that were all nipple. (A terrific advantage on the basketball court, as in life.) In fact, if it weren't for her long, Farrah Fawcett hair and accompanying makeup, Irene could easily have been taken for a boy.

There were two schools of thought on eye shadow when I was in high school: some girls meticulously matched it to their outfits, being sure that their highlights—above the lid and below the eyebrow—corresponded to the contrasting color in their clothes. Others matched makeup with eye color, varying only the intensity of the shade. Irene was a renegade, defying both traditions, insisting on sky blue—despite her brown hair and eyes and rainbow assortment of J Crew polos. Irene's rebellion stopped here; in all else she was the standard bearer and enforcer of the status quo.

Irene also played more like your average high school point guard than Kate did. She was completely self-absorbed and unconscious of the rest of us. Irene shot whenever she had the ball. She dribbled too much (even if well) and she wouldn't pass. She tried endlessly to go in for lay-ups. She didn't think. Irene played like a one-person team, dribbling and shooting, dribbling and shooting. Of course, she got good at both because she had so much practice, but she was lousy to play with.

Friday afternoon after our first week of practice, Sr. Bernadette told us who would play where. We sat, as we had all week, far apart from each other on the bleachers of the gym listening to her comments about our play. She read without looking up from the notes she had taken on her coach's clipboard. We each had a towel and were conscientiously wiping away the day's sweat. Only Kate was still. She sat with her endless legs apart, one planted—knee bent—on the bleacher on which she sat, the other stretched out in front of her, ankle resting on the next, lower tier. Her freckled arms wrapped around the near leg, securing it to the seat. Sr. Bernadette looked up when she got to the end of her notes.

"Starting lineup will be as follows: Pat Gallagher, forward; Peggy Gallagher, forward; Theresa Meagher, center; Irene Fahey, off guard; Kate Malone, point guard. These are not lifetime memberships. If you play well, you keep your spot; if you don't, you rest awhile. It goes without saying that everyone will play."

Before Sr. Bernadette finished her last sentence, Irene was in the showers. Her little body was rigid as she hightailed it across the gym, but her large mouth was open and slack, mumbling things we all tried not to hear.

Sr. Bernadette was the best coach I'd ever had. And the coolest teacher. Unlike most of the other nuns at Immaculata, she was post–Vatican II, which meant she didn't wear a habit and she smiled at you when she spoke. But Sr. Bernadette was the most post–Vatican II nun I ever knew. She wore her hair short, but not severe. It was thick and black, stylishly cut in a shag. She had bright black eyes and smooth, almost-brown skin. During the day she wore jeans, and at practice she wore shorts and a tee shirt. Hers are the only nun's knees I've ever seen. She talked nonstop about basketball, and she shouted when she was angry or excited. She said "pissed off." She ran. Her last name was Romanelli, which was a big deal at the time because Irish people dominated the Catholic league then, and because what you were, like which church you belonged to, mattered.

Her office was at the far end of the girls' locker room, next to the exit doors. Its walls were half wood, half glass, and you could see her working away at her desk as we got dressed to leave. The glass was opaque, with a bubbly texture, so you could see her outline. Sometimes girls went in to talk with her after practice if they were having trouble, or if Irene had said something particularly mean to them. I liked to take my time getting dressed so I could watch her move around her office.

There was a lot of talk about Kate's past. Particularly from Irene. Of special interest was why she had been bounced from five Catholic schools. Kate always left practice immediately, without showering; as soon as the door shut behind her, the discussion began. Irene would parade around the dressing room still pink-faced from practice, wet from the shower, and wrapped in a thick white towel. She would stop at practically every stall, grab on to the chrome curtain rod overhead, and swing into our rooms unannounced as we changed.

"My cousin Mary Louise was at Our Lady of Mercy with Kate two years ago and she says Kate was expelled for refusing to go to religion class and disrespecting the nuns. She wouldn't even go to Mass."

Irene would pause, release one hand from the chrome bar to readjust the tuck and tightness of her towel, which was arranged to give the appearance of a bust, and continue talking and swinging one-armed.

"But my mother says her mother's just too cheap to pay tuition. Each year they pay half in September and promise to pay the rest by Christmas vacation. But never do. Can you imagine that, your mother lying to the nuns? Jesus Fucking Christ that's gross."

The first time Irene popped uninvited into my dressing room, I was mis-stepping into my underwear, damp from a hurried toweling-off. She stared at my body as I fumbled with leg holes.

"What do you think, Saint Theresa?" Irene always called me that. "I heard that our star player did it with black boys when she was at Sacred Heart."

Irene's mouth stayed open in a question mark as she surveyed my nakedness. I pulled on my jeans before answering. Somehow Irene always asked you questions that made you a jerk for just thinking about answering them. Her eyes traveled from my (now covered) thighs to my bare breasts. The stall was too small for me to go anyplace, so I stood there growing red, trying to come up with an answer I could live with. Irene was discovering that I had the biggest breasts on the team.

"Jesus Fucking Christ you've got big tits," Irene said. "Hey,

Frances! Maura! Did you realize what big fucking tits Saint Theresa has?" A small crowd gathered. My dad says that people like Irene are a form of penance.

Our first game was against Irene's alma mater, Perpetual Faith. We all were quiet on the bus ride over except Irene; she gave us a pregame scouting report on her old teammates. We learned what everyone's shooting percentage was and who shaved her armpits.

When we climbed down off the bus at Perpetual Faith we could see the other team watching us, but we pretended not to. They were peering out of the small rectangular windows set high in the walls of the gym. We knew that they had to be on tiptoe, standing on top of the bleachers; we knew because we did the same thing when the teams came to play us at Immaculata. I could picture their stretched arches as they leaned against the glass. They were sizing us up, gauging their strength, laughing at the shrimpy girls, worrying about the tall ones.

Sr. Bernadette had told us to look at the back of the head of the girl in front of us as we filed into the gym. Kate led the processional, followed immediately by Irene. Perpetual Faith's players were shooting when we entered, spread out in a fan underneath the basket. Most of them knew Kate by sight, having lost to her in the past. You could see them pulling aside the new players to explain.

"No, no, the tallest girl's the point guard. The other one, the next-to-tallest, she plays center. Watch out for the guard, that's Kate Malone."

I was self-conscious, not being the tallest and playing center. I knew I got the job because I was tall enough and because busing had brought us only forwards and guards. I would have been happier hiding out as a forward; I would have felt less responsible. One of the Gallagher twins could have played center, they were good enough, they were better than me. But Peggy and Pat had played as forwards together all their lives. Choosing one as center over the other would have disturbed their equilibrium.

I wished I was a star center, the way Kate would have been. Lots of people thought that using her as a guard was a waste. But Sr. Bernadette knew that if Kate played center, Irene would be point guard, which meant that nobody but Irene (least of all Kate) would touch the ball.

My biggest shortcoming was that I wasn't aggressive enough, wasn't mean. I was taller than most of the centers I played, and I regularly got good position. I was a decent rebounder, although I've never been a great jumper, and frequently got outjumped by some little but elastic girls. Offensively I was a nightmare. No guts. Most of my opportunities to score came from one-on-one matchups: me versus the other center in the middle of the key, smack underneath the basket. I was easily intimidated. If a girl played me close, if she bumped me or perhaps pushed me a little, just to let me know she was there, I would back right off. I would pass back out of the key, move the ball farther away from the basket. I was exasperating, really. Irene said so, right to my face, at practice. I guess I sabotaged a lot of good plays that way, by panicking.

I got constant advice from my teammates and Sr. Bernadette about posting-up, which is hoopster language for these one-on-one battles I kept avoiding. I got advice about staying firm, and wanting it bad enough, and going straight up or going up strong, and even mixing it up with the big girls. But it was useless; the language alone confused me. Mixing what up? With whom? People assumed I couldn't post-up because I was afraid of the other girl, afraid she would hurt or humiliate me. But it wasn't true.

I played the entire first quarter on the verge of puking, praying no one would pass me the ball. Defensively, I was solid enough: mostly I just stood there and let girls run into me. Irene and Kate shot from everywhere. Swish, swish, swish, went the ball through the hoop. I didn't come close to scoring until the second half, when they substituted in a new center.

Kate and Irene had brought the ball up, and were weaving in and out of the key. I was directly underneath the basket, hands up, my back to the other center. She looked familiar, but I couldn't quite place her. I heard nothing but the sound of my own heartbeat and breathing. Sr. Bernadette waved wildly from the sidelines and I could see her mouthing directions. A play and then several plays unfolded around me. I tried to stay focused on the ball. My opponent and I do-si-doed for position. Finally, I heard a sound that didn't belong to me: the chink chink of Mary Jude McGlaughlin's cross and Virgin medallion hitting against each other.

Mary Jude was a friend of my cousin Anne, and from what Anne used to tell me, she was shy, devout, not overly intellectual, extremely sweet, and oppressively pretty. She had been warming the bench for Perpetual Faith for three years, and had scored twice during brief cameos, once for the opposing team. Mary Jude touched my soaked back lightly, just above my hip, with the tips of three fingers on her right hand. Her breathing was soft and even, and although I couldn't see her face, I knew she was smiling: Mary Jude never didn't smile.

I sighed. Here it was again. How could I possibly compete against such goodness? How could I fake left, all the while knowing that I would be moving to my right, digging my shoulder into Mary Jude as I pivoted, and lightly pushing the ball into the basket? How could I leave her standing there, as people had so often left me, mouth agape, embarrassed, wondering what had just happened? How could I press my advantage knowing the punishment she would take from her teammates, punishment I knew only too well? Worst of all, Mary Jude would smile through it all. This registered as sin to me. Something I would have to purge from my soul in order to receive Communion next Sunday. Something, if left unattended, I would burn in hell for. So I didn't.

When the ball finally came to me, I was a knot of anxiety. I turned and faced Mary Jude. I held the ball high, above her head, and discovered I was right about her smile. She beamed at me. I smiled back. She had huge brown eyes. In the half second before I was going to pass the ball back to Kate, one of Mary Jude's teammates whacked the ball out of my hands and into the hands of their point guard. They scored before I turned around.

Irene was all over me.

"Jesus Fucking Christ, what was that? You plan to just give them the ball all day? Whose side are you on anyway?"

I blanched. The one legitimate basket Mary Jude had scored in the last three years was against me: I let her. It was as if I had no choice: it meant so much to her. I was terrified that Irene had figured it out; that she would tell about Mary Jude and the others like her. And there were others. Lots of others. I guess I knew the other centers wanted to win as much as I did, and I couldn't stand the thought of taking that away from them. It wasn't that I liked to lose; I hated to lose. But I guess I hated making other people lose worse. And besides, I was used to it.

I knew that this weakness was ten times worse than plain cowardice. I was My Own Worst Enemy. And now, potentially, the team's.

We won anyway. The first in an endless season of wins. We beat Perpetual Faith 59 to 36. Kate scored 23 points; Irene hit for 19. The team was ecstatic. Sr. Bernadette lectured us on the bus on the way home. I sat as far away from Irene as possible. Sr. Bernadette crouched in the aisle between the seats, pivoting left and right, facing each of us directly as she spoke. Sr. Bernadette had a custom of grabbing your shoulder or your knee or whatever was handy when she talked to you, so she was impossible to ignore. That day on the bus she got so close to me I could feel her breath on my face. I didn't hear a word she said, but I remember how she looked up close. Her hair was damp and limp from all the perspiring she had done during our game, her face glistened and the muscles on her neck stood out. Her black eyes were as black as her missing habit, and luminous.

Usually I hated the bus rides. If I could have, I would have sat right by Kate, who took the seat directly behind the bus driver and across the aisle from Sr. Bernadette. I was dying to be included in their conversations, to listen to Kate talk basketball, and to be on the receiving end of Sr. Bernadette's intensity. They sat at a slight angle to each other so that their knees touched, and Kate held the playbook on her lap. Sr. Bernadette gestured from the book to the air in front of them, with one hand going back periodically to Kate's shoulder to confirm her understanding. Kate stared closely at the invisible drawings in the air between them.

Irene occupied the very last bus seat by the emergency exit; the rest of us were staggered in the seats just before her. The cooler you were the farther back you sat and the closer to Irene you positioned yourself. I sat alone, as far away from Irene as I could get without leaving the group entirely. She talked nonstop about Kate. My ears burned red as I slumped forward in my seat pretending not to hear her, pretending to read the book in my lap, stealing glances at the front of the bus.

But I was, I knew, as guilty as Irene. Like her, I was obsessed with Kate. I wanted to know everything: what her family was like, why she kept changing schools, where she learned to play so well, whether she liked us, whether she liked me. In retrospect, I was infatuated with her, and it was my first big, stomach-wrenching infatuation. But I didn't know to call it that. I didn't even know enough to be embarrassed. Although, thank God, I knew enough to keep it from Irene.

I listened very closely to the horrible things Irene said. Each day she had a new story explaining Kate. Kate was on drugs; she was a kleptomaniac; her mother was a prostitute; her family was on welfare; they were really Protestant Irish; her father was a Jew; Kate was on the Pill; and, the worst possible slander for our immaculate ears, she had had two abortions. Everyone knew that Kate lived alone with her mother, and this in itself was extremely suspect. Some kids at Immaculata had as many as ten brothers and sisters; most of us had at least four. I had never met an only child; Sr. Agnes said they were sins. And Catholic families were not families without fathers.

If Kate knew about the rumors Irene spread, she never let on. Kate rarely spoke. She had no friends on the team, or at Immaculata, as far as I could tell. When Kate spoke it was b-ball talk. At practice she doubled as Sr. Bernadette's assistant coach, showing us moves and illustrating plays. One week Kate was assigned to demonstrate posting-up to the centers and forwards. That Monday we gathered around her underneath one basket, while Sr. Bernadette hollered at the guards at the opposite end of the court.

"First you have to find out where you are. Establish some territory. Take up some space. Back your butt into the other girl. See how much room she'll give you. Once you know where she is and how much she'll take, then you're ready. The first rule in posting-up is wanting it. Even if your hands are up like this for the ball, no guard's gonna pass it unless your face says you want it. The second rule is not thinking about it too much. Get ready and go. The longer you wait, the more likely it'll be taken away."

Was she talking just to me? Did she know? Had Irene told her something, or was I that transparent?

"Get out of your head, Theresa," Kate said on Tuesday. "I can see you thinking. Get out of your head."

"How?" I asked. "How can you see me thinking?" And to myself: *What can you see me thinking?*

"I just can." She shrugged. "And if I can, so can they. So lose it, whatever it is."

I struggled to empty my face. I struggled to eliminate Mary Jude and the others from my consciousness.

"Well, you don't have to look like an idiot." Kate smiled at my vacant expression. The other girls laughed, and I was giddy with the attention. Emboldened, I asked her how come she knew so much about basketball.

"I don't really know," she said, completely serious. "It's like I was born knowing."

"Did your father teach you?" I ventured. "Or your brothers?" Heads turned; ears pricked expectantly.

She shook her head, No. Now her face emptied. End of conversation.

But I couldn't let it go. After practice, I followed her to her locker. She hadn't heard my footsteps over the noise of the girls taking showers, so she jumped when I said loudly into her left ear, "Uncles or cousins?"

"Uncles or cousins, what?" She looked angry.

I had never been this close to Kate, and now I saw the details of her face for the first time. Her skin was pale—red-head pale—and a pattern of soft brown freckles ran across the bridge of her nose and splashed onto her cheeks. Her eyes were clear blue. They widened with shock and anger as I persisted.

"Did your uncles or cousins teach you to play?"

"Why are you so anxious to know who taught me what? Maybe I taught myself. Maybe, like I said, I was born knowing. Maybe I couldn't help but learn. What's it to you?" She crossed her long arms in front of her chest and grew two inches. Her thin Irish lips pursed.

"I was just curious. Thought maybe if I knew what you did to get so good, I could learn a little faster. You know." Sweat collected on my eyelids.

"Look, lemme give you a tip, save you some time. The thing you need to do more than anything else is be in your body. I've seen it before. Lots of girls play in their heads. Get back here." One of her extraordinary arms flashed out and smacked me in the roundest part of my belly. The spot she touched burned, and I could feel little waves of heat fan out until my fingertips were warm. I knew the color was draining from my face. I nodded and bent forward a little, in an unintentional bow, and got stuck there. I tried to smile my thanks, but I couldn't move my muscles the way I wanted. Finally, I just backed away. We didn't speak again until Friday.

"Terry, come here."

Terry? No one called me Terry. It was always Theresa. I looked behind me; perhaps there was a new girl I didn't know.

"Yes, you, Terry. Come here. Come guard me."

We had had a week of posting-up lessons—we had practiced both offensive and defensive positions—and it was time to show Sr. Bernadette what we had learned. I couldn't move.

"Quit stalling, Terry. Get over here."

Terry. I said it over to myself. Kate had a name for me.

Slowly, anxiously, I got in position behind her. She grew taller and wider until I could see nothing but her muscled back and clump of braided hair. All week I had practiced against the Gallaghers and lost. How could I possibly defend against Kate?

She inched me back toward the basket with her butt. Her shoulders twisted left, then right, then left again. Finally Kate stepped away from me, turned, and shot. When I could at last see the ball, I started moving toward it, straight up into the air. My shoulder left its socket, released my arm, which floated up to touch the ball, and returned. Before I knew it, we were all three back on the ground.

"Not bad, Terry. Not bad at all." Kate looked surprised, but not displeased. "Now just stay there." She slapped one arm onto my shoulder, retrieved the ball with her free hand, and pumped it into my stomach. "Don't think about what you did, just stay here. In your body."

But I was already out, thinking about my new name, afraid of what I'd just done.


As we won more and more, I grew increasingly frustrated with my inability to score. I wanted to be part of the team in a way that I wasn't. I wanted to slap hands with everyone, triumphant, after an especially tough basket. Or, more truthfully, I wanted everyone to slap my hand, the way they slapped Kate's and Irene's. I wanted to be sought after. I wanted Kate to congratulate me in the same expressionless, monotone manner in which she congratulated Irene. I wanted the cool indifference of excellence.

So at the halfway point in the season, after we'd won twelve straight games, and we were looking like we couldn't lose, I began practicing on my own, mornings, before school. An hour and a half of shooting and dribbling (I set up those fluorescent orange cones and did figure eights around them) every day. I got a little better and a lot bored. Playing alone had its limitations; it's one thing to shoot from eight feet out, it's another thing to shoot from anywhere with someone's hand in your face. And I had no one to post-up against. So I started looking for a morning pickup game.

All the league stars played mornings. Many of them played

nights, too, after regular practice or games, after dinner, under streetlights that had been rigged with hoops. I knew that Irene played early mornings in the school playground with a bunch of girls from Perpetual Faith. Girls-room girls. Smokers. They all wore eye shadow that matched their sweatpants and tons of St. Christopher medals and gold crosses that were constantly being tucked into ironed, white tee shirts. Irene was the best athlete there, and she tenaciously maintained possession of the ball, so after a few wasted efforts I decided to try a boys' game. I went to several boys' Catholic school playgrounds and found as many games. It didn't work. I realized that a girl's ability was always a problem for boys. If I wasn't as good as they were, they humiliated me by never passing me the ball; if I was as good, they humiliated me by never passing me the ball. Only girls who were as talented as Kate could play with boys without humiliation. Finally, I got up the courage to ask Sr. Bernadette. I tapped on the bubble glass of her office door one day after practice, after everyone had gone.

"Come in," she hollered, and swiveled in her chair. The office was warm and smelled of leather from balls and gloves and cleats. I stood with my hands behind my back, one hand still on the doorknob.

"What's up, Theresa?" She smiled. She looked even smaller sitting down; her feet swung an inch above the ground.

"I, umm, I was wondering if you, umm, knew of a game I could play in mornings. Other than Irene's game." I turned the knob in my hand. It was slippery.

"What about my game?" she offered immediately.

"What about your game?" I was confused.

"My game." Sr. Bernadette stood up and jammed her hands in her sweatpants pockets.

"You coach a game? I'm looking for a pickup game, not another team." I leaned back into the door.

"No, I play in a game. A pickup game." She was still smiling.

"You play in a pickup game?" I didn't know nuns could do that. After all she had played in college before she took her vows.

"Theresa, what's the problem? Am I not being clear? I can't imagine being any more clear, really." Sr. Bernadette's smile waned and she seemed a little exasperated.

"No. It's just that, what do you mean, a game?"

"Jesus. I mean I play in a morning pickup game and would you like to play with us?"

For Christ's sake, I had made a nun swear. I opened the office door and took a half step out. "Well, yes, I mean, are you sure it's OK?"

"It's OK," Sr. Bernadette sighed. "Where are you going?"

"Then OK. All right. See you there. Where is it?" I was outside her office now. Only my head stuck into the warmth.

"Dorchester." Sr. Bernadette stepped toward me.

"Dorchester. OK. No problem. See you then. Tomorrow OK?" I closed the door. Then opened it. "How do I get there?"

Sr. Bernadette laughed and sat back down. "You can catch the bus on Randolph Avenue, right in front of Immaculata."

"No problem," I lied and shut her door for good. I couldn't believe it! Sr. Bernadette invited me to her personal game. Her very own private game. I floated home. Maybe now I could sit in the school bus with her and Kate. Maybe now I would be protected from Irene.

The next morning I had to take two different buses to get there, and I had to lie to my parents about where I was going. Dorchester was off-limits.

. . .

I jumped off the bus three blocks too soon. My stomach knotted. It was a big, public school playground with several hoops. A handful of men played at the near corner. I stood by the fence in front of them, hidden by their moving bodies. I could see Sr. Bernadette and her friends warming up at the far end of the concrete park. I had imagined the way they might look several times: last night I dreamed that they played in full habits. My mind pictured every possible combination of athlete and cleric on the court. But I never guessed they would be a mixed group, even in Dorchester. I didn't know any black people, none of my friends knew any black people, so I hadn't imagined them in Sr. Bernadette's basketball game. I waited for everyone to start playing before I walked over.

Kate was there! I gasped at the sight of her, exhilarated and disappointed. Sr. Bernadette had invited another person from our team to share in her private life. I was not so special after all. I wondered how long they had been playing together, and if they had become friends. The knot in my stomach tightened.

There were ten women playing ball, including Kate and Bernie—which is what they called Sr. Bernadette. Two more women sat next to me on a green wooden bench that was rooted into the cement a few feet behind one of the hoops. I was sweating so much that my thighs slid off the bench and little pieces of green paint stuck to me when I stood up. The women at my side watched the game closely, calling out encouragements.

The first play I witnessed was a court-length pass to Kate, who was waiting underneath the basket. It took three seconds. They tried the exact same thing next possession but someone on the other team leapt into the air and stole away the play. I was out of breath just watching them.

They fought hard for rebounds and loose balls, and sometimes knocked each other down. One woman got roughed up three times in three consecutive plays. She was a forward and a very aggressive rebounder. She had the same coloring as Sr. Bernadette; another Italian I guessed. Her dark hair stood out every which way. Each time she hit the cement, whoever knocked her down helped her up. By the third fall everyone was laughing. She even smiled, although you could see she was hurt. Someone said it was a good thing she had so much padding, and they all laughed louder. The well-padded woman walked stiffly around the court, rubbing her behind. The others stopped to catch their breath, bending completely over, resting their hands on their knees so that their elbows jutted out and made shelves of their arms. Everyone's tee shirt was stuck to them.

After a minute or two, one of the point guards approached the injured forward and spoke to her. She massaged the woman's butt like it was her shoulder or something. They walked slowly over to the bench. We all stood up.

"Sub," said the guard, looking at me. "We need a forward."

The injured player lay out flat on the ground in front of the bench. She brought one knee up to her chest and held it there tightly. Her sore cheek lifted off the ground. One of the women who had been calling encouragements hustled onto the court.

"You sure look like a forward." The guard shrugged, letting her eyes travel up and down my full length. I felt that same funny heat wave I felt when Kate touched my stomach that time after practice.

"Center," I whispered.

"No kidding?" She smiled. "You're gonna play against Katie?" She shook her head. "Aren't you the brave one. I'd be whispering that too, if I were you." She sped back to the game.

I hadn't even noticed that Kate was playing center. I wondered if it was because they needed a center, or because there were guards who played better than Kate. I had never seen a guard better than Kate, so I watched the friendly woman play.

She reminded me of Irene—except that she was more friendly and she was black—they had the same build and the same jauntiness. She was everywhere at once. It was the kind of attitude you hate in people you don't like. It didn't bother me so much in her. She stole the ball five times in about eight tries.

I was used to seeing people steal a lot. Kate and Irene did it all the time, but against lesser players. This guard was something else again. The women she stole from were no pushovers; they could handle the ball, every single one of them. Where she edged them out was in speed and desire. Just a millisecond faster: she would attack the ball the instant after it was released from her opponent's hand, but before it touched the ground. She didn't grab the ball with both hands: that would have been too awkward, and too easy to defend against. She just tapped it lightly to one side and was gone. Like that. Desire so overwhelming you couldn't see it happening.

My dad had a drill test for desire. He said that desire was the most important thing in an athlete. Only he called it playing with heart. That's how he picked his starters: the five guys with the most heart played. At home, he would roll a basketball on the ground away from me and Tim. When it was a few feet out, he'd blow his coach's whistle and we'd lunge for it. On the cement driveway. We'd dive and grovel and kick for the ball. That was what I thought desire looked like. Desperation and skinned knees. I had trouble recognizing the smiling guard's desire: desire that left no room for alternatives. Desire that brought pleasure.

She was having a great time. Everyone was.

They were a strange-looking bunch. All different sizes and colors and abilities. I had expected them all to be the same.

They were not. The guard who reminded me of Irene was 5 foot, 4 inches tall. The other point guard was equally as small, but had legs the thickness of fire hydrants. She could touch the rim of the basket; she could alley-oop.

There was something peculiar about them. Something I couldn't quite name. They were women, not girls. For the first time I saw the difference. I realized that this was what made Kate stand out so at Immaculata; and that this, somehow, was why she had been thrown out of five Catholic schools. There was a sturdiness about them, a sense of commitment to life, like at one point they each had made a conscious decision to stay alive. They had made choices.

The longer I watched them play, the more inexplicable they seemed. I had never met women like them before. My mother, none of my friends' mothers, were like these women. Yet deep in my stomach they were familiar. I began to suspect I'd met them before and searched my brain for a memory. Nothing.

Kate was playing against a tall light-skinned black woman named Toni, who was as skinny as she was long. Kate seemed thickset by comparison. They spent most of their time about a hair's width apart, exchanging bruises. Fifteen minutes into the game, Kate elbowed her in the head, accidentally, while pulling down a rebound. It smarted. Toni staggered toward the bench, holding her head in her hands. "Sub," she hollered. Everyone else stopped moving.

"Toni, Toni, you okay? Talk to me, Toni." Kate's face was a mask of concern.

Toni turned to them, fingering the growing lump on her head. "You playing football out there, Malone, or what? No finesse, I tell you, Irish girls got no finesse."

Everyone smiled; a few giggles escaped. Kate tried not to laugh.

"Your concern is underwhelming, Malone, underwhelming." Toni resumed her stagger toward the bench and plowed directly into me. "Who are you? More Irish, I see. I need a sub. Go play against your cousin, will ya. You can beat up each other for a while." She shoved me onto the court.

Irene's look-alike came immediately to my rescue. She grabbed me by the shoulder.

"No problem, no problem. Maureen's here, and she's gonna take care of you. Mo's gonna help you out. What's your name, sweetheart? If you're gonna play with us, we need to know your name."

"Theres—Terry," I said, looking away from Kate. "Terry Meagher."

"Okay, Terry Meagher, it's two-one-two zone." She dragged me over to my new teammates. "You just stand in the middle with your arms up like this, okay?" Mo threw both of her arms into the air, her little body making a giant X. "Me and Bernie are your guards, Merril and Sam are behind you. Got that?" She stood frozen in a half–jumping jack. I nodded.

Everyone grunted hello, and Bernie—Sr. Bernadette— winked at me. Mo flung one arm over my shoulder and pulled me to her. She covered her mouth with her free hand and whispered loud enough for everyone to hear: "Don't let Katie get inside, okay? You're finished if she gets inside. Foul her if you have to."

I looked into Mo's eyes. Dark brown eyes in a dark brown face. Irene came to mind: how like Mo she was. How she would hate that. I thought about Mom and Dad. How grateful they were to have sent me to Catholic school, years ago, before it all started, before yellow school buses meant anything more than transportation. I pictured the busload of black second-graders that got stoned. I remembered the TV news clip my parents had kept me from watching; before they shut it off, I had recognized an Irish flag waving behind the mob of white parents.

Mo's left hand hung pink and brown over my shoulder, an inch from my face. I reached up and pressed it with both of my sweaty hands. "Cold hands." I smiled at Mo.

"They're always that way, even when I play." Mo looked directly at me.

"Cold hands, warm heart," I offered, and was instantly embarrassed. "It's an old Irish saying," I backtracked. What was I doing?

But Mo seemed charmed. "I like that. Cold hands, warm heart. Good for you. I like that. You're gonna do just fine. Well, let's go, Terry Meagher. And watch out for these cold-hearted women with hot shots." She laughed and shook her head.

The rest of the game seemed to go in slow motion. I knew it was faster than any other game I'd ever played in, but I could see every detail like it wasn't, like I was watching it under a magnifying glass.

I kept one eye on Kate, one eye on the ball, and one eye on Mo, who was never far from the ball. Then it happened. I was in the middle of the key, with Kate at my back. Mo brought the ball up and charged around me, into the key, making like she was going in for a lay-up. But instead of shooting, she dropped the ball back for me. Her move drew everyone with her, over to the right side of the key. Well, almost everyone. I was just left of center, with Kate between me and the basket.

So I did what Kate taught me. Fake right-left-right, turn, and up into the air. Kate was there, matching everything. A long, strong arm shot into the air and slapped the ball a second after it left my fingertips. We three thudded to the ground. The ball bounced hard, back into my hands. I held my breath. Kate was huge in front of me. Left-right-left, this time and up again, knees bent, arms stretched. Kate's arm grew longer than mine. She slammed the ball. We crashed down. People began murmuring encouragements. I heard my name. This time the ball dropped to Mo. She fired it back to me. I was shocked. She was closer to the basket than either Kate or me. Mo smiled and rolled her eyes up to the clouds. So I went up again, no fakes, just straight up into the air, Kate following.

She would beat me like this every time, I knew, so without ever having done it before, and a little off-balance, I hooked the ball. I had seen people do it before, mostly smaller players who were trying to get over big girls. Irene could hook, Sr. Bernadette could hook, and I had seen Mo do it once early that morning. But I myself had never tried it, not even in practice. It wasn't really a conscious decision, my right elbow just bent, all by itself, and let the ball go. It cleared Kate's fingers, smacked the backboard a little too hard, and fell into the hoop. This time we both landed on our butts.

From the ground, everything finally made sense. I knew what Kate meant by being in one's body: I was in mine. I looked up at the calves and thighs surrounding me. These women were in every inch of theirs. They seemed completely without fear: of their bodies, of each other, of their desires. I could see that they even liked their bodies, which is what at first seemed so peculiar. I had never met a woman who liked her own body.

I stayed on the ground, not wanting to get up. I knew that being in my body meant choosing myself. And choosing desire. So few women I knew had chosen themselves: Sr. Bernadette, Kate, and in her own evil way, Irene.

Sr. Bernadette walked over to Kate, who was still flat on her back, and extended both of her hands. Kate grabbed hold and Sr. Bernadette yanked her to her feet. Kate seemed about eight feet tall standing so close to Sr. Bernadette. They just looked at each other, and I could tell that they were, indeed, friends. But somehow it didn't bother me so much now.

Kate let go of Sr. Bernadette's hands and stepped over to me. She reached out one hand and pulled me up. She dusted my behind and shrugged, indifferent: "Nice move . . . Who taught you that?"

"No one," I said. "No one taught me that." And she nodded.

# POEM FOR MY YOUTH/
# POEM FOR YOUNG WOMEN

eloise klein healy

**M**y eyes sometimes bounce up quickly I look away seeing
you see me and seeing me and seeing me and not knowing
  what to cover
I cover everything even imagining someday when I'm older

my eyes will anticipate and pick up quick the ball scooting
across a hard infield and knowing what to focus I'll focus
everything my body will move to it with the logic of strength
and good equipment and I will plant my feet knowing the
  slight
slide before the grab and hold and there will be no mistake

about it, the throw and I'll follow through with everything
my legs know about direction and the tight fit of muscles to
  skin
to the speed of reacting and reacting right my quickness
is about youth but already I see it is not young.

# FROM *LADY LOBO*

## kristen garrett

The warm-ups ended with a flurry of slamma-jammas from both teams, both backboards rocking, each team trying to show they were bigger and stronger and meaner than the other, both teams with three wins in the week, knowing only one would finish the week with four wins. Both head coaches were at the scorer's table, pointing fingers, talking nonstop, working on the refs, wanting every call to go their way, working on each other, too, laying the mental groundwork in case they met again in the National Tournament at the end of the year.

The public address announcer said the CBS cameras were coming on the air and for everyone to make noise, but nothing changed because the noise was already deafening, in the hundred-decibel range, everyone screaming their heads off, the band pounding out Rocky Top.

Knoxville, Tennessee. In the mountains of east Tennessee. Fifty miles north of Chatsworth.

Home.

Thompson-Boling Arena was huge, seating almost twenty-five thousand. It was one of the new sanitary basketball arenas. It was sold out for the doubleheader.

When Casey was a kid it was a big treat, the biggest thrill

| 61

of her life, the times Dad and Mom took her to Knoxville to watch the Lady Vols play. She couldn't count the number of nights she'd lain in her bed, smiling and thinking about growing up and playing for the Lady Vols, wearing the Big Orange, playing in front of twenty-five thousand screaming fans. When she fell asleep she'd dream it was all true, she was wearing the Big Orange, hearing her name over the public address system, running through the corridor of players while the twenty-five thousand people screamed and the band played "Rocky Top."

All those thoughts and dreams had come true. She was playing in Thompson-Boling Arena, she was hearing twenty-five thousand people screaming, she would hear her name over the public address system, she would run through the corridor of players in an orange uniform.

But it wasn't Tennessee orange she was wearing.

"At guard, from Chatsworth, Tennessee, number three—"

She didn't hear anything else. The boos started and got louder and louder. She ran through the corridor of players, burst into the open, stood in the center of Thompson-Boling Arena, and the boos rained down on her like hailstones.

She didn't know where Dad was with his Camcorder or Mom with her wet eyes or the rest of her family and friends were sitting; she couldn't see them but she knew they could see her, could hear her getting booed like a dog. The only sign of friendship she could see was a big white poster board sign bouncing way up at the top of the arena, *We Love You, Case. Katie And A Twin Sandwich.* And her teammates. Muttering to themselves, angry looks on their faces.

She wanted to cry. She wasn't the local girl done good and come home. She was a traitor, instead. She wanted to scream at all twenty-five thousand people, "I would've picked Tennessee in a second over Tech, but Tennessee didn't want me. Tennessee didn't even come watch me play in high school.

Well, screw you! I would've picked Tennessee then, but I wouldn't now. I'm an Okie now!"

But she couldn't scream. Nobody would hear her. So she waved. And the booing got louder. Alysa trotted out, threw an arm around Casey's shoulders and rumbled, "I don't think these crackers like us, Lower Case. Ain't no big thing. I don't like them, either. Do you?"

Before the tip, the Tennessee players started slapping each other's hands, ignoring the hands the Tech players were offering, and shouting, "Their fighting game won't work here! If they try it we'll give it back to 'em!"

"Go on with your bad selves," Alysa rumbled, pulling her hand back, looking furious, an awe-inspiring sight. "We left our fighter at home. We don't need her for the likes of you."

Everyone got in each other's faces, waving arms and talking trash, seeing who would back down from the intimidation first, Alysa and Weatherly exchanging, "Muh-thuh-fuck yo-selves," with the Tennessee trees, everyone's eyes feverish, jazzed half-insane by the quality of the competition and the big crowd and the CBS cameras and the national audience.

The head ref shrieked her whistle and shouted, "I'll start this game by ejecting both first-teams if I have to!"

Everyone shut up and took their positions around the circle, tight-lipped and grim-faced.

The first three times Casey got her hands on the ball, the crowd taunted her, singsonging, "Ca-sey! Ca-sey! Ca-sey!" The first three times she got her hands on the ball, she squared to the basket and fired, ignoring everyone else, ignoring Coach Murphy's game plan, ignoring everything except wanting to score and score and score and shove the booing up everyone's butt.

Her first shot was an air-ball. Her second shot bounced off the front of the rim. Her third shot was another air-ball and the taunts turned to laughs. Tennessee converted all of her missed shots into easy baskets, the third one drawing Casey a hacking foul, a tomahawk job on one of the Lady Vols, committed from pure frustration.

"Cheap-shot bitch!" the Lady Vol shouted, picking herself up from the floor, rubbing her forehead where Casey's forearm had landed.

"The hell with you!" Casey shouted. "The hell with you and fuck you and fuck everything about this place!"

She was spitting fire, but she felt cold inside because she knew what was going to happen.

Coach Murphy benched her.

It was the most humiliating moment in Casey's life. Trotting off the court, everyone booing and laughing their heads off, everyone knowing she was getting benched for losing her grip, knowing herself she'd lost her grip and let the crowd get to her and rattle her. And all her family and friends watching.

Two minutes into the game: Lady Vols 8, Lady Lobos 0.

Casey sat at the far end of the bench, as far away from the people and TV cameras as she could get. As far away from Coach Murphy as she could get. She grabbed a towel and covered her face because her chin was trembling and she knew in a second her face would screw up and she'd start crying. She felt someone squatting in front of her, felt a hand on her knee, heard Coach Murphy's calm voice.

"Casey, look at me."

"I can't," Casey said. She'd dug a huge hole for the Lady Lobos, a hole they wouldn't be able to crawl out of. She'd let everybody down. Let all her teammates down.

"I understand," Coach Murphy said. "Composure, Casey." She walked away.

Casey got put back in ninety seconds later.

.   .   .

Casey was the first one showered and dressed. She grabbed her gym bag and left the locker room, going to the players' entrance where she could be alone except for one bored-looking security guard standing around. She sat on a bench and thought of all the dreams, all the wants, all the needs. Childish dreams and wants and needs. All coming down to one shot.

One simple shot.

A shot she'd made on countless playgrounds, in countless gyms, in countless practices, in countless games. A shot she'd nailed hundreds of times in her parents' driveway on cool autumn afternoons, shooting at the regulation hoop Dad had put up, dribbling and nailing the same shot over and over again until it got dark and cold and Mom opened the front door and called for her to come inside and drink some hot chocolate and get warm.

That's what it's all about, babe. Choking in clutch plays. Succumbing to your puckered butt. Major-college ball.

A missed ten-footer.

Lady Vols 81, Lady Lobos 80.

Memories of watching a ten-foot shot bounce off the front of the rim, dropping to her knees, pounding the floor with her fists, seeing the Lady Vols mobbing each other at half-court, calm-looking Coach Murphy walking to the Tennessee bench to shake hands with the Lady Vols' coach, remembering where she was, remembering the booing, the TV cameras, standing, fighting through her teammates trying to console her, screaming, "Choke-choke-choke!" and running into the locker room, "The Good-Bye Song" echoing in her head no matter how tightly she pressed her hands against her ears . . .

Casey looked out the window at the parking lot. The team bus was sitting outside the door in the twilight, parking lights on, luggage compartments open, smoke puffing from the tail pipe.

There were two girls standing just outside the door. One looked about ten years old, the other twelve or thirteen. They were wearing heavy coats and ski caps, breath steaming from their mouths, stomping their feet to keep warm, clutching game programs and pens in their mittened hands. Two adults, a man and a woman, huddled together in the background, talking between themselves, hands jammed in their coat pockets.

Casey remembered the times Dad and Mom brought her to Lady Vols games, how they'd waited patiently while she stood outside the players' entrance, hoping to get an autograph or a glimpse of one of her heroines. Autographs that were meaningless now, she'd misplaced them years ago. Or lost them. Or thrown them away.

She stepped to the door and opened it. "I don't know when the Tennessee players will come out. Do you want to come in and wait?"

"You're Casey," one of the girls breathed. "We're waiting to see you. We're from Chatsworth."

"Want to come in and I'll autograph your programs?"

The girls looked at their parents. "Please, Daddy," one said. "Can we? Please?"

The father nodded. Casey signed their programs. Then she opened her gym bag and gave each of the girls a pair of orange and black sweatbands and a roll of athletic tape. One of the girls said, "Is this real tape? Just like the players use?"

Casey nodded. "It's J-and-J. The same as I use."

"You're famous," one of the girls said. "We read about you in the paper all the time. The paper says you play on a mean team, but I don't believe it. I'm a guard just like you."

"I'm not," the other girl said. "I'm a center because I'm tall."

"You're not tall," the first girl said. "You're just growing faster than everyone else."

They left, walking across the parking lot, walking faster and faster until they started running, holding their hands out to show their parents what they'd gotten. Casey went outside, threw her gym bag into the luggage compartment, and got on the bus. She sat in the very back, turning her back and staring out the window at the mountains and bare trees and thinking about her childish wants and needs and dreams.

# SPORTS FIELD

judith wright

Naked all night the field
breathed its dew until
the great gold ball of day
sprang up from the dark hill.

Now as the children come
the field and they are met.
Their day is measured and marked,
its lanes and tapes are set;

and the children gilt by the sun
shoulder one another;
crouch at the marks to run,
and spring, and run together—

the children pledged and matched,
and built to win or lose,
who grow, while no one watches,
the selves in their sidelong eyes.

The watchers love them in vain.
What's real here is the field,
the starter's gun, the lane,
the ball dropped or held;

and set towards the future
they run like running water,
for only the pride of winning,
the pain the losers suffer,

till the day's great golden ball
that no one ever catches,
drops; and at its fall
runners and watchers

pick up their pride and pain
won out of the measured field
and turn away again
while the star-dewed night comes cold.

# FROM *ALL THE WAY HOME*

1984

ellen cooney

**A**vis sighed heavily. She was nearly fifty years old, a woman with grown children, and she was just as much at odds with herself and her moods as if she were still fifteen. They came out of the blue, no easier to control than the weather: it couldn't be; it mustn't be, that in the space of not more than five or ten minutes she was catapulted from the heights of pleasure to the bottom of despair, or was that in itself just exaggeration, one more intemperate mood, another emotion that altered not only the way she leaned back sadly against the door of the car, but the way she looked at her husband, her sister sitting quietly in the back seat, the houses they were driving past, the trees, the telephone poles, the blue uncloudy sky that even as it arched and stretched, serene and passive, seemed to be bouncing right back in her face her own leaden ponderous immense sense of—sense of what? She could not even say for herself what it was, this troubled mood that knit her bones together and pushed up against the back of her eyes: she could only grit her teeth and say to herself that she was almost fifty years old, she was practically an old woman, she was ripping apart a perfectly ordinary Saturday afternoon when there was shopping to do, and sheets to wash, and a house to air, and for what?

She was an old woman dressed up for a game of softball. In itself a thing of ridicule, it was all the more awful when she considered how she had let herself forget herself: surely she could not have been in her right mind earlier that day when she went for a run along the river, when her blood was steaming and elation ran just behind her like a frantic puppy nipping at her heels; no, she had not been herself at all since the day Augusta Cabrini came barging into her life with her scarred face and her fiery eyes and the quiet commanding dignified way she came into a room, leaning on her cane with an air not of injury but of strength; and putting out her hand to meet the hand that was offered, Avis took one long look at the big broad girl and immediately fell under a spell. Within three days she had stopped eating except at mealtimes. In a week she was shutting all the window shades in her house and turning on the record player to play her children's records: she was exercising, she was doing sit-ups and push-ups and stretches and bends; she was running in place as the furniture shook and jumping rope as the plates rattled in the cabinets, and in the morning when she awakened in stiffness and pain she heaved herself out of bed to get up and do it again.

It was too, too foolish. Her children mocked her and her husband had nothing for her but badly hidden pity. Oh, they had tried to humor her all along: Angela telephoned weekly with recipes she took from ladies' magazines; Mary-Susan sent home piles of rhythm-heavy records she collected from the girls in her dorm; the boys visited regularly to supervise her workouts, full of advice on isometrics and the proper way to pump half her weight in iron. But behind her back they shook their heads and clucked their tongues, fleeing to their own lives to tell their friends how comical it was, how pathetic and even repugnant it was to have for a mother a woman who spent all her free time learning how to whack a ball with a bat and run around three bases without dropping dead from exhaustion.

Leo could say all he liked about how happy the whole business made him; but the truth was that Leo was every bit as embarrassed as if his wife suddenly took up a new religion or dyed her hair bright orange: Avis was sure of it.

As the car pulled up to the high school and swerved toward the parking lot where the band was already in formation, Avis slid down a bit lower in her seat, vowing to herself that no power on earth could make her get out of the car. Leo put on the brakes. His door sprang open. Birdey leaned forward to check her lipstick in the rearview mirror. Leo got out of the car to look at the band. Birdey slipped out after him, calling her sister to follow.

"In a minute," said Avis. She locked both doors against the wild, colorful scene outside. Women in purple and white were greeting each other as their children ran in and out of the rows of the band. Photographers waved cameras, and a man with a whistle around his neck waved his arms. Rollie the Fist wandered about with his tape recorder. The Little League All-Stars and the Girl Scouts and the Ivan A. Tolland Memorial Baton Corps shoved each other into lines that rippled and swayed in long trembling fingers of sunlight; and as the clamor of the crowd and the booms of the drums and the bleats of the horns and the toots of the man with the whistle blended all together in one stunning splash of sound that drove Avis flat down on the seat with her hands to her ears, there came a polite but insistent rapping against the window. She looked up.

They were flushed and out of breath but they were smiling. Her two daughters, arm in arm, peered into the car and gestured for her to roll down the window. She knew what would come next. Their consciences uneasy, they had followed her here to say that they loved her but they wanted her to turn the car around and go back home. Angela was about to say: After all, Mother, you're nearly fifty!

But here was Mary-Susan, poking her head in with a kiss and a hug around her mother's neck. And here was Angela, holding out in her open palm a small silver medal attached to a safety pin. The medal bore the face and torso of the Virgin Mary. Her hands were upon her heart. Her eyes were turned upward. Angela turned it over and Avis read the inscription. *Avis from June, Good Luck!*

"Mrs. Campbell stopped by while you were upstairs getting dressed," explained Angela. "In all the confusion, we forgot to tell you."

"Put it on, Mother," urged Mary-Susan. "Mrs. Campbell said to tell you she's proud of you."

"She *should* be," beamed Angela, adding softly that so were they all; and fixing it in place inside the neckline of her shirt, Avis had to pause a moment to let her eyes uncloud; and stepping out of the car, her spirits clacking back to life like engines she gathered up her cap and her cleats, gave her daughters a squeeze each, threw back her shoulders, and marched off to join the rest of her team.

# MORNING ATHLETES

1982

marge piercy

Most mornings we go running side by side
two women in mid-lives jogging, awkward
in our baggy improvisations, two
bundles of rejects from the thrift shop.
Men in their zippy outfits run in packs
on the road where we park, meet
like lovers on the wood's edge and walk
sedately around the corner out of sight
to our own hardened clay road, High Toss.
Slowly we shuffle, serious, panting
but talking as we trot, our old honorable
wounds in knee and back and ankle paining
us, short, fleshy, dark haired, Italian
and Jew, with our full breasts carefully
confined. We are rich earthy cooks
both of us and the flesh we are working
off was put on with grave pleasure. We
appreciate each other's cooking, each
other's art, photographer and poet, jogging
in the chill and wet and green, in the blaze
of young sun, talking over our work,

our plans, our men, our ideas, watching
each other like a pot that might boil dry
for that sign of too harsh fatigue.

It is not the running I love, thump
thump with my leaden feet that only
infrequently are winged and prancing,
but the light that glints off the cattails
as the wind furrows them, the rum cherries
reddening leaf and fruit, the way the pines
blacken the sunlight on their bristles,
the hawk circling, stooping, floating
low over beige grasses,
                              and your company
as we trot, two friendly dogs leaving
tracks in the sands. The geese call
on the river wandering lost in sedges
and we talk and pant, pant and talk
in the morning early and busy together.

# COMPETITION

mariah burton nelson

I like to swim naked
I like to swim fast
swimming next to you I swim faster
shed more layers of flesh
learn your rhythms as well as my own
Each time I breathe I see you
breathe
stroke
breathe
stroke
and see you again
You can tell by my stroke that I need you
you can tell by my stroke
by the way that I breathe
that I need your stroke, your breath
that to be my best I need you
swimming beside me

# OCTOBER 1968,
# MEXICO CITY
# (FROM *AQUAMARINE*)

1992

## carol anshaw

**F**or a few supersaturated moments, Jesse feels and sees and smells and hears everything. The crushing heat, the Mexican sky white with a flat sun, pressing like an iron against the roll of her shoulders. The rising scent of chlorine and baby oil and something that's not sweat exactly, but an aquatic analog, something swimmers give off in the last few minutes before an event, a jazzy mix of excitement and fear and wanting. The crowd, riled up as though they are going to swim this race themselves.

Except for her godmother, who sits in the stands, unruffled, unflapped—a midwestern Buddha, here by way of two days and a long night on a Trailways bus from Missouri. With her is Jesse's brother, bouncing a little in his seat, twiddling his hands like a haywire backup singer, a Temptation gone ka-flooey. There's so much else going on, though, that for once he draws no particular attention.

Down at pool level with Jesse is Bud Freeman, coach of the American women's team, a crew-cut fireplug several inches shorter than Jesse, at the moment casually peppering her arm with light jabs of his thick finger, reminding her that Marty Finch is a splash-out-and-die girl, not to worry about her in the first fifty meters. His mouth is so close to Jesse's face she can smell his breath, which is like oranges. She nods and tongues the insides of her goggles and looks over his shoulder at Marty, who is doing leg stretches against the next starting block, not looking at Jesse. Which is smart. Jesse shouldn't be looking at her either, not now.

Jesse stands next to the Lane 4 starting block. She's still nodding at whatever Bud is saying, although she has stopped listening, doesn't really need to. She has swum this race in her head every day since she was fourteen. For most of those three years' worth of days, her body has been through fifteen thousand meters, so it will know on its own precisely how to take these hundred. Today she will really just be going along with herself for the ride.

It's time to take to the blocks. In this instant, the wave she was riding—absorbing everything at once—crashes onto the shore of her self, and she whites out into a space at her dead center. She loses Bud, the crowd, the sun. All there is is her and the water stretching out in front of her, to be gotten through. Fifty meters up. Flip. Fifty meters back. A quick trip.

She stretches the strap of her goggles around the back of her head, lets it snap. Fiddles with the eye cups, tugs at the strap ends until she's sure she has a seal. She crouches and swings her arms behind her, then forward, just short of losing her balance. She's ready. She doesn't even need to see the starter to know he's raising the pistol. She can feel the event approaching, feel herself moving into it.

"Swimmers, take your marks." The metallic command comes through the public address horns, taking the event out of the dimension of not-happening, onto the plane of about-to-happen.

She hyperventilates to expand her lungs, flattens her soles against the roughed surface of the block. Now comes the critical moment, the one in which she needs to leave even herself behind and become purely what she can do, translate matter into energy, become velocity. In the hundreds of events she has swum on the way to this one, this split second in which she can see the race ahead completely, and see herself winning it, has given her an edge.

This time, though, the power of belief slips away, just a little. Just for the microslice of the second it takes for her to look over at Marty. Who does, for a flash instant, look back. But, through her goggles and then Marty's, and with the sun behind her blacking her out, Jesse can't read her face. She is still trying to decipher it, to pull some important message off it, still trying to link today with last night, to figure out the connection between those events and this one. While she is temporarily lost in this constellation of fear and exhilaration and squeezed hope, the starter's pistol, which she is supposed to respond to instinctively, as though it's inside her, goes off in some very faraway place. Taking her completely by surprise.

And so Jesse Austin leaps out, hangs suspended for a freeze-frame moment, and enters Olympic waters one tenth of a second later than she should. She can't curse the lapse. There's no time. The next minute is an aquamarine blur. The color shattered into a million wavy panes as the water prisms the sunlight that hits the pool bottom. Aquamarine and the deep blue of the wide stripe she follows down the center of the lane, tucking into her flip turn where the stripe dead-ends in a T. The touch of painted concrete against the balls of her feet as she pushes off. And then the last fifty. She knows she's swimming fast, maybe faster than she ever has. She feels an infinitesimal difference. It's as though the water has given in, is letting her through.

And then, there's the slick slap of tile on the palm of her hand as she finishes where she started. She comes up fast and flushed and eating air. She corkscrews out of the water, ripping off her goggles, looking around wildly for signs. To her left, in Lane 5, Marty has also touched. She's pulling off her cap with a rubbery squeak, bending back, her hair catching the water like white seagrass. Jesse watches this for a moment; it's a part of the too much happening all at once. She's still looking for the word to come down.

Then Bud is crouching on the rim of the pool just above her, shaking his head, holding up two fingers. She has come in second, taken the silver. Won something, but it's the loss that hits her first. She feels as though great weights are dragging her under. She looks over and watches Marty catch the good news from Ian Travers, the Australian coach. She has taken the gold. She's tossing her cap and goggles into the air and smiling with her whole body. And then she looks around and reaches outside the perimeter of her victory, over the lane markers to wrap an arm around Jesse's shoulders. It's a cross-chest carry of sorts, a gesture to bring Jesse up with her.

Amazingly, it works. Jesse can feel her spirit grabbing onto Marty's, and for this moment at least believes *they've* won, that together they've beat out the competition, that the two of them are laughing together in the hilarious ozone just above the plane of regular mortals. They go under, somersault, come up, and shoot out of the water, trailing arcs of spray behind them.

Jesse feels they have attained a great height, as though glory is a wide, flat place they will inhabit forever, rather than a sharp peak that will eventually slide them down another side, to ground level. But she isn't looking down now, only out, toward the limitless possibilities implicit in having attained this one.

She can feel their breezes rushing over her, lightly.

# FROM "CANDY BUTCHER"

1936

### fannie hurst

For the twenty years of her life, Geraldine Schmalz had awakened every morning in a small, wall-papered room in a packing-case house on an unpretty street in the township (of all places!) of Coney Island. And now, as the *Empress Eugenie* steamed into New York Harbor, a city of six million souls was waiting to greet this same Geraldine Schmalz . . .

Call it what you will—fate doing a handspring, destiny turning cartwheels—Geraldine, who up to six months ago had never seen her name in print except in her swimming club bulletin and on those tin plates which drop out of a penny-in-the-slot machine if you press the proper letters, was now seeing that name a headline on every front page as she steamed along the Brooklyn shore line of the city of her nativity, toward a metropolis about to smother her beneath a welcome of bracelets, shields, and ticker tape . . .

"Tell us, Miss Schmalz, what were your thoughts during the last ten minutes of your fourteen-and-one-half-hour swim?"

"Gentlemen, my child don't like to remember them."

"Not exactly that, Pops. You see, I really don't know. I think I had kind of lost track of time and space and distance and everything except—I guess just getting there. Of course I knew that I wanted terribly to make it. But it wasn't as if I knew it with my mind. Sort of with my pain, if you know what I mean. I was just something churning and pushing and shoving my way through that great big Channel."

"Great! Go on."

"I—oh—I've tried to tell. The reporters over there too kept wanting to know. You see, it was just sort of an accident that I ever even got the chance to qualify for the International Swim. I was just a pretty good amateur, having lived at Coney Island all my life, where my Pops has a business. The Channel-swim part of it didn't enter my head, until I got over there and saw swimmers without my endurance or record trying it."

"Tell them, daughter, how you felt the blood vessel burst in your eye and how you got water on the ear."

"Father has reference to this red spot you see in my eye. It's better now. Almost cleared."

"No, it is not yet clear. Open wide, daughter, and show it."

"I had been in the water about five hours, I guess it was, using every inch of all there was in me. A choppy sea was beginning to slow me more than I liked, but before I started I had said to Pops here, 'As long as I can see your old bald head, Pops, in the follow-up boat, I'm unbeatable.' "

"Just like that, she said it to me! 'Keep your old bald head in sight, Pops.' "

"Well, I'm doing a side stroke, my eye on Pops, and all of a sudden I can feel something go bang, like a small gun explosion, in my right eye. That's the red spot you see in the white, and the funny part of it is, coincidence I guess, that minute I felt the sea running into my right ear and— Gracious, what's that! Is it the ringing in my ears, or bells or whistles or what?"

"We're in!"

"Those are bells *and* whistles, and they're not in your ears, young lady. They are in your honor! Attaboy, keep to your stateroom, Miss Schmalz! They've got to throw cordons around that crowd down there. Look at that pier, will you? I'm an old ship news reporter, but this is history! Say, does this town like girls who swim channels!"

Really it was terrific. It was so terrific that the heart felt strained from its moorings precisely as on that last mile of Channel it had pulled and groaned and seemed to sweat like an exhausted rower who could not make shore.

At the base of the gangplank of the *S.S. Empress Eugenie*, a city, pressing to welcome Jerry Schmalz, blocked disembarkation so that finally police on mounts had to charge through the human blockade, clearing a precarious path.

Straight up through the narrow grand-canyon of lower Broadway, where a hundred times, as an undistinguished miss on undistinguished mission bent, she had hurried along as any pedestrian in a crowd, the cheering human phantasmagoria now followed the triumphal entry of Geraldine Schmalz.

Buildings were like monkey trees, alive with chattering faces. Buildings *were* monkey trees, incredibly agog with antics, confetti, and ticker tape.

"Attagirl, Jerry. Handed it to them, didn't you? Didya dance with the Prince of Wales? Where is the rosette he gave you? Show us how you showed them. It took an American girl to show them how to do it. Whoopee, there goes the gal who put the English Channel on the map. Whoopee, Jerry. We want Jerry—we wa-an-t Jer-ry!"

Bow right. Bow left. Bow center. Bow up. Bow down. Bow center.

There was clean going ahead, along a line whizzed open by the motorcycles! And the prancing of the mounts of the riding police kept back the bulging side lines. Bow right. Bow left . . .

Four high hats in the open car, and Pops' bald pate, and the slim, browned girl who had been hoisted to the back of the seat, where she kept herself balanced by one hand on Pops' bald pate. Bow right. Bow left. Bow . . .

The chattering of the monkey trees! Lunacy of the colored paper and the shouting and the tangling ticker tape through which they had to move slowly as it caught them across throat and eyes.

"Pops," she screamed, "can you believe it's us?"

And Pops, unable to hear a word through the bedlam, pushed with his great soft body against her knees as she sat perched behind him, and because her throat was contracted, she kissed him behind his ear, and left a wet mark.

It was such a strange time to keep remembering her mama, whom she had never known. But if only the bit of bone of her lying in her carefully remembered grave could know something of all this splendor which had had its beginnings in that unpretentious birth which had taken place twenty years before, in an upstairs room of a narrow packing-case of a house on a quite unpretty street in Coney Island.

"Mama," she could feel herself saying silently through the din, "this is your Geraldine. Just think of that, Mama, this is your Geraldine. Pops said to me, 'Jerry, you could beat them all.' And I knew what he meant and tried the cross-Channel swim. I never meant to when I left America. But Pops and I said to ourselves considering all my endurance swimming—well, anyway, here we are, Mama!"

City Hall! The wide steps covered with more massed humanity and loud speakers and news photographers and the Mayor of the City of New York standing bareheaded in the center of the bedlam, waiting!

# THE LADY PITCHER

1980

### cynthia macdonald

It is the last of the ninth, two down, bases loaded, seventh
Game of the Series and here she comes, walking
On water,
Promising miracles. What a relief
Pitcher she has been all year.
Will she win it all now or will this be the big bust which
She secures in wire and net beneath her uniform,
Wire and net like a double
Vision version
Of the sandlot homeplate backstop in Indiana where
She became known as Flameball Millie.

She rears back and fires from that cocked pistol, her arm.
Strike one.
Dom, the catcher, gives her the crossed fingers sign,
Air, but she shakes it off and waits for fire.
Strike two.
Then the old familiar cry, "Show them you got balls, Millie."
But she knows you should strike while the iron is hot
Even though the manager has fined her
Sixteen times for disobeying

The hard and fast one:
A ball after two strikes.
She shoots it out so fast
It draws
An orange stripe on that greensward.
Strike three.

In the locker room they hoist her up and pour champagne
All over her peach satin, lace-frilled robe.
She feels what she has felt before,
The flame of victory and being loved
Moves through her, but this time
It's the Series and the conflagration matches
The occasion.

In the off-season she dreams of victories and marriage,
Knowing she will have them and probably not it.
Men whisper, in wet moments of passion,
"My little Lowestoft," or, "My curvy Spode," and
They stroke her handle, but she is afraid that yielding means
Being filled with milk and put on
The shelf;
So she closes herself off,
Wisecracking.
When she is alone again she looks at the china skin
Of her body, the crazing, the cracks she put there
To make sure
She couldn't
Hold anything for long.

# REVENGE

ellen gilchrist

I t was the summer of the Broad Jump Pit.

The Broad Jump Pit, how shall I describe it! It was a bright orange rectangle in the middle of a green pasture. It was three feet deep, filled with river sand and sawdust. A real cinder track led up to it, ending where tall poles for pole-vaulting rose forever in the still Delta air.

I am looking through the old binoculars. I am watching Bunky coming at a run down the cinder path, pausing expertly at the jump-off line, then rising into the air, heels stretched far out in front of him, landing in the sawdust. Before the dust has settled Saint John comes running with the tape, calling out measurements in his high, excitable voice.

Next comes my thirteen-year-old brother, Dudley, coming at a brisk jog down the track, the pole-vaulting pole held lightly in his delicate hands, then vaulting, high into the sky. His skinny tanned legs make a last, desperate surge, and he is clear and over.

Think how it looked from my lonely exile atop the chicken house. I was ten years old, the only girl in a house full of cousins. There were six of us, shipped to the Delta for the summer, dumped on my grandmother right in the middle of a world war.

They built this wonder in answer to a V-Mail letter from my father in Europe. The war was going well, my father wrote, within a year the Allies would triumph over the forces of evil, the world would be at peace, and the Olympic torch would again be brought down from its mountain and carried to Zurich or Amsterdam or London or Mexico City, wherever free men lived and worshiped sports. My father had been a participant in an Olympic event when he was young.

Therefore, the letter continued, Dudley and Bunky and Philip and Saint John and Oliver were to begin training. The United States would need athletes now, not soldiers.

They were to train for broad jumping and pole-vaulting and discus throwing, for fifty-, one-hundred-, and four-hundred-yard dashes, for high and low hurdles. The letter included instructions for building the pit, for making pole-vaulting poles out of cane, and for converting ordinary sawhorses into hurdles. It ended with a page of tips for proper eating and admonished Dudley to take good care of me as I was my father's own dear sweet little girl.

The letter came one afternoon. Early the next morning they began construction. Around noon I wandered out to the pasture to see how they were coming along. I picked up a shovel.

"Put that down, Rhoda," Dudley said. "Don't bother us now. We're working."

"I know it," I said. "I'm going to help."

"No, you're not," Bunky said. "This is the Broad Jump Pit. We're starting our training."

"I'm going to do it too," I said. "I'm going to be in training."

"Get out of here now," Dudley said. "This is only for boys, Rhoda. This isn't a game."

"I'm going to dig it if I want to," I said, picking up a shovelful of dirt and throwing it on Philip. On second thought I picked up another shovelful and threw it on Bunky.

"Get out of here, Ratface," Philip yelled at me. "You German spy." He was referring to the initials on my Girl Scout uniform.

"You goddamn niggers," I yelled. "You niggers. I'm digging this if I want to and you can't stop me, you nasty niggers, you Japs, you Jews." I was throwing dirt on everyone now. Dudley grabbed the shovel and wrestled me to the ground. He held my arms down in the coarse grass and peered into my face.

"Rhoda, you're not having anything to do with this Broad Jump Pit. And if you set foot inside this pasture or come around here and touch anything we will break your legs and drown you in the bayou with a crowbar around your neck." He was twisting my leg until it creaked at the joints. "Do you get it, Rhoda? Do you understand me?"

"Let me up." I was screaming, my rage threatening to split open my skull. "Let me up, you goddamn nigger, you Jap, you spy. I'm telling Grannie and you're going to get the worst whipping of your life. And you better quit digging this hole for the horses to fall in. Let me up, let me up. Let me go."

"You've been ruining everything we've thought up all summer," Dudley said, "and you're not setting foot inside this pasture."

In the end they dragged me back to the house, and I ran screaming into the kitchen where Grannie and Calvin, the black man who did the cooking, tried to comfort me, feeding me pound cake and offering to let me help with the mayonnaise.

"You be a sweet girl, Rhoda," my grandmother said, "and this afternoon we'll go over to Eisenglas Plantation to play with Miss Ann Wentzel."

"I don't want to play with Miss Ann Wentzel," I screamed. "I hate Miss Ann Wentzel. She's fat and she calls me a Yankee. She said my socks were ugly."

"Why, Rhoda," my grandmother said. "I'm surprised at you. Miss Ann Wentzel is your own sweet friend. Her momma was your momma's roommate at All Saint's. How can you talk like that?"

"She's a nigger," I screamed. "She's a goddamned nigger German spy."

"Now it's coming. Here comes the temper," Calvin said, rolling his eyes back in their sockets to make me madder. I threw my second fit of the morning, beating my fists into a door frame. My grandmother seized me in soft arms. She led me to a bedroom where I sobbed myself to sleep in a sea of down pillows.


The construction went on for several weeks. As soon as they finished breakfast every morning they started out for the pasture. Wood had to be burned to make cinders, sawdust brought from the sawmill, sand hauled up from the riverbank by wheelbarrow.

When the pit was finished the savage training began. From my several vantage points I watched them. Up and down, up and down they ran, dove, flew, sprinted. Drenched with sweat they wrestled each other to the ground in bitter feuds over distances and times and fractions of inches.

Dudley was their self-appointed leader. He drove them like a demon. They began each morning by running around the edge of the pasture several times, then practicing their hurdles and dashes, then on to discus throwing and calisthenics. Then on to the Broad Jump Pit with its endless challenges.

They even pressed the old mare into service. Saint John was

from New Orleans and knew the British ambassador and was thinking of being a polo player. Up and down the pasture he drove the poor old creature, leaning far out of the saddle, swatting a basketball with my grandaddy's cane.

I spied on them from the swing that went out over the bayou, and from the roof of the chicken house, and sometimes from the pasture fence itself, calling out insults or attempts to make them jealous.

"Guess what," I would yell, "I'm going to town to the Chinaman's store." "Guess what, I'm getting to go to the beauty parlor." "Doctor Biggs says you're adopted."

They ignored me. At meals they sat together at one end of the table, making jokes about my temper and my red hair, opening their mouths so I could see their half-chewed food, burping loudly in my direction.

At night they pulled their cots together on the sleeping porch, plotting against me while I slept beneath my grandmother's window, listening to the soft assurance of her snoring.

I began to pray the Japs would win the war, would come marching into Issaquena County and take them prisoners, starving and torturing them, sticking bamboo splinters under their fingernails. I saw myself in the Japanese colonel's office, turning them in, writing their names down, myself being treated like an honored guest, drinking tea from tiny blue cups like the ones the Chinaman had in his store.

They would be outside, tied up with wire. There would be Dudley, begging for mercy. What good to him now his loyal gang, his photographic memory, his trick magnet dogs, his perfect pitch, his camp shorts, his Baby Brownie camera.

I prayed they would get polio, would be consigned forever to iron lungs. I put myself to sleep at night imagining their labored breathing, their five little wheelchairs lined up by the store as I drove by in my father's Packard, my arm around the jacket of his blue uniform, on my way to Hollywood for my screen test.

Meanwhile, I practiced dancing. My grandmother had a black housekeeper named Baby Doll who was a wonderful dancer. In the mornings I followed her around while she dusted, begging for dancing lessons. She was a big woman, as tall as a man, and gave off a dark rich smell, an unforgettable incense, a combination of Evening in Paris and the sweet perfume of the cabins.

Baby Doll wore bright skirts and on her blouses a pin that said REMEMBER, then a real pearl, then HARBOR. She was engaged to a sailor and was going to California to be rich as soon as the war was over.

I would put a stack of heavy, scratched records on the record player, and Baby Doll and I would dance through the parlors to the music of Glenn Miller or Guy Lombardo or Tommy Dorsey.

Sometimes I stood on a stool in front of the fireplace and made up lyrics while Baby Doll acted them out, moving lightly across the old dark rugs, turning and swooping and shaking and gliding.

Outside, the summer sun beat down on the Delta, beating down a million volts a minute, feeding the soybeans and cotton and clover, sucking Steele's Bayou up into the clouds, beating down on the road and the store, on the pecans and elms and magnolias, on the men at work in the fields, on the athletes at work in the pasture.

Inside, Baby Doll and I would be dancing. Or Guy Lombardo would be playing "Begin the Beguine" and I would be belting out lyrics.

*"Oh, let them begin . . . we don't care,*
*America all . . . ways does its share,*
*We'll be there with plenty of ammo,*
*Allies . . . don't ever despair . . ."*

Baby Doll thought I was a genius. If I was having an especially creative morning she would go running out to the kitchen and bring anyone she could find to hear me.

"Oh, let them begin any warrr . . ." I would be singing, tapping one foot against the fireplace tiles, waving my arms around like a conductor.

*"Uncle Sam will fight*
*for the underrr . . . doggg.*
*Never fear, Allies, never fear."*

A new record would drop. Baby Doll would swoop me into her fragrant arms, and we would break into an improvisation on Tommy Dorsey's "Boogie-Woogie."

But the Broad Jump Pit would not go away. It loomed in my dreams. If I walked to the store I had to pass the pasture. If I stood on the porch or looked out my grandmother's window, there it was, shimmering in the sunlight, constantly guarded by one of the Olympians.

Things went from bad to worse between me and Dudley. If we so much as passed each other in the hall a fight began. He would hold up his fists and dance around, trying to look like a fighter. When I came flailing at him he would reach underneath my arms and punch me in the stomach.

I considered poisoning him. There was a box of white powder in the toolshed with a skull and crossbones above the label.

Several times I took it down and held it in my hands, shuddering at the power it gave me. Only the thought of the electric chair kept me from using it.

Every day Dudley gathered his troops and headed out for the pasture. Every day my hatred grew and festered. Then, just about the time I could stand it no longer, a diversion occurred.

One afternoon about four o'clock an official-looking sedan clattered across the bridge and came roaring down the road to the house.

It was my cousin, Lauralee Manning, wearing her WAVE uniform and smoking Camels in an ivory holder. Lauralee had been widowed at the beginning of the war when her young husband crashed his Navy training plane into the Pacific.

Lauralee dried her tears, joined the WAVES, and went off to avenge his death. I had not seen this paragon since I was a small child, but I had memorized the photograph Miss Onnie Maud, who was Lauralee's mother, kept on her dresser. It was a photograph of Lauralee leaning against the rail of a destroyer.

Not that Lauralee ever went to sea on a destroyer. She was spending the war in Pensacola, Florida, being secretary to an admiral.

Now, out of a clear blue sky, here was Lauralee, home on leave with a two-carat diamond ring and the news that she was getting married.

"You might have called and given some warning," Miss Onnie Maud said, turning Lauralee into a mass of wrinkles with her embraces. "You could have softened the blow with a letter."

"Who's the groom?" my grandmother said. "I only hope he's not a pilot."

"Is he an admiral?" I said. "Or a colonel or a major or a commander?"

"My fiancé's not in uniform, Honey," Lauralee said. "He's in real estate. He runs the war-bond effort for the whole state of Florida. Last year he collected half a million dollars."

"In real estate!" Miss Onnie Maud said, gasping. "What religion is he?"

"He's Unitarian," she said. "His name is Donald Marcus. He's best friends with Admiral Semmes, that's how I met him. And he's coming a week from Saturday, and that's all the time we have to get ready for the wedding."

"Unitarian!" Miss Onnie Maud said. "I don't think I've ever met a Unitarian."

"Why isn't he in uniform?" I insisted.

"He has flat feet," Lauralee said gaily. "But you'll love him when you see him."

Later that afternoon Lauralee took me off by myself for a ride in the sedan.

"Your mother is my favorite cousin," she said, touching my face with gentle fingers. "You'll look just like her when you grow up and get your figure."

I moved closer, admiring the brass buttons on her starched uniform and the brisk way she shifted and braked and put in the clutch and accelerated.

We drove down the river road and out to the bootlegger's shack where Lauralee bought a pint of Jack Daniel's and two Cokes. She poured out half of her Coke, filled it with whiskey, and we roared off down the road with the radio playing.

We drove along in the lengthening day. Lauralee was chain-smoking, lighting one Camel after another, tossing the butts out the window, taking sips from her bourbon and Coke. I sat beside her, pretending to smoke a piece of rolled-up paper, making little noises into the mouth of my Coke bottle.

We drove up to a picnic spot on the levee and sat under a tree to look out at the river.

"I miss this old river," she said. "When I'm sad I dream about it licking the tops of the levees."

I didn't know what to say to that. To tell the truth I was afraid to say much of anything to Lauralee. She seemed so splendid. It was enough to be allowed to sit by her on the levee.

"Now, Rhoda," she said, "your mother was matron of honor in my wedding to Buddy, and I want you, her own little daughter, to be maid of honor in my second wedding."

I could hardly believe my ears! While I was trying to think of something to say to this wonderful news I saw that Lauralee was crying, great tears were forming in her blue eyes.

"Under this very tree is where Buddy and I got engaged," she said. Now the tears were really starting to roll, falling all over the front of her uniform. "He gave me my ring right where we're sitting."

"The maid of honor?" I said, patting her on the shoulder, trying to be of some comfort. "You really mean the maid of honor?"

"Now he's gone from the world," she continued, "and I'm marrying a wonderful man, but that doesn't make it any easier. Oh, Rhoda, they never even found his body, never even found his body."

I was patting her on the head now, afraid she would forget her offer in the midst of her sorrow.

"You mean I get to be the real maid of honor?"

"Oh, yes, Rhoda, Honey," she said. "The maid of honor, my only attendant." She blew her nose on a lace-trimmed handkerchief and sat up straighter, taking a drink from the Coke bottle.

"Not only that, but I have decided to let you pick out your own dress. We'll go to Greenville and you can try on every dress at Nell's and Blum's and you can have the one you like the most."

I threw my arms around her, burning with happiness, smelling her whiskey and Camels and the dark Tabu perfume that was her signature. Over her shoulder and through the low branches of the trees the afternoon sun was going down in an orgy of reds and blues and purples and violets, falling from sight, going all the way to China.

Let them keep their nasty Broad Jump Pit, I thought. Wait till they hear about this. Wait till they find out I'm maid of honor in a military wedding.

Finding the dress was another matter. Early the next morning Miss Onnie Maud and my grandmother and Lauralee and I set out for Greenville.

As we passed the pasture I hung out the back window making faces at the athletes. This time they only pretended to ignore me. They couldn't ignore this wedding. It was going to be in the parlor instead of the church so they wouldn't even get to be altar boys. They wouldn't get to light a candle.

"I don't know why you care what's going on in that pasture," my grandmother said. "Even if they let you play with them all it would do is make you a lot of ugly muscles."

"Then you'd have big old ugly arms like Weegie Toler," Miss Onnie Maud said. "Lauralee, you remember Weegie Toler, that was a swimmer. Her arms got so big no one would take her to a dance, much less marry her."

"Well, I don't want to get married anyway," I said. "I'm never getting married. I'm going to New York City and be a lawyer."

"Where does she get those ideas?" Miss Onnie Maud said.

"When you get older you'll want to get married," Lauralee said. "Look at how much fun you're having being in my wedding."

"Well, I'm never getting married," I said. "And I'm never

having any children. I'm going to New York and be a lawyer and save people from the electric chair."

"It's the movies," Miss Onnie Maud said. "They let her watch anything she likes in Indiana."

We walked into Nell's and Blum's Department Store and took up the largest dressing room. My grandmother and Miss Onnie Maud were seated on brocade chairs and every saleslady in the store came crowding around trying to get in on the wedding.

I refused to even consider the dresses they brought from the "girls'" department.

"I told her she could wear whatever she wanted," Lauralee said, "and I'm keeping my promise."

"Well, she's not wearing green satin or I'm not coming," my grandmother said, indicating the dress I had found on a rack and was clutching against me.

"At least let her try it on," Lauralee said. "Let her see for herself." She zipped me into the green satin. It came down to my ankles and fit around my midsection like a girdle, making my waist seem smaller than my stomach. I admired myself in the mirror. It was almost perfect. I looked exactly like a night-club singer.

"This one's fine," I said. "This is the one I want."

"It looks marvelous, Rhoda," Lauralee said, "but it's the wrong color for the wedding. Remember I'm wearing blue."

"I believe the child's color-blind," Miss Onnie Maud said. "It runs in her father's family."

"I am not color-blind," I said, reaching behind me and un-zipping the dress. "I have twenty-twenty vision."

"Let her try on some more," Lauralee said. "Let her try on everything in the store."

I proceeded to do just that, with the salesladies getting grumpier and grumpier. I tried on a gold gabardine dress with a rhinestone-studded cummerbund. I tried on a pink ballerina-length formal and a lavender voile tea dress and several silk suits. Somehow nothing looked right.

"Maybe we'll have to make her something," my grandmother said.

"But there's no time," Miss Onnie Maud said. "Besides first we'd have to find out what she wants. Rhoda, please tell us what you're looking for."

Their faces all turned to mine, waiting for an answer. But I didn't know the answer.

The dress I wanted was a secret. The dress I wanted was dark and tall and thin as a reed. There was a word for what I wanted, a word I had seen in magazines. But what was that word? I could not remember.

"I want something dark," I said at last. "Something dark and silky."

"Wait right there," the saleslady said. "Wait just a minute." Then, from out of a prewar storage closet she brought a black-watch plaid recital dress with spaghetti straps and a white piqué jacket. It was made of taffeta and rustled when I touched it. There was a label sewn into the collar of the jacket. *Little Miss Sophisticate*, it said. *Sophisticate*, that was the word I was seeking.

I put on the dress and stood triumphant in a sea of ladies and dresses and hangers.

"This is the dress," I said. "This is the dress I'm wearing."

"It's perfect," Lauralee said. "Start hemming it up. She'll be the prettiest maid of honor in the whole world."

All the way home I held the box on my lap thinking about how I would look in the dress. Wait till they see me like this, I was thinking. Wait till they see what I really look like.

I fell in love with the groom. The moment I laid eyes on him I forgot he was flat-footed. He arrived bearing gifts of music and perfume and candy, a warm dark-skinned man with eyes the color of walnuts.

He laughed out loud when he saw me, standing on the porch with my hands on my hips.

"This must be Rhoda," he exclaimed, "the famous red-haired maid of honor." He came running up the steps, gave me a slow, exciting hug, and presented me with a whole album of Xavier Cugat records. I had never owned a record of my own, much less an album.

Before the evening was over I put on a red formal I found in a trunk and did a South American dance for him to Xavier Cugat's "Poinciana." He said he had never seen anything like it in his whole life.

The wedding itself was a disappointment. No one came but the immediate family and there was no aisle to march down and the only music was Onnie Maud playing "Liebestraum."

Dudley and Philip and Saint John and Oliver and Bunky were dressed in long pants and white shirts and ties. They had fresh military crew cuts and looked like a nest of new birds, huddled together on the blue velvet sofa, trying to keep their hands to themselves, trying to figure out how to act at a wedding.

The elderly Episcopal priest read out the ceremony in a gravelly smoker's voice, ruining all the good parts by coughing. He was in a bad mood because Lauralee and Mr. Marcus hadn't found time to come to him for marriage instruction.

Still, I got to hold the bride's flowers while he gave her the ring and stood so close to her during the ceremony I could hear her breathing.

The reception was better. People came from all over the Delta. There were tables with candles set up around the porches and sprays of greenery in every corner. There were gentlemen sweating in linen suits and the record player playing every minute. In the back hall Calvin had set up a real professional bar with tall, permanently frosted glasses and ice and mint and lemons and every kind of whiskey and liqueur in the world.

I stood in the receiving line getting compliments on my dress, then wandered around the rooms eating cake and letting people hug me. After a while I got bored with that and went out to the back hall and began to fix myself a drink at the bar.

I took one of the frosted glasses and began filling it from different bottles, tasting as I went along. I used plenty of crème de menthe and soon had something that tasted heavenly. I filled the glass with crushed ice, added three straws, and went out to sit on the back steps and cool off.

I was feeling wonderful. A full moon was caught like a kite in the pecan trees across the river. I sipped along on my drink. Then, without planning it, I did something I had never dreamed of doing. I left the porch alone at night. Usually I was in terror of the dark. My grandmother had told me that alligators come out of the bayou to eat children who wander alone at night.

I walked out across the yard, the huge moon giving so much light I almost cast a shadow. When I was nearly to the water's edge I turned and looked back toward the house. It shimmered in the moonlight like a jukebox alive in a meadow, seemed to pulsate with music and laughter and people, beautiful and foreign, not a part of me.

I looked out at the water, then down the road to the pasture. The Broad Jump Pit! There it was, perfect and unguarded. Why had I never thought of doing this before?

I began to run toward the road. I ran as fast as my Mary Jane pumps would allow me. I pulled my dress up around my waist and climbed the fence in one motion, dropping lightly down on the other side. I was sweating heavily, alone with the moon and my wonderful courage.

I knew exactly what to do first. I picked up the pole and hoisted it over my head. It felt solid and balanced and alive. I hoisted it up and down a few times as I had seen Dudley do, getting the feel of it.

Then I laid it ceremoniously down on the ground, reached behind me, and unhooked the plaid formal. I left it lying in a heap on the ground. There I stood, in my cotton underpants, ready to take up pole-vaulting.

I lifted the pole and carried it back to the end of the cinder path. I ran slowly down the path, stuck the pole in the wooden cup, and attempted throwing my body into the air, using it as a lever.

Something was wrong. It was more difficult than it appeared from a distance. I tried again. Nothing happened. I sat down with the pole across my legs to think things over.

Then I remembered something I had watched Dudley doing through the binoculars. He measured down from the end of the pole with his fingers spread wide. That was it, I had to hold it closer to the end.

I tried it again. This time the pole lifted me several feet off the ground. My body sailed across the grass in a neat arc and I landed on my toes. I was a natural!

I do not know how long I was out there, running up and down the cinder path, thrusting my body further and further through space, tossing myself into the pit like a mussel shell thrown across the bayou.

At last I decided I was ready for the real test. I had to vault over a cane barrier. I examined the pegs on the wooden poles and chose one that came up to my shoulder.

I put the barrier pole in place, spit over my left shoulder, and marched back to the end of the path. Suck up your guts,

I told myself. It's only a pole. It won't get stuck in your stomach and tear out your insides. It won't kill you.

I stood at the end of the path eyeballing the barrier. Then, above the incessant racket of the crickets, I heard my name being called. Rhoda . . . the voices were calling. Rhoda . . . Rhoda . . . Rhoda . . . Rhoda.

I turned toward the house and saw them coming. Mr. Marcus and Dudley and Bunky and Calvin and Lauralee and what looked like half the wedding. They were climbing the fence, calling my name, and coming to get me. Rhoda . . . they called out. Where on earth have you been? What on earth are you doing?

I hoisted the pole up to my shoulders and began to run down the path, running into the light from the moon. I picked up speed, thrust the pole into the cup, and threw myself into the sky, into the still Delta night. I sailed up and was clear and over the barrier.

I let go of the pole and began my fall, which seemed to last a long, long time. It was like falling through clear water. I dropped into the sawdust and lay very still, waiting for them to reach me.

Sometimes I think whatever has happened since has been of no real interest to me.

# TO THROW LIKE A BOY

1992

nancy boutilier

**D**espite appropriate estrogen levels,
I learned at an early age
to throw like a boy.

When Billy Lester cried
for being chosen last
the other boys called him a girl.

As we grew older
our language grew richer.
"You woman," hissed Brad Seeley
when David Matsumura walked away from a fight.
I was better versed in cussing
than body parts by the time I was
singing the neighborhood slang.

"You pussy," I screamed at my brother
when he refused to play me one-on-one.
Although he had 6 inches and 40 pounds on me,
he cringed at the insult, accepted my challenge,
and I stood my ground when he drove to the hoop.
I don't remember slamming asphalt,

but I came to hearing the compliment
"Man, your sister sure has balls."

Such flattery ran dry
when I hit the age of Kotex.
Without words for rhythms
my body understood
I had to choose
between exile into womanhood
or their loudest praise of me,
inclusion as one of the guys.

Unsexing myself was easy at fourteen,
but fourteen lasts only one year
and the swelling of breasts
tingling between thighs
put me at war with my body.
Too much ambition, too little food—
going to every extreme to avoid being
without balls, a pussy, a woman.

# WHEN I AM 98

1996

carolyn kremers

When I am 98
I want to remember
this: how I ran
inside the old college gym building
over arrows,
from the locker room,
down the hallway,
past the ski team bulletin board,
around the corner,
past the ROTC classroom
and the military posters—
Be All You Can Be,
Army ROTC Got Me the Job—
past the indoor rifle range, up the stairs,
down the hallway, past the weight room,
around the corner with mirrors,
past the hockey banner
and the basketball banner
and the vigorous young women
playing volleyball,
past the free telephone in its booth,

and the other weight room,
down the stairs, back to

the locker room, around
and around, up and down
stairs, again, down hallways,
over arrows (2 orange cones:
CAUTION—Runners Ahead)
my hand waving
at friends, my shoulders
passing other runners,
legs and arms pumping blood
and oxygen, drinking
the stale indoor air
of Fairbanks in winter, the shorter
steps of someone behind
pushing me to run
harder, faster, longer
strides, 1 for each of his 2,
my heart pumping, pumping, a laugh
escaping as he says from behind,
"You're too fast," and I stay ahead,
2 more laps around the hallways,
up and down stairs,
my black plastic watch
approaching 30 minutes, then
his gray head,
green running shorts,
pixie legs, Frank Williams,
Dean of Engineering,
passing at last,
            and I am alone,
again, still running, but slower,

catching my breath, remembering
this same oxygen debt
in races, how one runs
like a waterfall, like a fox
on the tundra, like there's no time
to lose, running
until my watch says 42.

And I want to remember
after, stretched out
like a corpse
on the thick red padded board
in the weight room,
AM rock music pulsing
on someone's boom box, the creaks
of weights and pulleys, men and women
pushing, lifting, grunting, and my body
long in a white T-shirt and shiny black tights,
tucking my Nike Air toes under the strap,
graywhitebrown hair wet, stuck
to the red board, how it feels
to close my eyes in this live room
and listen
        to a heartbeat,
        the brink of breath,
do 39 sit-ups,
then walk
down the dim
hallway, dizzy
with youth
and its thin
promises.

# ATALANTA IN CAPE FAIR

1939

jessie rehder

In the front bedroom of the Prokosch house, where her grandmother's pine bed stood in the corner, plainer than the chintz chair and gate-legged table her mother had bought recently, Joanna began to dress. With agile fingers the girl jerked the blouse over her head, rumpling the straw-colored hair above her high forehead, not troubling to smooth it down. When she grabbed the bloomers from the bed she handled them as though they were armor, thrusting her long, straight legs through the black serge in one motion. Near the mirror she paused, glancing at her face with puzzled eyes, wishing it were less freckled now that she was sixteen.

When Joanna leaned down to tie her shoe she forgot her aversion to her own face and began thinking of the basket-ball game ahead of her to-night. Already she could smell the acrid odor of sweat that would pervade the gymnasium and hear the raw voices of the crowd lifted to the rafters in the nonsense of high-school cheers. These shouts were exciting when the game lagged and her own team was ahead; but when the contest was a close one she did not even hear them. Then the long hurrahs could sift down from the gallery, the boys on the side-lines could stamp their feet like cattle, but nothing mattered except the way the ball went.

The game to-night, the last she would play in Cape Fair before going away to college next year, would be a close one, but Joanna knew her team would win. They always won when her fingers were as cold as they were now and her stomach quivered under her blouse. She wished, however, that the score were already on the blackboard and the game behind her. She wanted people to slap her on the back and tell her how well she had played. She needed the triumphant shouts that went with victory. Then she could see it as a thing accomplished, without the isolated element of doubt that stuck in her throat like a crumb.

"Mother," she called, her voice tense. "Is my sweater mended? It's time to go."

Her mother came through the door, carrying the sweater at arm's length, as though it were a fish she had just caught. For a moment she looked at Joanna, her eyes moving over the girl's proud shoulders. Then, with a sigh, she handed over the garment.

"Since to-night is the last game, and everybody in town will be there, I think you ought to take your new sweater."

"I don't like my new one," Joanna replied.

She stamped her foot against the floor like a pony, staring belligerently at her mother, disturbed by the other's inability to understand that without this garment the contest to-night, a championship game, would be lost before it began. Passionately she pulled the sweater to her, grabbing it from her mother's hands. This faded piece of blue wool, with its worn or broken strands, had been her companion in so many successes it had long ago become the symbol of her own invincibility.

"I wish you could come to the game," the girl said, drawing on her mittens.

"You know that I'd like to come."

"Won't you?"

"I have to stay here with Stephen."

The mother glanced over her shoulder at the bedroom behind where her youngest son lay in his iron crib. Then her eyes returned to Joanna.

"You can tell me about the game after you come home from the party," she said.

"I suppose I've got to go to the party."

The girl frowned and sat down on the bed again and stared at the floor, filled with sudden panic. Her face lost the intense, concentrated look it had worn during the day, when the contest ahead, glittering like a light at the end of the corridor, had been her only thought. The dance at the country club, which was to be given after the game for the players, must soon be faced. The contest over, she must change to her evening dress and drive with her eldest brother along the road through the pines to the squat bungalow where the party was to be held. With an effort Joanna smothered her distrust of a gathering where slick-haired boys and Southern girls with tea-rose faces would be predominant.

"Your evening dress is ready," the mother said.

Freddie, the eldest Prokosch boy, came to the door. He stood in the lamplight, his long form bonier and more impressive than Joanna's now that he had begun to grow up.

"You hate parties and I hate basketball games," he said with his wide grin. "Especially when my sister's the star. Come along. I've brought the car round from the garage. It's time to go."

Joanna kissed her mother good-by and followed Freddie from the house. She trailed the taller form of her brother along the sidewalk to the car, the rubber soles of her shoes sucking against the concrete pavement. With the winter air on her cheeks and the scent of the night in her nostrils, the girl forgot the party and began to think of the game again. She climbed into the seat, her eyes crackling, her mouth a straight line. While the Ford jogged along the dark streets, with winter rushing through the cracks in the windshield, she sat with her hands folded between her knees to keep them warm. Silhouetted against the street lights, her profile had a relentless air of youth about it. She was like an Atalanta, cold, virginal, with no thought except victory.

"Get out." Freddie prodded his sister. "We're here."

Joanna followed her brother across the brick sidewalk and into the dusty lobby of the high school where the game was to be played. The muscles in her stomach were tighter than before, and as she walked her feet seemed hardly to touch the floor. The objects she noticed every day when she came to school—the picture of Washington crossing the Delaware, the statue of Poe's Raven that was more like an owl, did not exist for her to-night. She saw only the bright lights of the gymnasium down the hall, heard nothing but the voices of the players as they shouted to one another while they practiced.

"They've started." Freddie began to climb the steps that led to the gallery. "You'd better hurry."

The girl rushed through the door and joined the other players on the court. The ball in her hands, she lost all thought except of the thing she was doing. Under the harsh lights of the gymnasium, with the crowd hanging over the rail above her like clothes from a line, the girl raced through practice with joy in her eyes. She tossed shots from the foul line, caught the ball her team-mates threw her, and boomeranged it back to them, dribbled down the black-marked floor for a trick shot, twirling the ball into the net over her shoulder. In every move Joanna had a finer precision than the other players, but she was too absorbed in the power of her body to be conscious of her own superiority.

"Yea . . . team . . . ray . . . team. Sis, boom, bah. Off to the races, hah, hah!"

The clamor pressed against the glass skylight as the practice ended and the players trooped off the field to the dressing room. In this cubicle, which was filled with broken tennis rackets and old sweat shirts, Joanna sat by herself in the corner listening impersonally to the admonitions of Miss Alligood, the bespectacled supervisor of athletics.

"The championship of the State is at stake," the teacher began in her high, timorous voice, which sounded frightened even while she was exhorting her charges to smash their opponents off the floor. "The girls on the other team are bigger than we are, so everybody must do her best—I want fair play, mind you, but above all things, we must keep the cup in Cape Fair where I am sure"—she lost the thread of conversation but managed to pick it up again—"where I am sure it rightfully belongs. And now let us pray."

"Do we have to pray to-night?" A young Jewish girl with a serious face and eyes like violets spoke up and retreated in the same breath. "If just this once—"

"Be quiet, Hulda." Sally Peters, a large forward with tousled hair, interrupted fiercely. "Let's get it over."

The team came together, including Hulda, who entered the circle hesitantly. The girls put their arms round one another's shoulders and bent their heads toward the floor as though one of them had lost something and they had all decided to look for it together. Joanna waited until the others were assembled, then left the bench in the corner and crossed the room toward the group with long strides.

"Our Father," Miss Alligood began, in a tone of not being sure whom she was addressing, "help us to play to-night as we have never played before."

Joanna cleared her throat uncomfortably. She had always felt that the prayer was something to be got over before the game began. From the corner of her eye she glanced at the Jewish girl, wishing she knew her better. Something about Hulda's face, the proud arch of the eyebrows, the deep solemnity of the mouth, made Joanna feel almost humble.

"In Jesus' name, amen."

As the prayer ended, someone threw open the door to the gymnasium. Bright light fell over the group of players. A chill of excitement went through Joanna. She forgot the prayer, the Jewish girl, and began listening to the voices of the crowd waiting for the game to start. When play began, the great force that had been building up inside of her would be unloosed like rushing water. Ever since she could remember, it had always been that way. A whistle sounded and she jerked to attention, eyes bright, legs trembling.

"Ready—play!"

The white-trousered referee threw the ball into the air and the opposing centers leaped for it. When it fell in her direction Joanna went down the field, passing the ball, receiving it again, working toward the goal. She feinted, pivoted, backed away from a guard, and finally with a flip of the wrist tossed the ball at the basket where it hovered over the rim and then swished through the net for the first score of the evening.

"Pop corn, hot air—our team's Cape Fair. Yea, Prokosch!"

Joanna heard her own name vaguely and the cheers not at all. They were like a satire on a Greek chorus, performed by people who did not belong in the play. As the game progressed they rose spontaneously with every lull in the action, their echoes lingering against the ceiling after the words had died away.

Near the end of the half, when the Cape Fair team was in the lead, the cheering crowd in the balcony changed its mood and took on the tense expectancy of people watching an execution and wondering just how terrible the slaughter would be. The students in their striped sweaters clenched their hands over the iron rail that circled the oval bowl in the gallery and looked with hardened eyes at the court below where the game progressed. The players settled into geometric patterns and then broke into chaos again, but more than one watched Joanna rather than the shifting figures. She played with magnificent abandon, twirling the ball toward the basket from acute angles, running up the field for another, still another, impossibly achieved goal.

"Half—half!" The harassed umpire blew the whistle desperately, looking at Joanna as though he were uncertain whether she would obey the signal.

The girl came to a perfectly timed stop and walked to the bench. The color was high in her cheeks but under the freckles her skin was as smooth as cream. A faint line of perspiration sat like dew on her upper lip but she did not bother to wipe it off. She sat very still on the hard bench, too aglow with action to be aware of anything except the control she was exercising over her own body.

At first she was like a person in a fog, but when the mist before her eyes cleared she began to see the gymnasium and the people who filled it with a detached interest. At one end of the gallery were a group of girls known as the "Dizzy Dozen," who were recognized as the social arbiters of the high school. Joanna looked curiously at their modish dresses and the pink finger-nails. When she saw these things she felt a vague curiosity, but as she looked into their faces, so different from her own face, with the bones close to the skin, the tilted nose, the eager mouth, she turned away deliberately.

"Oh, Miss Prokosch!" The voice from the gallery had a roll like surf against the shore.

Joanna looked up and saw Mr. Bellamy, the town alderman, who always came to the game. She wanted to look away again, for she hated his tobacco-stained mouth and hearty manners; but she knew that she must be polite. Rising from the bench, she walked out on the court and lifted her head toward the gallery, tossing the hair away from her eyes. From her non-chalant pose and relaxed arms nobody would have suspected how much she disliked the beefy man who leaned down to speak with her, his striped necktie dangling in the air like a stick of peppermint.

"Keep up the good work," he called stentoriously. "Get in there and sock 'em."

Joanna nodded, not bothering to reply. When Bellamy's head had disappeared she sat down on the bench and began looking at the people in the crowd again. Her eyes went past the mother of Alice Peters, who always brought her knitting to the game, over the acid form of Miss Alligood, and came at last to the violet-eyed Jewish girl who had objected to the prayer. Hulda sat on the bench with the other substitutes, look-ing at the coach with a faint hope in her eyes that Miss Alli-good would decide to let her play in the last half of the game. Joanna watched the Jewish girl for a long time, finding it hard to believe that anyone should want to play and not have the power for it. To throw a ball better than anyone else, to swim a channel, or smash a tennis ball down the base-line, as she had once said to her mother, were as simple as breathing.

"I never felt that way," her mother had replied. "But I know how you feel. I'm glad you're interested in games," she had added, "but at college you'll find there are other, more im-portant, things to do."

Joanna wiggled uncomfortably on the hard bench. Could anything be more important than basket-ball, she wondered, knotting the sweat-shirt tighter about her neck. And would she ever do anything as well as she played this game? Her parents were not sending her away to college to become an athlete. They were sending her so that she could learn solid geometry and more history. She liked history, but geometry—Joanna shook her head. It was easier to throw a basket-ball from the exact center of the floor than to square the hypotenuse. Suddenly she wondered whether she would ever be able to do anything well except play this game.

Jumping to her feet, she walked down the side-lines, trying to recapture her former feeling of security by exercising her legs. She glanced impatiently at the umpire's table where the referee and the score-keeper were huddled together, going over the record for the first half of the game. Her only desire was for them to finish what they were doing and blow the whistle that would start the action again. To be caught up in the hard contact the contest brought, to lose herself in a sudden rush down the field, to leap high in the air after the ball would be like ascending to heaven.

"The half won't start for ten minutes," someone said over her shoulder. "The way you're going, Joanna, you'll wear yourself out before it begins."

She turned and saw Jim Brandon, the tall captain of the football team, who had come across the court and was leaning nonchalantly against the wall.

"Hello, Jim," Joanna said shyly.

"Nice game you're playing." He stared at his fingernails.

Joanna stood up so that she could talk with him. The two leaned against the wall, their shoulders close, like figures in a frieze. Jim towered above Joanna but in her own way the girl was as perfect as he. His blunt fingers might have twisted an iron bar, while hers, which were also strong, had a delicacy about them that would make a flower safe. When she moved she was quicker than Brandon too and not so clumsy.

"Put on your sweater or you'll go stiff," Jim said.

The boy touched his own red jacket with the football letters sewed triumphantly across the front of it in a gesture that was almost defiant. "Look," he might have been saying, "these letters show how much stronger I am than you are." There was humor in his gesture too but Joanna did not see that. She saw only his superior smile, which made her feel more uncertain than she had been before she started thinking about the geometry she would have to take at college.

"I'm warm enough, Jim," she said. "I won't get stiff."

"Stay away from the basket during the next half. Keep close to the middle of the floor." Now Brandon's voice had the detachment of a master who speaks to a pupil. "The other team's on to your short shots and will stop them."

"Do you think so?" Joanna asked.

"Sure they are. They'll bunch their guards under the basket and keep them there. So play wide. Even if you miss it's better than getting nowhere."

"All right," Joanna replied.

"And say—I just saw that brother of yours. He told me you were going to the party with him. I'll take you instead, Joanna."

As Brandon walked nonchalantly away Joanna pulled her sweater closer over her shoulders, staring at him with eyes that were almost frightened. Jim knew the right thing to say about the game, the party, about everything. And no matter what happened he was never ruffled. That night a week ago when they had driven down the sound road in his new car and he had tried to kiss her, it had been she, rather than he, who was upset.

"You're a little girl, Joanna." She could hear him saying it now in that soft voice of his. "Some day you'll know how much fun this is."

It would be fun with a boy who loved you, Joanna thought, sitting down again. But Jim only wanted her because she was the best basket-ball player in Cape Fair. Or was it that? Sometimes when he looked at her she felt that he liked her for the kind of person she was. If that were true, some night she would draw him to her instead of pushing him away. But he changed so often that she could never be sure, and that evening a week ago on the sound road, with the pine branches soughing above her, she had been less certain than ever.

She wanted to be as sure of herself as Jim was, not only when they were making love but while she did geometry or when she was at a party. Brandon would be the most popular boy at the country club to-night. Joanna could almost see him waltzing across the pine floor, dancing with the apple-cheeked girls, having a fine time. While she—well, she would be dancing with one, then another of the wet-haired boys with the fuzz still on their cheeks, but she would not feel right about it any more than she felt right about kissing Jim, or wearing the party dress her mother had bought for her, or slipping her toes into the high-heeled shoes that glittered on the floor of the Prokosch closet.

Joanna looked down at the heavy rubber-bottoms that encased her feet. She wriggled her toes inside the canvas, feeling the high arch of the bones, wishing she was as much at home in patent leather as in Keds. She wished too, with a sudden desperation, that the dance were over and that she were safe at home in her own bed. She thought with longing of the way Freddie's shoes sounded when he dropped them on the floor and of the gentle whimpers her youngest brother made when he had dreams he did not like.

The party behind her, it would be fun to lie between cool sheets and listen to the wind in the willow tree outside of her window. Then she would be comfortable, not excited as she was when she twirled a basket-ball toward the net, or unlike herself as she felt in evening dress. When she lay in her grandmother's bed, all that mattered was the sweet, night wind and the tired feeling that began to come over her. It would be good to lie there, with warmth creeping deliciously up from her toes until only the tip of her nose was cold. Finally she would slide into a sleep so profound that not even the noise of her father's alarm clock, going off with a jangle at five in the morning, could awaken her.

The referee's whistle shrilled the news that the half was about to begin, and Joanna jumped to her feet. Stripping off her sweater with a fierce alacrity, she ran out on the court, forgetting everything in a hard excitement. While she practiced her shots, the gymnasium shrunk around her until it became a world in miniature. In this small universe she was a goddess who could not be overthrown. With every practice shot she became more sure of herself. The harsh, blue lights in the gallery, the singsong voices of the crowd, the new springiness in her legs, made her want to laugh aloud, bringing her a superb physical delight.

"Ray—ray—lack-a-day. Cape Fair!"

The sound of the cheering faded and the second half began. Although Joanna was unconscious of what she was doing, the way she played fell into the most perfect pattern imaginable. Every movement was a blend of instinct with the purest physical power. Her body responded before her mind instructed it; her fingers, knowing which way the ball would go, reached for it before the sphere came in her direction. Once she had the ball in her hands and was passing it back and forth she went down the field to the best spot for a goal so fast that she shook her opponents away from her as though they were flies.

Everything about the game Joanna had ever known returned to her. The long afternoons in the gymnasium when she had stayed after the others went home and tossed the ball through the shadows until she learned to know where it was going without following it with her eyes, fused into this moment. She was not one girl but all the girls she had been from that first moment four years ago when she walked across the court with her rapid stride, picked up the ball, and threw it at the goal to watch it drop perfectly through the net.

As the half progressed, Joanna began to feel vaguely that she was playing in a rhythm of her own. She lost the sense of the forms of her fellow-players round her, forgot the passage of time, and moved down the field with a classic grace that brought the spectators to their tip-toes and made the brightly sweatered boys in the gallery break into raucous cheers. The pink-cheeked girls too forgot their restraint and let small noises escape from their red-tipped mouths. But Joanna had stopped thinking of them. She sped down the court below the balcony, oblivious to everything but the delight that coursed through her body.

She kept clear of the goal, where the guards hovered with upraised hands, and moved nearer the center circle, shooting the ball from her chest. Afraid to leave the goal free, the guards stood in their positions while Joanna moved before them like a ballet dancer. A few of her shots went wild, rattling off the backboard into waiting hands, but more often the ball rolled around the rim and dropped into the net. She kept working back, always closer to the center, until she was in a space by herself, so far away from the goal that nobody believed there was any chance of her making a shot successfully.

The instant before the whistle that ended the half blew she tossed a long goal from the exact center of the field. The ball arched through the air like a bird, going so high that for a moment it looked as though it would break through the sky-light and disappear. Before it began to fall Joanna lost interest in it. With the superb nonchalance that comes only when a person knows he has done a thing perfectly, she turned and walked away without glancing back at the goal. As the ball swished through the net, the final whistle blew. In the gallery people beat one another across the shoulders, on the court the referee hugged the umpire. Everyone went slightly mad except Joanna, who stood near the center circle breathing regularly as though the game were about to begin.

"Joanna!" Freddie wiggled through the crowd to his sister's side. "You were tops," he yelled. "Tops!"

The girl turned, but before she could speak to her brother, Mr. Bellamy, the town alderman, cigar still in his mouth, came down from the gallery like a whirlwind. Brushing Freddie aside, he grabbed Joanna's shoulder.

"Grandstand playing!" Bellamy beat the girl wildly between her shoulder blades. "That last shot beats anything I ever saw. Should be in the New York papers. I know you were thinking of the gallery but that don't matter. A sensational feat!"

Joanna stood very quiet, still thinking of the party ahead.

# WOMEN'S TUG OF WAR AT LOUGH ARROW

tess gallagher

In a borrowed field they dig in their feet
and clasp the rope. Balanced
against neighboring women, they hold
the ground by the little gained
and leaning like boatmen rowing into
the damp earth, they pull
to themselves the invisible waves, waters
overcalmed by desertion
or the narrow look trained to a brow.

The steady rain has made girls of them,
their hair in ringlets. Now they haul
the live weight to the cries
of husbands and children, until the rope
runs slack, runs free
and all are bound again by the arms
of those who held them, not until, but so
they gave.

# WET

1974

laurie colwin

Lucy had been swimming all her life: she had been in the water at three months and was swimming without water wings at the age of two. She grew up in Minnesota, and her family summered at Stone Boy Lake, named for an outcropping of boulders that from a distance looked like a gingerbread man. The lake was two miles long, ringed by dense firs and overshadowed by timber mountains. It was almost gothically dark, except at high noon when the sun cut straight down onto the water, like the beam of a klieg light. At Stone Boy Lake, you swam to your friends, and it was not uncommon for Lucy to swim several miles a day, climbing onto mossy jetties, where there would be a towel waiting. She and her friends swam from mooring to mooring, and they put towels out for one another. In the winter, when you could skate across the lake, she swam in the pool at Mallard Academy in St. Paul. At college, she swam every day in the college pool, although she hated chlorine. She swam through the seasons, through exams, through broken love affairs.

She met Carl Wilmott in Cambridge, and they were married three years later. Carl was getting his doctorate and Lucy was a researcher for the law review. They lived in a light, sparse apartment in Cambridge, and when an assistantship suddenly came up for Carl at Chicago, they were packed in two days. They moved three days after New Year's and were settled within a week.

Lucy was middle-sized and lean. She had craggy features, but they were small, as if a large, rough-hewn statue had been reduced to human scale. When she smiled, her eyes almost disappeared behind her cheekbones, and the skin around her eyes was so translucently white you could see the veins beneath it.

Carl, who was ruddy, large grained, and reddish, was often stricken with the thought that she would die. Her sparseness and paleness evoked fragility, and he was constantly amazed at how tough she was. Even her clothing was delicate and yacht-like. Carl's sports were squash and handball and he watched with wonder as his delicate wife dived from boulders into mountain pools so cold they shocked his entire body if he put so much as a foot in. She leaped into the ocean at Maine in October while he sat on the beach wrapped in a blanket with two sweaters underneath. He watched her slide down the steep rocks of waterfalls wearing a T-shirt against scrapes. She cut through the water, making a greenish arc. She stood on the highest diving boards, spreading her arms like a dancer, or warrior, or the angel of death.

The first day of their life in the new apartment, Carl went to a faculty meeting. Lucy called university information to find out where there was a pool, and was told that she could swim at McWerter Hall, which was nine blocks away.

It was below freezing. Her toes ached in their boots before she had walked half a block. She had not lived with this kind of cold for ten years, and her body had forgotten. When the inside of her nose began to stiffen, she was afraid her eyes would freeze. It was suicidal to take off a glove. By the time she got to McWerter, she could not feel her feet.

The guard pointed the way to the ladies' locker room, where

she was told she would need a pass, and when she explained that her husband was new faculty, she was given a temporary card and filled out the forms for her official pass.

When she got to the pool, there were two girls sitting with their feet in the water: their voices bounced off the walls and were squashed by the high ceiling into a soft, eerie hush. Their bathing suits were bone dry. A flat cloud of steam hung above the water and she dived through it from the high board. She dived and swam for two hours, and when she got out, there was nobody there. In the locker room she combed her lank hair in front of a fogged mirror, and by the time she had walked a block, even with a hat and scarf, the front of her hair was frozen.

In February it stopped snowing, but it got colder. The coal trucks unloaded in the streets and the ice turned black. Brakes on cars and bicycles froze, and children coming home from school at lunchtime skated on the jet-colored humps of ice that formed in the middle of the street. In the dead, arctic air, they played with their heads down, and walked backward against the wind. People passed each other on the street, their eyes streaming. When the wind let up, they brushed the tears off with their gloves, as if suffering from secret heartbreak.

Every day, after his two o'clock class, Carl met for coffee with Johnny Esterhazy, who had been his friend in Cambridge. They were both New Yorkers, and the cold exhausted them.

"I saw Lucy yesterday," Johnny said. "I really admire her. The front of her hair was all frozen."

"You admire her because her hair was frozen?"

"What I mean is, it takes courage to swim in this kind of weather. I told her I thought she was crazy, but she said she'd been in the pool every day since you got here."

Carl drank his coffee in silence and watched a group of girls go by, packed so tightly in their layers of clothing they could hardly walk. He knew Lucy swam all summer, but he had no idea that she swam in the winter too. The fact that she did, and that he didn't know, shocked him so deeply that he could hardly speak. He had no idea where the university pool was, and was about to ask Johnny, but it seemed to him that to ask was admission of some terrible ignorance, like asking an old family friend meekly for the address of a parent. It set off in his mind steep, painful doubts. On the way home, he decided he would ask her, but could not arrange a question in his mind. He could not find a tone of voice that was neither accusatory nor whimpering, and he was amazed at how profoundly the thought of Lucy's swimming, which was a perfectly natural thing for her to do, affected him.

When he got home, it all seemed inappropriate and out of proportion. Her hair wasn't wet. It didn't smell of chlorine. Her face was cool when she kissed him, but it always was. They sat down to a large, cheering dinner, after which Carl read and Lucy played the piano. At midnight they yawned, and with their arms around each other, went to bed.


In March, the cold began to crack and the black ice softened, forming deep, muddy puddles. When it snowed, the snow was light and fine. Then it sleeted, and by the beginning of April it only rained. Tiny green swells began to appear on the stunted hedges.

Finally it was clear, cold spring. Lucy walked toward the lake through the park, where the grass was still brown and scorched. There was a slight halo around the Museum of Science and Industry. She walked over the bridge above the Outer Drive and onto the rocks by the lake. Under her blue jeans, sweater, and coat she had on a bathing suit, and in her book bag was a towel. Johnny Esterhazy had told her that Lake Michigan was polluted, but it was clear enough for her to see the rocks beneath the water. Whatever it had in it, it did not have chlorine: it was a lake, not an indoor pool. She stripped to her bathing suit, and her knees almost buckled from the cold. There was not a soul around. She climbed from rock to rock until she was standing in water up to her knees, and then she jumped.

Over dinner, Carl and Lucy reviewed their days. Johnny Esterhazy and his fiancée were coming for dinner on Friday. The head of the department had invited them to a cocktail party. Lucy had sent off applications to the law school, and had had an interview at the law library. She was waiting for an opening. They had rediscovered some people they knew from Cambridge and had made friends with Ted and Ellie Lifter, a pair of sociologists who lived downstairs, and they talked about the easy, friendly shape their life was taking. But she never said she swam—it was not included in her list of the day's proceedings—and it seemed to Carl that his shock had been some aberration, but he could never find a place in their talk to ask. She only said: "It'll be nice at the lake when it gets warm."

When he looked at her over the dinner table, her pale, fair hair and skin, her pale eyes, and the vein that divided her forehead, or when she smiled and her cheekbones diminished her eyes, he looked for any sign of deception—he had come to think of her swimming as something she purposely hid from him—but there was nothing but openness and affection. Lucy, in a way that was neat and efficient, was very loving. Her home, her clothes, her possessions were neat as a pin and he could not help but know that she loved him in a way that was steady and unblinking.

At night, her long thighs were cool and the insides of her arms were cold. While she slept, Carl thought how fragile and transparent she looked, and how rugged she actually was. At times he was overwhelmed by the fact that she swam every day and didn't tell him; it seemed monstrous to him that she kept this part of her life shut off from him, if that was what she was doing. He knew that all he had to do was ask, and she would smile her wide smile and explain that she always swam, that it was so natural to her that she simply assumed he knew. But he could not bear to admit that he was so remote that what was second nature to her had been news to him. Johnny Esterhazy had said: "Lucy's incredible. She told me that out of her entire life the days she hasn't been swimming add up to about a month. That's devotion." But she had never said that to him, and it meant that the whole five years in Cambridge she had arranged a part of her life away from him and had gone swimming in it. In the summers they went to his parents in Maine, or to hers at Stone Boy Lake, and they often swam together, but this was different: in Cambridge, and now in Chicago, they were apart for most of the day and she had taken a couple of secret hours every day and used them secretly. It seemed so deliberate, so contrived and concealed it broke his heart to think about it. But then he would think that his vision was distorted. Lucy was a born swimmer. It was as natural and necessary to her as breathing, and people don't discuss their breathing. He knew Lucy. She was his wife. They had been together for five years. Her swimming was something he knew he was meant to assume, but at night it looked like sabotage.

On the day of a heavy rainstorm, he saw her from the window of his office, walking under her golf umbrella toward

McWerter, and he followed her. He climbed the stairs to the bleacher and waited until she came through a door and walked to the edge of the pool. Mist had formed on his jacket and he was sweating under his collar. He could feel his hair collecting wetness. Through the steam and haze, he saw his wife on the low board. She dived through the water like a bird and emerged at the shallow end like a white seal. He thought to call out to her, but didn't, and since she never looked up, she didn't see him. She tossed her hair back and he could see that her eyes were ringed with red and unfocused from the chlorine.

There was a catch in his throat as he watched her walk the perimeter of the pool to the high board, leaving no footprints on the wet tiles. She stood on the tip and sprang, and as she connected with the water, it seemed to slice his heart. For an instant he hated all the water she moved so easily through and left no mark on.

His arms were stifling under the heavy tweed, but he was afraid that if he took his jacket off she would hear him.

She did a swan dive off the low board and he watched her sleek racing crawl for ten laps. Then she climbed onto the high board, framed by a window the width of the room. The sky was the color of faded ink, the wind flung leaves against the glass, and the rain affixed them. Carl felt absurd in his clothes. He would have liked to go downstairs and get into a suit and swim with her, but it would have been betrayal. Instead, he watched her do a half gainer, and when she was under water, he left by the side door.

At dinner, over coffee, he said abruptly: "I want to go swimming with you tomorrow." He was that desperate.

Lucy smiled and her eyes disappeared. It was a truly open smile.

"Sure," she said. "That would be nice. I'm going around three-thirty."

That was the end of the conversation. It was all right. He had mistaken everything. She assumed he knew she swam every day. They were going to swim together: the spell was broken. After dinner she went to play the piano, and he put the garbage outside. When the wind hit him suddenly, he leaned against the banister and, to his own amazement, wept.

He was at the pool at three-thirty and she was already in the water, swimming slow laps. The bleak light glared through the window. She lifted her head to the side, performing her determined crawl; her eyes seemed albino.

Carl played in the water, did surface dives, stood on his head in the shallow end. He jack-knifed from the low board and then he and Lucy swam six laps of side stroke together. They performed a little water ballet, and kissed at the bottom of the deep end. Then he sat on the edge of the pool, glazed from the water, and watched. She was not swimming for fun, or exercise, or habit. She had never joined a swimming team, not even in high school. It was like the air for her: she was amphibious.

Then she got out and sat beside him. Her feet were long, like blades.

"That was really nice, wasn't it?" she said.

"It'll probably be nicer in Lake Michigan," Carl said.

"It *is* nicer in the lake," she said. "I was in a couple of weeks ago."

Whatever spell he had broken by coming swimming reformed. A couple of weeks ago it had been cold, and she had been in the lake. Surely that was unusual enough to tell him about, yet she had never said. The skin around her nails was slightly grainy and her hair was flat against her head. Drops ran from her bangs to her nose, and down her cheeks, like effortless tears. He watched their separate feet, spookily luminescent in the blue water.

As the weather got warmer, the air became light. It was prairie spring and the flowers came up. In Jackson Park, school children were being taken on nature walks, and riders appeared on the bridle path. Carl walked under a little bridge in the park and across the wet grass till he came to the rocks. When the park lights came on, there was a haze around him. The traffic from the drive sounded like an ocean in the distance. He climbed down the rocks to the lake and put his hand in the cold water. Mossy algae waved back and forth with the current.

When he got home, his bones felt light and he took a nap on the couch with the window wide open. The air seemed to breathe on him. He was awakened by Lucy's cool hand on his forehead. In her other hand she was holding a brandy snifter full of water.

"Look," she said. "Snails." In the bottom of the snifter were some small stones covered with algae. Two snails sat on the stones, and three clung to the side of the glass.

"I got them today. They're all over the rocks at the point. I went snorkeling," she said.


They had a quiet dinner, read the papers, and then played a transcription of Mozart's fortieth symphony for four hands, but they hadn't played it for a long time and were badly out of practice.

The windows in the bedroom were open, and the air was sweet and infantile. Carl was awake, but Lucy slept without a sound. He had his arms around her and he put his cheek next to her damp hair. Her sides, as always, were cold, as if under her skin her bones were cold. He watched her sleep and thought that, even with his arms around her, she was dreaming in private. He kissed the top of her head, resting his chin on her hair. It gave up a heavy, sweet, slightly burnt smell. She was drying. A lock of damp hair fell across his wrist. Her hair was warm and steamy against him. Every day of her life, she would be, at some point, damp, and for one solid time every day, as long as she lived, wet.

# FROM *WATER DANCER*

1982

### jenifer levin

**W**ater sucked at land, at the rocks along it. It churned everything up and laid down a new surface, then crept back before the next surge. It made rocks smaller and smoother by microscopic measurements every minute of every day. It swept firm earth into soaked chaos. This was cold water that made you numb. This was water in which average human beings did not live for very long. It was rough water. Saltwater.

Dorey stepped into the water.

She took another step, slowly. Began to feel her toes again. Then she stopped just to look. It was that beautiful clear green-gray tint that made you remember warm things. Dorey stepped deeper, up to the knees. Shallow now, and receding. The tide would take her out past the breakers. This water made you think of coral reefs and sun and still it was so cold you almost couldn't believe it existed in the same world as the sun, on the same day, under the same sky. She stepped again. Ilana, she said. Then she wanted to jump out backward to warmth, seventy degrees and rising, and the land where Ilana was. The place she was going Ilana couldn't be in, so with each step she lost her more and more.

Then something inside her clicked, the door to all that shut and was securely latched. Dorey breathed. Felt good. A little underweight, she'd have preferred to weigh another ten pounds . . . She breathed deeply, went forward until water crept up her thighs. It was calm here near shore. The alphabet. She'd start out with the alphabet this time and run through that for the first two hours just to establish pace. She'd planned it all carefully. Alphabets for the first one hundred and twenty minutes and then she would do numbers up to three thousand. Then there was the tape Tycho'd sent up. She'd memorized it through those earphones. The tape was forty-seven minutes long. If she went through it song by song once, filled in the remaining thirteen minutes by calculating flip turns to every tenth stroke, that took her another hour and by then it was time for feeding. Then alphabets again. And later she'd be dreaming somewhere else anyway, no need for alphabets. Cold. She stepped waist-deep. She was ready. She had to walk out a way, feel it get shallower, then the suck of breakers on sandbars, then the pull tugging her towards them and she went along for the ride, sidestepped whitecaps, caught a swell and was no longer on her feet but kicking, lifting the right arm high, all of her in water . . .

Of all the planets spinning that day through the planetary system, only one had on it the vast collections of liquid water called oceans. Descending to a certain depth, the human body would begin to compress. Eventually the external pressure of increasingly dense water would force the body to cave in. This was long, long before it hit bottom—the ocean floor—a longer distance than up Everest and longer than the 10 K. At bottom the floor was in a state of constant geological change. Shelves were crumbling, valleys deepening, plains and ridges shifting. The changes echoed up through pitch-dark cold, past levels where plants grew bleak white without sun, and sucking fish swallowed molecular configurations of plankton that glowed in perpetual night. The echoes bumped off ascending layers of shelf sloping into dry-topped continents. They spun up in zig-zags, rumbled through decreasing blackness and density towards the first gray glimmerings of light. Bouncing, enmeshed in one another, the echoes of change sliced through to water surface. There they met air, sun, wind, and rain that fed water to the water. Meeting this, the echoes struggled along the surface as currents. Like the floor from which they'd ascended, they were in a state of constant change. So the current that ran parallel to the mainland shore of the San Antonio Strait could not be predicted long-range. It was subject to forces other than wind, or rain. All it did was writhe around itself, each of its multitudinous echoes struggling, snaking brutally along the ocean surface in a long, south-flowing stream.

At four minutes past ten in the morning on September 14, Dorey Thomas was swimming along the ocean surface at a rate of about two miles an hour—which, considering surface temperature and relative turbulence, was damned good time to be making. So she had swum nearly eight miles into the strait of San Antonio, heading east from Punta Provechosa. Another eight miles away, just about mid-channel, the current waited. It meandered. It would take her longer than just another four hours to reach there because, although she did not know it, the water temperature would soon drop by one degree and that would slow her down. Her change in pace would at first be unnoticeable, but by infinitesimal increments she would continue to slow until, at nightfall, her pace would appear drastically altered . . .

Well, Dorey told herself, see, you should have put on more weight. You're already cold.

She told herself she'd been colder before. Quebec. That year at Lac Louie. Or Ontario some days, sure. D breathe E F breathe G H breathe I J.

There was one sound in the world. It was flesh on water, each splash the same. It rang against the layers on her ears. S T breathe U V breathe. Each hand already numb. One of those hands would touch sand tomorrow and she wouldn't feel it at first it would be so numb but then a quick jolting sensation would quiver up the arm of the hand that was first to touch. K L breathe M N breathe O P.

Colder before and weighed less. How many fingers? Burns used to say as a joke. If you can count to ten you're okay in my book. Which direction you going? Know that and you're all right. Keep going that way that's all that counts, he said, I don't care if you freeze your butt off. Keep that pace and concentrate on where you're heading. Keep that pace and worry about yourself, forget the rest of those jokers in there. Let the water take care of them, you concentrate on where you're going and the water you're in.

U V breathe W X breathe Y Z breathe A B. That stroke of yours, Burns shook his head, distance stroke, distance, that's what you're doing there in this measly little pool. Maybe the 800 this year they'd said. Said that to Carol. The 800. Q R breathe S T breathe. No. She wouldn't slip back to then. Not to childhood or triumph. Not to despair either. This was it— now. Only now, the now was all that mattered. No backsliding. Not yet. Now was just the getting there, stroke, stroke, breath, numbers and the alphabets. No pools here no mothers here. No books here no lovers. Not now. Then was before. There was no past here, only water. Water always shifting, always in the present. Breathe. Don't slip back. Not now. Not yet. A B breathe C D. Burns. Remember. Old guy. Mean old guy. Said women were the tops at this stuff in his book, more endurance, less complaints.

*Carol. It's cold.*

No, she told herself, no you can't go back to then. Not now. Too early. Stay here. K L breathe M N breathe O P breathe Q R breathe and she caught herself, shivered smiles to herself, she could count to ten and go A to Z breathe A B breathe C D breathe and she knew, she was sure, of the direction. East. She was swimming the San Antonio Strait, she was going to cross it and touch land at the end. S T breathe U V. Pale lovely Pacific. It was frozen green-gray and not a fish in sight.

D breathe E F breathe G H breathe I J. Time for her feeding now. She stopped to tread and then the whistle shrilled once twice three times, up to five so she backstroked and was treading again. Cold but it was all right. You're okay, she said. You know where you're going, where you're crossing to.

It was five after one in the afternoon. She grabbed for the cup . . .


You're hungry and you ought to eat, it said. Here, eat this. She did. Couldn't see her hand reach for the liquid but knew it was out there somewhere, heading in the right direction and shuddering uncontrollably like her teeth. What went down hurt her lips and tongue. They were puffy with salt and raw.

Remember where you're going, it said. East. Remember stay here for a while because you haven't hit that current yet. Important. Stay.

*Carol.*

Not yet.

It was cold.

*When the moon goes high in the—*

Stay.

She did. Lifted the right arm, stroked, stroked, breathed to her right. She swallowed saltwater. Then something forced its way up from her stomach, all the heat vomiting out of her. She had to stop. Rolled over on her back, shaking. Couldn't keep it down. I'm sick, she said. Sarge I'm sick. Oh come on, it said. It was a voice she'd heard before. Come on, don't be a crybaby. You're just fine. You know the story. You're strong, so stop sniveling.

She rolled back over quickly, lifted the right arm, the left, breathed, again. Swimming. There now, see, that's better, that's the way it is meant to be. You're doing well, see how well.

Who are you? she asked.

Dorey Thomas.

Well it's good to meet you. Thank you. Thanks a lot. Dorey Thomas the swimmer?

The swimmer. Listen. Let me tell you a secret. All these terrible things, they aren't happening to you. The cold. The sick feeling. These things are not happening. Not to you. They are happening to me. So relax.

I'm sick.

Stop complaining. Come on. Faster. Don't you want to make good time? Well then. Let's get moving.

Here, all here. Hands arms neck head, bench press, lats.

What about your legs?

Leg press. Hamstrings quadriceps. Not much good at it.

That's okay. Keep kicking, you know you're strong.

Yes. Well I do. Thanks. When the moon goes high in the sky I also rise and my eyes are tired from so much looking at the sea. No. That's not the way it goes. Before dawn I also rise and my eyes. Breathe. Are tired. Breathe. Okay now. Sure I'm still crossing the San Antonio Strait, I am in water. They said try the 800, Carol, just try—

*Not yet. Stay here. You have to.*

—the *800*, the Regionals. See how she does at—

Get back here.

—and they were surprised weren't they.

Dorey! Dorey Thomas! Stay awhile.

She did. One two three four up to ten. Alphabet once more, one more time just to make sure. Hands arms shoulders neck all right. Breathe. Torso yes. Breathe. Thighs calves breathe. Toes count them. How many, Burns? Count to ten and where are you heading? East in the strait of San Antonio. To touch sand tomorrow. Uh-huh.

She was okay. She knew where she was and where she was going to and there was someone out in the fog now, telling her try this, this is broth. Broth and a vanilla cookie, try it, champ. She did. It was three o'clock . . .

Ilana watched the sun's progress. It was west in the sky now, worst afternoon heat over, and though she'd been drinking plenty of water she felt numbed by the sun, a little dazed. Maybe it was simply that she'd been focusing on that white dot swimming through water for so many hours. Focus on anything long enough and you went somewhere else . . .

"Hello." When she touched Sarge's shoulder he turned. "Tired?"

He shook his head. "Thinking."

"It's almost four."

"Right."

"I can feed her this time, Sarge, if you're tired. I'd like to."

Minutes later, she'd changed clothes. Ilana imagined herself sliding along aluminum, feeling for a grip. Would it be like climbing cliffs. She'd balance the feeding stick and hot cup in one hand. If there were cookies or any other solid food it would be wrapped in plastic. She focused on the image of herself doing this. Once she had a clear picture of how she would appear, she knew she could do it easily. It was a matter of visual cognizance—for her, all movement was.

She stepped down rope rungs.

That's when she felt the cold. Spraying against the bared top of her chest it was salty and numbing. Gasping, she'd forgotten what it was like. She took her time before crouching to sit, slide along those few feet out to the pontoon's end with careful balance while her legs hung, feelingless, in water. The waves had diminished during the last hour. None washed over her. Still, it was cold . . .

Braced against the drum, she looked up. The face staring blindly in her direction, bobbing between waves, could have been anyone's. Could have been but was not. Somewhere, in the blank line of the nose, the opened mouth, Ilana searched out a lover. Thought maybe she'd found her. Then she was leaning over to reach, extending the cup-tipped feeding stick across water. She spoke clearly. Had to repeat everything until the words stopped making sense, but finally she was heard.

"Ilana?"

She was relieved. Yes, she said, yes it's me. What Dorey said next was unrecognizable. The sound came out all swollen. I don't understand, Ilana said, again please, tell me again. Dorey did. Finally Ilana thought she understood.

"You're okay?"

"Okay."

"Drink this, Dorey. Here. To your right. Your right. To the right. Drink this. All of it. To the right."

"I'm a little crazy now, Ilana."

What, Ilana said, tell me again, I'm listening. Listening. I am. Tell me. Again. I'm sorry, one more time. Once more. Crazy? You are? Crazy but okay?

"Uh-huh."

"Good. That's good. It's the best way to be."

Ilana, I'm a little crazy now, it happens like this a lot but I'm okay. Still here. There was something I wanted to tell you. Can't talk. Feel sick. Well, a little. Still here. Something I'd like to tell you now while I'm still here in the water.

"Later."

Ilana understood. She began the slow slide back to ship. Around the midriff of the feeding stick, her fingers shook with cold.

. . . By the time the eastern sky'd begun to darken they were heading nearly due north. In the west the sun was dark orange and just starting its fade. Air temperature was sixty-eight degrees and falling. Water temperature was fifty-two point three degrees Fahrenheit and winds were with them this time, blowing from the southwest. Waves were erratic. Some five-footers. Still they were, like the winds, slamming along in the right direction.

Just before twilight was the time when ghosts rode echoes right up to the surface of the San Antonio Strait. They were the strait's lost spirits, and most had left their bodies behind in its water over a century ago. Along the perimeters of the current they hovered silently, huddled close together without touching in the deepening gray.

There's another, one said in Spanish. Pointed soundlessly. Dorey looked up. They were conferring about something, it seemed. Her. She didn't understand the Spanish, it was being spoken too quickly. Still she caught a couple of words.

Another what?

*Otro nadador.* Another swimmer.

But this one's a woman.

*Nadadora. Estará lo mismo.*

No. Perhaps it won't be the same.

Perhaps.

They were silent again. Looking up, she thought she'd caught a hint of her name being spoken but no. Only gray tranquillity that clamped over her now like a snow-cold glove. What was there in the world but the sound of water, those relentless splashes ringing against both her ears until she almost did not hear them because everything had become them. Her arms stroking water. Her arms causing splashes. Arms rendering her ears deaf. Watching, the spirits stepped from their perch atop waves. One sat on her shoulders.

Knock knock.

Go away.

Knock knock.

Who's there, she sobbed.

Guess.

Go away.

No I won't. Guess.

I don't know.

Do you want me to tell you? Do you?

Please, she said, you don't understand. I have to concentrate now.

Knock knock.

Who's there?

Matt.

Who?

You know. Matt Olssen, me. Remember me? I beat you in Quebec.

Not by much.

Hah. Want to shake hands?

The hand crawled over her shoulder. It caressed the raw line of her neck. Fingers found her lips and pried them apart to poke into her mouth. The fingers were salt-tasting. They were bone. She screamed and kept swimming. Then the weight on her shoulders lifted, mouth emptied, she'd thrown up again and was swimming north, chattering teeth biting once in a while into her tongue. Her toes were gone.

She concentrated.

Now came a noticeable tug from the east, water just slightly more turbulent and its direction confused. Closer. Getting closer. The skin along her spine burned. Its burning was a bright line of flame in ice, a tingle of expectation. That current. She swallowed more water, threw up the rest of last hour's feeding.

Fog on her goggles darkened with evening. North. She concentrated. Counted each splash up to ten and then started over. In front of her yawned an enormous mouth. Its lips were full, slime-smeared, its insides black and cavernous and it had no teeth. Whoosh, it went. Sucking. It sucked her to the east now, lips glistening. She fought to keep heading north and it laughed. So little, it mocked. You're so little.

Who are you?

Water.

Oh, she said. She was afraid.

Someone else was talking, that swimmer. Better concentrate. Just concentrate now, that's right. Keep the pace.

But the water.

Keep that pace. Cut out all this whining, huh? Remember this isn't happening to you, it is happening to me. Remember.

*Dorey Thomas.* She wanted to cry with relief.

Right. Let's get going. We can do it.

Too small.

No you're not.

She paused, confused. Small. But you're bigger than me, are you a giant?

No, said Dorey, I'm something better now, don't you remember?

I'm sorry, she cried, I forgot.

Think a minute. Let's swim now. Uh-huh. Just think.

Something better? No. Well, I don't know. Tell me.

You haven't really forgotten. Do you want me to tell you anyway?

What? she stroked. Stroked. Breathed. What are you?

Dorey smiled. I—she glowed proudly—am a water dancer.

She breathed. Then wanted to throw open her arms with a burst of recognition. Ah, she said. A water dancer. Well, so am I.

Well then, *concentrate.*

She did.

It was five o'clock . . .


Sometimes what she imagined was a beam of light attached to the topmost cap emanating from her forehead. It was similar to the kind worn by coal-miners, spotlighting the dismal route ahead.

Sometimes she worried about sharks, then remembered that none had ever been spotted here. This was the San Antonio Strait. She guessed they preferred less difficult water.

Sometimes what happened was the cold went completely through her, pierced her chest, and rode out somewhere in the vicinity of her spine. It came in waves like gusts of wind. Each wave of ice was electric shock.

She'd slowed again to less than a mile an hour. South-flowing, the current pushed them . . .

"Here, dear. Here's some food."

The voice's faint sound filled her with longing, and a sense of expectation for which she could not account.

"Who's there?"

"Ilana. This is Ilana."

She stopped. Tried to think. Then she had it and gave a

grin that split her lips but they were too numb to feel it. "Ah. Are you my lover?"

"Yes."

"Still?"

"Yes," Ilana lied.

Dorey swallowed some liquid and spat out the rest. Blindly, she backstroked a little. Water swirled into her mouth, she felt it creep down her throat and mix unsettled with what she'd just consumed. Most of it water anyway. *Lover*. Why not. Bugs had them. Sharks had them. Animals had them men had them and so would she. A lover. For a second she felt part of what she floated in, inside of it as it was inside her, integral aspect of the water-covered world. For a second, there was peace. She felt her eyelids sink down and she turned suddenly, listened carefully, heard the whistles signaling which direction. Bear left, the signals said. Arm raised, muscles felt torn. Arm raised. Breathe. She went on ahead . . .


"Ilana!"

At one in the morning she was treading, trying bleakly to yell.

"Ilana!"

Ilana stepped down the rope. On metal she balanced. Something rang dully in her head and at first she thought it was the incessant rhythm of exhaustion but after a while she knew that, no, it was something else altogether, some realization she was wavering at the edge of. When water washed over her thighs she shuddered. Fifty-three degrees and steady was cold enough. Personally she liked it in the eighties.

Out along the pontoon she'd left a boat behind. Whatever she was heading for was different, she knew, than anything she had done in the past. And perhaps it was weariness that brought these tears to her eyes now, here, in the middle of an ocean at an hour past midnight, but she didn't think so.

"I'm here."

"Ilana."

"Yes."

Features blanched, swollen, unfamiliar, the swimmer faced her by instinct and reached, hand dropped weakly, splashed the water.

"Ilana, what time is it?"

Ilana thought before answering. When she spoke it was with care. "Oh, don't worry about the time. You're doing fine."

"One o'clock? It's only one o'clock?"

"No. I don't know."

"Then," the voice slurred, "how do you know it's not?"

Ilana took deep breaths. "Because," she said, "you are almost there."

"What?"

"You're almost there. Get going now, don't you feel good about that?"

*"Liar."*

In the head-splitting light, Ilana rubbed her cheek with those long fingers of hers. The fingers came away wet, whether with sea or tears she didn't know and didn't care.

"Liar. You're lying to me."

"Dorey. I've never lied to you. Not ever, remember?"

Dorey paused silently, treading. Well, it was true. Then it could not be one o'clock and still the middle of the strait if she were almost there, could it. Maybe the stars had already faded. And it was nearly dawn. Well, maybe. Ilana was there. She reached. No, they hadn't lied to each other. She remembered. No betrayal.

Almost there, Ilana coaxed. Almost there, so don't you worry about the time now, not now, you just concentrate on swimming. Just swim now, all right? You're fine, you're doing very well, believe me.

Dorey believed her. It was Ilana saying these things, after all, Ilana who didn't lie. She ate part of a cookie they'd crumbled in liquid but threw it up. She guessed if she were almost there she had just better swim. Ilana was right. Sure.

So somewhere after one o'clock in the morning Dorey Thomas, more than halfway across the strait of San Antonio, gave up on time. She let it leave her. Realized, once she felt it slough off, how much energy she'd been expending keeping track of alphabets and Spanish words of songs, keeping track of feedings and what they meant in relation to distance. Now that she was no longer spending precious calories on thoughts of time, she could concentrate on one thing alone: stroking through water, maintaining the specific rhythm of a pace she'd worked towards all her life. There was no further purpose in this—no goal of time towards which the strokes could be counted because she'd lost track of time and, losing time, lost sight of all specificity. The space between where she was each instant and the shoreline she struggled to approach was now immeasurable. The only goal left her—if it could indeed be called a goal—was the rhythmic continuation of strokes through water.

She concentrated.

Each stroke an end in itself. There was no other purpose in the world than this, she knew, to stroke through water and that way keep going. Every stroke the same, so every stroke was an infinity of strokes, in the dead of night each infinity measured by the sound of a splash . . .


Carol, remember that day. I was little . . .

Remember at the beach. I climbed on your shoulders. That way I was over the waves. You bounced. You played horse.

Dorey reached for sun. Just as it was about to envelop her it faded. Something sat on her shoulders. It seemed a weight from outside, like a leaden shoe. She wondered who was stepping against her back. Wasn't fair.

Carol?

Think we're there yet?

The weight got heavier. Much more of that and her shoulders would cave in, she knew. No more giant. Back when she was a giant maybe she could have carried it. Maybe. No. Because she'd been a giant, and even then all it took was one wave. One wave and poof. Giant broke in two. Humpty Dumpty.

Well, I tried, Carol. For you. To be that strong. See. You needed it. But it wasn't possible. I was barely strong enough for one. See, when you stop being a giant it's so lonely. Lonely. Still lonely. All right. But I can touch now. Getting there. Stronger now, I guess. I know. And no giant. No. Just going for it. Going for broke. Free, you said, it is possible to be free. That's the part I liked. Believed. Still do.

That frozen feeling in the center of her chest seemed to waver then, massive glacier teetering on the edge of some vast cavern before it tipped, crumbled, dissolved, and she reached, reached, breathed easier now from the center of her chest where the sun glowed hot, bright, unsmothered by ice. Still the weight crouched, gripped with monkey hands on her shoulders. She breathed out sun and heard the hiss of melting ice down in the cavern there. It was a sound almost of lament, far-off wails heard in some jungle, a dark female cry. Dorey listened carefully. Her right, she knew, to stop for just this second and understand something. The glacier had been water after all. Frozen water. Not permanent. Not indestructible. At least she was less destructible than ice. Hot blood inside stronger than the cold. For now. Strong. She could breathe easier. And it was her right to listen, to hear the dark sounds of dying. Or, pounding against it, her own pulse-beat. Dancing. And know she was alive.

The lie. It was a lie, Carol. That I was doing it for you. Sure. It was for that glow. What's left under everything. Get rid of everything else and you feel it. The glow. Not giving up. Making it through. That's all. Alive. Cold but feel that, that glow. Alive.

The weight pressed down. Everything hurt.

How much longer?

Remember? What you told me once. What I believed?

By the beach. I was twelve. You told me that day. You can be free, darling, it is possible if only you're willing to pay the price, and the price is very high. Simply a choice. You must need it more than anything. You must want it more than love.

It was too cold to feel anymore. She'd dropped down below the earth into water and was starving, filthy, no chance to clean right now and no strength left to stop. Just keep going. She'd dropped down below where people didn't go unless they had to, where nothing changed but the wind and time didn't exist. But something sat right there on her shoulders, crying, insistent. Sounded like an infant. Dorey pulled out the scissors. Sorry, she said, I am sorry. She'd have cried but nothing left. Sorry. I would carry you now, Carol, if I had the strength. Except I'm not a giant anymore. Just enough left for me. Forgive me. Forgive me. I have to make it. Carol, it's what you wanted.

She cut.

The scissors dropped, sank out of sight. From below rose blade-shaped traces of blood, and between Dorey's shoulders the cord flapped, spliced, oozing, with nothing at its other end. She picked up the pace slightly. With each stroke the cord shriveled and dried until it was nothing but dessicated, unneeded skin, and the skin washed away from her by salt-water.

"How much longer?"

"Not much. You're almost there."

Perched on the pontoon, she said it mechanically. It was four o'clock and stars had died, moon vanished in an ash-colored sky.

"But how much? How long?"

"Keep going," she said, "you're almost there."

In clammy predawn, Ilana felt her shoulders droop. The lines on her face she could just about feel through her skin. How deeply they'd etched themselves. Winds had calmed to nothing, so what shrouded the water now was a vast stillness. Even their voices seemed muted by it, echoes nonexistent. Parallel to them the *Lazarilla* had slowed. If you squinted from deck you could make out figures standing still, watching. They hung there over the rails. They froze like shadows in the dark.

"Almost," Ilana whispered. "Almost there."

It was true. When the sun rose they'd see the mainland shore and see it was close. Now, though, it was hard to believe things were on the verge of dawn. They seemed, instead, to be on the edge of some black well, a sewer of ink into which the world would slide.

"Go away," she sobbed. Her tongue filled her mouth. "I don't believe you anymore."

Ilana leaned far over. She shoved the half-finished cup back towards the face. "Please believe me. Keep going. You're almost there."

Dorey rolled over. Hands reached for goggles. Then she slid into a backstroke before rolling over again, faced the voice that hounded her right back into the cold, goggles intact, hands clenched below the surface.

"Ilana, what are you doing to me."

She started to swim again . . .

"Here, dear," said Ilana. "Here."

"Ah."

"You're almost there."

She inched her head forward. The cup waited, she could smell it. Lips tried to find the rim and they swelled around it.

"Almost there," said Ilana.

Sweet liquid burned down her throat, hurt her tongue, and she tried to scream. Another sip. Another. Had to. Then it hurt too much and brought back the nausea. She shook her head. No. No more. Too sick. Almost there, that's what Ilana said and Ilana wouldn't have lied. Well, she'd better not waste time then. Couldn't afford to throw up. Precious energy spent.

"Going," she said. Ilana understood. She looked to Sarge for reassurance and he nodded. Let her go. Believe it or not, she's all right.

Dorey stroked sideways in the water, then she'd stopped and was treading again, facing the pontoon. Ilana leaned forward. The repetition was patient, methodical. Ilana listened harder. She could feel her ears straining as if both were hands reaching for something just beyond reasonable grasp. In the patience, the repetitious care with which the words were repeated for her, she got a glimpse of something familiar and of something enduring and realized that, apparent or not, this enduring center was alive in the body speaking before her. It was what had pushed so far, so hard, for more than a day now, had done so without sleep or the relief of being warmed by touch. Dorey, she said. Ilana smiled, relieved, finally recognizing her. She listened. Then she had it.

"Ilana. Do you know me now?"

"Yes," said Ilana, "I am proud."

"See you," Dorey blurted.

When she began to swim again, Ilana let her head sink tiredly to her hand. She was older physically and irrevocably. Hair all gray. Too old to bear children. Too much of that water inside had dried up by now. Still, what she'd recognized in Dorey—or what she'd finally recognized as Dorey—was there in her, too, she knew. What was it but a capacity for some incessant kind of behavior. An incessance that made you put one foot before the other when you no longer wanted to, or made you send one arm stroking when nothing was left to propel it. As if the instinct to survive lived deeper in them than desire itself, deeper than consciousness. That was what she'd recognized, this instinct as base as blood, and like blood it ran through both of them . . .

In the last mile, the water calmed to a lovely stillness. It reflected a cloudless sky, tinted the sky's reflected image slightly green. Flame-gold sun crawled above the horizon. It was a perfect day.

The closer they got to shore, the more the air changed. It was heavier, less pure. It was sweeter. Gulls swooped against the sky, struck water for fish. They'd rise, small catch flapping in beaks, their wings fluffed to shake off water. Sometimes they'd circle. One would break away, torpedo the water with a scream of triumph.

Dorey heard one thing now, one series of sounds. It was the breathe, stroke, stroke that coincided with the boom, thump, thump of her heart. That heart constituted a powerful sort of engine. Fifty beats, normally, was what it took to propel her through a minute. Sometimes less. And now it seemed to her to have slowed considerably, immeasurable time stretching between each pulsation, each pause delineated by the suck of a breath. There was nothing else in the world but this. Each stroke took her farther away from what she'd been before. One stroke a lover. One stroke a giant. The strokes disappeared with the water they propelled through. She left them all behind. So what she headed towards was unknown, the land she touched would be a strange one. She'd arrive bereft of all the elements by which she could quantify the shape of a day, or qualify her place within it. Arrive stripped, therefore different . . .

"Keep your distance. Please." Sarge had to use a bullhorn. His voice was too raw. The closer they got, the more boats putted out to meet them. Not an overwhelming number of vessels but enough, hell of a lot more than he'd ever have thought of, and they were all shapes and sizes. Made him nervous. So he kept repeating that, keep your distance. Please. Keep your distance and be careful, she's pretty tired right now. They hung back, obedient. The faces on them were curious. Plenty were young faces but looked slightly worn, strained with a looming anticipation.

At 7:38 a.m. Dorey picked up pace a little. Water on the outside of her goggles had gotten lighter. She guessed sand. Then something inside her cracked open, bled out. Silently, breath spilling back into saltwater, she felt sounds coming from her totally muted by water. She was crying. She didn't know why. Just for the pain, maybe, that had turned to ice long ago, or for all those things that were now lost. Every stroke stripping more and more of it away. She was changing. That meant leaving skin behind. Her head wanted to bust open. Well, she'd sleep soon, once she got there, sleep and it would be okay then. Okay and maybe she'd never do this again, not ever, not unless she had to. Right. Only if she had to. She promised herself.

Muffled, Dorey was sobbing. It hurt. She needed to drink water. To bathe. She was hungry.

The water grew even lighter, goggles clouds in front of her that brightened the closer they got to the sun. She wasn't hungry anymore. Not dirty. Just trembling, she was just trembling all over with a happiness that seemed absolute, it was hot like fever, kept her moving in the foreign light of a strange kind of ecstasy. The 800, something whispered. Come on. You can do an 800.

She started to.

Come on. You are almost there, you know. Dorey. Keep going. Come on lady. Come on baby come on kid come on champ keep that pace come on. Too much for you? No. No, well, I'm glad to hear that. Glad, understand. Come on. You can do an 800.

She did.

What flew by her now were visions of sand. Her fingers clutched at sand and each time it was a mirage. She cried and kept going. Then her left hand hit a mirage and stuck. Fingers moved against the mirage. They burrowed in deep. Her fingers clawed at the grainy texture and squirmed with the unfamiliarity of it, this sense of touch. Other hand groped sightlessly forward. She reached and the right set of fingers touched too. She was on hands and knees in sand, head above water, and what washed over her back was sunlight.

"Did it," she said. The words squeezed out around her tongue.

There was noise. Voices. Splashing. She looked up, pinpointed one voice among many. Who? she asked.

"Dr. Gallagher here. John Gallagher. You've made it and it's a few feet to the beach. Would you like a hand?"

Uh-uh. She shook her head. Started to crawl. The water splashed with her. It swept up towards shore. She inched along and didn't stop until her hands touched sand that was dry and then she kept going, a little more, she told herself, just a little more, get those legs out of the water too. Her feet. Well, she thought she'd lost them long ago. But now they were touching sand too, and the sand was dry. She'd kept goggles on, so was effectively blind, but knew it by that touch. It was the sense of touch that distinguished her from fish, that set her apart from the water she'd been in. Had to be separate from something in order to touch it.

"May I?" Hands hovered at her goggle straps. She nodded.

Ilana removed them carefully. The eyes were almost shut. Light shot into them, blinding. Dorey reached to cover her eyes.

"Can you walk?"

She didn't know. She reached for Ilana's hand anyway and then she was standing. She looked awful. She was alternately bleached by salt and rubbed raw by it, swollen with water and nothing but skin and bones. The worn suits hung from her. She looked like some monster baby, crazed eyes half shut. Her tongue swelled out between her lips. She was shaking all over.

Record books would state that Dorey Thomas emerged on the mainland shore just before 8:15 a.m. The crossing had taken 26 hours, 9 minutes, 33 seconds.

A couple of journalists were there taking pictures. There'd be a big story in the local paper. There'd be a one-line mention in the *Times*, and a blurb in *SportsYear*.

Her feet left a couple of uncertain imprints in sand. Then she stopped, everything spinning. She let go of Ilana's hand. Took two steps on her own, then was falling forward. The bodies around her seemed far away . . .

She was overexposed, close to shock, sputtering breath. She looked just about dead. She was dripping water, and alive.

rina ferrarelli

During the third mile
not the eighteenth as expected
she surged ahead
leaving behind the press
of bodies, the breath
hot on her back
and set a pace
the experts claimed
she couldn't possibly keep
to the end.

Sure, determined,
moving to an inner rhythm
measuring herself against herself
alone in a field of fifty
she gained the twenty-six miles
of concrete, asphalt and humid weather
and burst into the roar of the crowd
to run the lap around the stadium
at the same pace
once to finish the race
and then again in victory

and she was still fresh
and not even out of breath
and standing.

# THE LOVELINESS OF THE LONG-DISTANCE RUNNER

### sara maitland

I sit at my desk and make a list of all the things I am not going to think about for the next four and half hours. Although it is still early the day is conducive to laziness—hot and golden. I am determined that I will not be lazy. The list reads:

1. My lover is running in an organized marathon race. I hate it.

2. Pheidippides, the Greek who ran the first marathon, dropped dead at the end of it. And his marathon was 4 miles shorter than hers is going to be. There is also heat stroke, torn Achilles tendons, shin splints and cramp. Any and all of which, including the first option, will serve her right. And will also break my heart.

3. The women who are going to support her, love her, pour water down her back and drinks down her throat are not me. I am jealous of them.

4. Marathon running is a goddam competitive, sexist, lousy thing to do.

5. My lover has the most beautiful body in the world. Because she runs. I fell in love with her because she had the most

beautiful body I had ever seen. What, when it comes down to it, is the difference between my devouring of her as a sex object and her competitive running? Anyway she says she does not run competitively. Anyway I say that I do not any longer love her just because she has the most beautiful body.

Now she will be doing her warm-up exercises. I know these well, as she does them every day. She was doing them the first time I saw her. I had gone to the country to stay the weekend with her sister, who's a lawyer colleague of mine and a good friend. We were doing some work together. We were sitting in her living room and she was feeding her baby and Jane came in, in running shorts, T-shirt and yards and yards of leg. Katy had often joked about her sister who was a games mistress in an all-girls school, and I assumed that this was she. Standing by the front door, with the sun on her hair, she started these amazing exercises. She stretched herself from the waist and put her hands flat on the floor; she took her slender foot in her hand and bent over backwards. The blue shorts strained slightly; there was nothing spare on her, just miles and miles of tight, hard, thin muscle. And as she exhibited all this peerless flesh she chatted casually of this and that—how's the baby, and where she was going to run. She disappeared through the door. I said to Katy,
    "Does she know I'm gay?"
    Katy grinned and said, "Oh, yes."
    "I feel set-up."
    "That's what they're called—setting-up exercises."
    I felt very angry. Katy laughed and said, "She is too."
    "Is what?" I asked.
    "Gay." I melted into a pool of desire.

· · ·

*It's better to have started. The pre-race excitement makes me feel a little sick. Tension. But also . . . people punching the air and shouting "Let's go, let's go." Psyching themselves up. Casing each other out. Who's better than who? Don't like it. Don't want to do it. Wish I hadn't worn this T-shirt. It has "I am a feminist jogger" on it. Beth and Emma gave it to me. Turns people on though. Men. Not on to me but on to beating me. I won't care. There's a high on starting though, crossing the line. Good to be going, good to have got here. Doesn't feel different because someone has called it a marathon, rather than a good long run. Keep it that way. But I would like to break three and a half hours. Step by step. Feel good. Fitter than I've ever been in my life, and I like it. Don't care what Sally says. Mad to despise body when she loves it so. Dualist. I like running. Like me running. Space and good feeling. Want to run clear of this crowd—too many people, too many paces. Want to find someone to run my own pace with. Have to wait. Pace; endurance; deferment of pleasure; patience; power. Sally ought to like it—likes the benefits alright. Bloke nearby wearing a T-shirt that reads "Runners make the best lovers." He grins at me. Bastard. I'll show him: run for the Women's Movement. A trick. Keep the rules. My number one rule is "run for yourself." But I bet I can run faster than him.*

*Hurt myself running once, because of that. Ran a 10-mile race, years ago, with Annie, meant to be a fun-run and no sweat. There was this jock; a real pig; he kept passing us, dawdling, letting us pass him, passing again. And every time these remarks—the Vaseline stains from our nipples, or women getting him too turned on to run. Stuff like that; and finally he runs off, all sprightly and tough, patronizing. We ran on. Came into the last mile or so and there he was in front of us, tiring. I could see he was tired. "Shall we?" I said to Annie, but she was tired too. "Go on then," she was laughing at me, and I did. Hitched up a gear or two, felt great, zoomed down the hill after him, cruised alongside, made it look easy, said, "Hello, sweetheart, you look tired," and sailed on.*

*Grinned back over my shoulder, he had to know who it was, and pulled a muscle in my neck. Didn't care—he was really pissed off. Glided over the finishing line and felt great for twenty minutes. Then I felt bad; should have known better—my neck hurt like hell, my legs cramped from over-running. But it wasn't just physical. Felt bad mentally. Playing those games.*

*Not today. Just run and feel good. Run into your own body and feel it. Feel road meeting foot, one by one, a good feeling. Wish Sally knew why I do it. Pray she'll come and see me finish. She won't. Stubborn bitch. Won't think about that. Just check leg muscles and pace and watch your ankles. Run.*

If she likes to run that much of course I don't mind. It's nice some evenings when she goes out, and comes back and lies in the bath. A good salty woman. A flavour that I like. But I can't accept this marathon business: who wants to run 26 miles and 385 yards, in a competitive race? Jane does. For the last three months at least our lives have been taken over by those 26 miles, what we eat, what we do, where we go, and I have learned to hate every one of them. I've tried. "Why?" I've asked over and over again; but she just says things like, "Because it's there, the ultimate." Or "Just once Sally, I'll never do it again." I *bet*, I think viciously. Sometimes she rationalizes: women have to do it. Or, it's important to the girls she teaches. Or, it has to be a race because nowhere else is set up for it: you need the other runners, the solidarity, the motivation. "Call it sisterhood. You can't do it alone. You need—" And I interrupt and say, "You need the competition; you need people to beat. Can't you see?" And she says, "You're wrong. You're also talking about something you know nothing about. So shut up. You'll just have to believe me: you need the other runners and mostly they need you and want you to finish. And the crowd wants you to finish, they say. I want to experience that solidarity, of other people wanting you to do what you want to do." Which is a slap in the face for me, because I don't want her to do what she wants to do.

And yet—I love the leanness of her, which is a gift to me from marathon training. I love what her body is and what it can do, and go on doing and not be tired by doing. She has the most beautiful legs, hard, stripped down, with no wastage, and her Achilles tendons are like flexible rock. Running does that for her. And then I think, damn, damn, damn. I will not love her for those reasons; but I will love her because she is tough and enduring and wryly ironic. Because she is clear about what she wants and prepared to go through great pain to get it; and because her mind is clear, careful and still open to complexity. She wants to stop being a Phys. Ed. teacher because now that women are getting as much money for athletic programmes the authorities suddenly demand that they should get into competition, winning trips. Whereas when she started it was for fun and for women being together as women, doing the things they had been laughed at for as children.

She says I'm a dualist and laughs at me. She says I want to separate body and soul while she runs them together. When she runs she thinks: not ABC like I think with my tidy well-trained mind, but in flashes—she'll trot out with some problem and run 12 or 15 miles and come home with the kinks smoothed out. She says that after 8 or 10 miles she hits a euphoric high—grows free—like meditation or something, but better. She tells me that I get steamed up through a combination of tension and inactivity. She can run out that stress and be perfectly relaxed while perfectly active. She comes clean. Ten or 12 miles at about eight minutes per mile: about where she'll be getting to now.

I have spent another half-hour thinking about the things I

was not going to think about. Tension and inactivity. I cannot concentrate the mind.


*When I bend my head forward and Emma squeezes the sponge on to my neck, I can feel each separate drop of water flow down my back or over my shoulders and down between my breasts. I listen to my heartbeat and it seems strong and sturdy. As I turn Emma's wrist to see her watch her blue veins seem translucent and fine. Mine seem like strong wires conducting energy. I don't feel I want to drink and have it lying there in my stomach, but I know I should. Obedient, giving over to Emma, I suck the bottle. Tell myself I owe it to her. Her parents did not want her to spend a hot Saturday afternoon nursing her games teacher. When I'm back in rhythm I feel the benefits of the drink. Emma is a good kid. Her parents' unnamed suspicions are correct. I was in love with a games teacher once. She was a big strong woman, full of energy. I pretended to share what the others thought and mocked her. We called her Tarzan and how I loved her. In secret dreams I wanted to be with her. "You Tarzan, me Jane," I would mutter, contemplating her badly shaved underarms, and would fly with her through green trees, swing on lianas of delight. She was my first love; she helped make me a strong woman. The beauty, the immensity of her. When we swam she would hover over the side of the pool and as I looked up through the broken sparkly waters there she would be hauling me through with her strength.*

*Like Sally hauls me through bad dreams, looming over me in the night as I breathe up through the broken darkness. She hauls me through muddle with her sparkly mind. Her mind floats, green with sequinned points of fire. Sally's mind. Lovely. My mind wears Nike running shoes with the neat white flash curling back on itself. It fits well and leaves room for my toes to flex. If I weren't a games teacher I could be a feminist chiropodist—or a midwife. Teach* other women the contours of their own bodies—show them the new places where their bodies can take them. Sally doesn't want to be taken—only in the head. Sex of course is hardly in her head. In the heart? My heart beats nearly twenty pulses a minute slower than hers: we test them together lying in the darkness, together. "You'll die, you shit," I want to yell at her. "You'll die and leave me. Your heart isn't strong enough." I never say it. Nice if your hearts matched. The Zulu warrior women could run 50 miles a day and fight at the end of it. Fifty miles together, perfectly in step, so the veldt drummed with it. Did their hearts beat as one? My heart can beat with theirs, slow and strong and efficient— pumping energy.

Jane de Chantal, after whom I was named, must have been a jogger. She first saw the Sacred Heart—how else could she have known that slow, rich stroke which is at the heart of everything? Especially back then when the idea of heart meant only emotions. But she was right. The body, the heart at the heart of it all: no brain, no clitoris without that strong slow heart. Thesis: was eighteenth-century nun the first jogger? Come on; this is rubbish. Think about footstrike and stride length. Not this garbage. Only one Swedish garbage collector, in the whole history of Swedish municipal rubbish collection, has ever worked through to retirement age—what perseverance, endurance. What a man. Person. Say garbage person. Sally says so. Love her. Damn her. She is my princess. I'm the younger son (say person) in the fairy story. But running is my wise animal. If I'm nice to my running it will give me good advice on how to win the princess. Float with it. Love it. Love her. There has to be a clue.

Emma is here again. Car? Bicycle? She can't have run it. She and Beth come out and give me another drink, wipe my face. Lovely hands. I come down and look around. After 20 miles they say there are two sorts of smiles among runners—the smiles of those who are suffering and the smiles of those who aren't. "You're running too fast," says Beth. "You're too high. Pace yourself, you silly twit. You're going to hurt." "No," I say, "I'm feeling good." But I know she's right. Discipline counts. Self-discipline, but Beth will help with that. "We need you to finish," says Emma. "Of course she'll finish," says Beth. I love them and I run away from them, my mouth feeling good with orange juice and soda water. Ought to have been Sally though. Source of sweetness. How could she do this to me? How could she leave me? Desert me in the desert. Make a desert. This is my quest—my princess should be here. Princess: she'd hate that. I hate that. Running is disgusting; makes you think those thoughts. I hurt. I hurt and I am tired. They have lots of advice for this point in a marathon. They say, think of all the months that are wasted if you stop now. But not wasted because I enjoyed them. They say, whoever wanted it to be easy? I did. They say, think of that man who runs marathons with only one leg. And that's meant to be inspirational? He's mad. We're all mad. There's no reason but pride. Well, pride then. Pride and the thought of Sally suppressing her gloating if I go home and say it hurt too much. I need a good reason to run into and through this tiredness.

Something stabs at my eyes. Nothing really hurt before and now it hurts. Takes me all of three paces to locate the hurt: cramp in the upper thighs. Sally's fault; I think of her and tense up. Ridiculous. But I'll be damned if I quit now. Run into the pain; I know it will go away and I don't believe it. Keep breathing steadily. It hurts. I know it hurts, shut up, shut up, shut up. Who cares if it hurts? I do. Don't do this. Seek out a shirt in front of you and look at the number. Keep looking at the number. 297. Do some sums with that. Can't think of any. Not divisible by 2, or 3, or 5. Nor 7. 9. 9 into 29 goes 3. 3 and carry 2. 9 into 27. Always works. If you can divide by something the cramp goes away. Is that where women go in childbirth—into the place of charms? All gay women should run marathons—gives them solidarity with

*their labouring sisters. I feel sick instead. I look ahead and there*
*is nothing but the long hill. Heartbreaking. I cannot.*

   *Shirt 297 belongs to a woman, a little older than me perhaps.*
*I run beside her; she is tired too. I feel better and we run together.*
*We exchange a smile. Ignore the fact that catching up with her*
*gives me a lift. We exchange another smile. She is slowing. She*
*grins and deliberately reduces her pace so that I can go ahead*
*without feeling bad. That's love. I love her. I want to turn round,*
*jog back and say, "I will leave my lover for you." "Dear Sally," I*
*will write, "I am leaving you for a lady who" (and Sally's mental*
*red pencil will correct to "whom") "I met during the marathon*
*and unlike you was nice and generous to me." Alternative letter,*
*"Dear Sally, I have quit because long-distance running brings you*
*up against difficulties and cramps and I cannot take the pain."*
*Perseverance, endurance, patience and accepting love are part of*
*running a marathon. She won't see it. Damn her.*

   *Must be getting near now because there's a crowd watching.*
*They'll laugh at me. "Use the crowd," say those who've been here*
*before. "They want you to finish. Use that." Lies. Sally doesn't*
*want me to finish. What sort of princess doesn't want the quest*
*finished? Wants things cool and easy? Well, pardon me, your Royal*
*Highness. Royal Highness: the marathon is 26 miles and 385 yards*
*long because some princess wanted to see the start of the 1908*
*Olympic Marathon from Windsor Palace and the finish from her*
*box in the White City Stadium. Two miles longer than before.*
*Now standardized. By appointment. Damn the Royal Princess.*
*Damn Sally.*


Finally I accept that I'm not going to do any work today. It
takes me several more minutes to accept what that means—
that I'm involved in that bloody race. People tend, I notice, to
equate accepting with liking—but it's not that simple. I don't

like it. But, accepting, I get the car out and drive to the shops and buy the most expensive bath oil I can find. It's so expensive that the box is perfectly modest—no advertising, no half-naked women. I like half-naked women as a matter of fact, but there are such things as principles. Impulsively I also buy some matching lotion, thinking that I will rub it on her feet tonight. Jane's long slender feet are one part of her body that owe nothing to running. This fact alone is enough to turn me into a foot fetishist.

After I have bought the stuff, I slaver a bit over the thought of rubbing it into her poor battered feet. I worked it out once. Each foot hits the ground about 800 times per mile. The force of the impact is three times her weight. 122 pounds times 800 times 26 miles. It does not bear thinking about. I realize the implications of rubbing sweet ointment into the tired feet of the beloved person. At first I am embarrassed and then I think, well, Mary Magdalene is one way through the sex object/true love dichotomy. Endurance, perseverance, love. She must have thought the crucifixion a bit mad too. Having got this far in acceptance I think that I might as well go down to the finish and make her happy. We've come a long way together. So I get back into the car and do just that.


*It is true, actually. In the last few miles the crowd holds you together. This is not the noble hero alone against the world. Did I want that? But this is better. A little kid ducked under the rope and gave me a half-eaten ice-lolly—raspberry flavour. Didn't want it. Couldn't refuse such an act of love. Took it. Felt fine. Smiled. She smiled back. It was a joy. Thank you sister. The people roar for you, hold you through the sweat and tears. They have no faces. The finishing line just is. Is there. You are meant to raise your arms and shout, "Rejoice, we conquer" as you cross it. Like*

*Pheidippides did when he entered Athens and history. And death. But all I think is, "Christ, I've let my anti-gravity muscles get tight." They hurt. Sally is here. I don't believe it. Beth drapes a towel over my shoulders without making me stop moving. Emma appears, squeaking, "Three hours, 26 and a half. That's great, that's bloody great." I don't care. Sally has cool soft arms. I look for them. They hold me. "This is a sentimental ending," I try to say. I'm dry. Beth gives me a beer. I cannot pour it properly. It flows over my chin, soft and gold, blissfully cold. I manage a grin and it spreads all over me. I feel great. I lean against Sally again. I say, "Never, never again." She grins back and, not without irony, says, "Rejoice, we conquer."*

# TO SWIM, TO BELIEVE

Centre College, Danville, Kentucky

maxine kumin

The beautiful excess of Jesus on the waters
is with me now in the Boles Natatorium.
This bud of me exults, giving witness:

these flippers that rose up to be arms.
These strings drawn to be fingers.
Legs plumped to make my useful fork.

Each time I tear this seam to enter,
all that I carry is taken from me,
shucked in the dive.

Lovers, children, even words go under.
Matters of dogma spin off in the freestyle
earning that mid-pool spurt, like faith.

Where have I come from? Where am I going?
What do I translate, gliding back and forth
erasing my own stitch marks in this lane?

Christ on the lake was not thinking
where the next heel-toe went.
God did him a dangerous favor
whereas Peter, the thinker, sank.

The secret is in the relenting,
the partnership. I let my body work

accepting the dangerous favor
from this king-size pool of waters.
Together I am supplicant. I am bride.

# TEAMWORK

lucy   jane   bledsoe

The first thing any of us noticed about Thalia Peterson was her legs. And I mean *legs*. The girl could play some serious ball too.

We all knew when she joined the team that there'd be changes. Not that we were blatant about anything, but when you work out together three to four hours a day, you get to reading each other intimately. You learn a lot about your team-mates. We all knew who liked girls, who did it with boys, who hated white girls and who thought black people were dumb. We had all those kinds of people on the team, but on a good ball team you learn to respect differences and keep your eye on the ball. You become so tightly woven into each other's lives by so much sweat, by so many wins and losses, fights and tears, and mid-game highs, that you can have all your homo-phobia, heterophobia, racism, and what have you, and still not be able to separate yourself from your teammates. On the court anyway.

Thalia Peterson was a southern white girl, big legged, with white teeth and a thick ponytail of smooth blond hair. Her eyes were both narrow-set and deep-set at the same time and had long dark lashes. She seemed farther back there than most people. I wondered if we'd ever be able to read her like we read one another. She wore make-up, too. Not that we weren't used to that. Both Kathy Jones and Amanda Severson wore make-up and of course that was their business, but Thalia's make-up was straight out of *Glamour* magazine, almost a lifestyle. She had the kind of looks boys made a point of turning and looking at, because if they didn't their manhood would be questioned. I knew she was pretty, but her looks weren't the kind I fell for. Just couldn't stomach those eyes.

Thalia Peterson was a junior like me. She'd been at the university for two years but hadn't come out for the team. End of her freshman year she pledged Phi Beta Pi, the snottiest sorority on campus, and got herself established there before revealing her jock talents. That was her business of course, though some say she waited two years just so she could blow everyone away when she did come out for the team.

At first we kind of liked her sorority connections because suddenly our home game crowds swelled full of her Phi Beta Pi sisters and their fraternity boyfriends. The fact was, people loved to watch Thalia Peterson play ball, and I couldn't blame them. She was a big girl, strong and tall, and damn near the most aggressive ball player I've ever seen. Get up under that basket for a rebound and *boom!* she'd block you out by throwing her powerful behind into you, more often than not sending you flying across the floor. She never got fouls called on her because the refs couldn't believe someone that feminine and pretty had any *umph*. You could see a quick puzzled look cross the ref's face before he decided that Thalia's opponent must have just fallen down. *She* couldn't have pushed that girl onto the floor. Truth was, in addition to a well-aimed elbow, Thalia Peterson was very skilled in getting her body in the right place at the right time.

There was something else about Thalia Peterson. She didn't

just like winning. She expected to win, even *lived* to win. In everything.

Most women on the team didn't enjoy her as much as the fans in the audience did. They didn't think it fair for Thalia to come out for the team her junior year when the rest of us had struggled up from junior varsity since freshman year. I didn't see that it mattered. But then, she didn't bump my position. I didn't have much of a position. I came off the bench as a guard when the game was clearly won or clearly lost. That was okay with me. Games scared me shitless. I played for the practices, the uniforms, the feeling of being on a team.

Some people cared a great deal about Thalia Peterson coming out her junior year. Kathy Jones for one. And Carson McDuffy for another. Kathy Jones, I already told you, wore make-up, was real skinny and gangly, and played center mostly. She was a fantastic shooter and great on boards, but inconsistent and definitely a bad ball handler. Carson McDuffy was hot. She could do everything—dribble, pass, shoot, and sometimes even rebound, though she was only five-foot-four. Her problem was that she played forward, insisted on it, in spite of her height. Her other problem was that she was hotheaded.

Carson was a very serious-minded ball player, hilarious off the court, singular in her likes and dislikes (luckily, I was one of her likes) and a lesbian. She had a medium-sized angular body, short scruffy brown hair and pale white skin. Carson had her goals set on making the Eastern Division All-Star team.

In the fall, on the first day of tryouts for the university team, Carson's confidence glowed. She made passes behind her back, crashed through a crowded key for lay-ups, and played as if the fast break was the only offensive option.

"Okay," I told her. "So you've been working out all summer. Easy on the rest of us okay?"

She fired me one of her try-and-stop-me grins and pressed

harder. The truth was she'd never looked better. I always took her with a grain of salt, she was so crazy, but her enthusiasm spurred the team on. I hoped almost as much as she did that she'd make the Eastern Division All-Star team this year.

Carson noticed Thalia Peterson during tryouts all right, and she planned on putting her in her place immediately. When Coach Montgomery shouted, "Pair up for one-on-one," Carson made her move. I saw her cock her finger, thumb up, at Thalia. "You," was all she said. Then she strode toward Thalia as if she was coming on to her. "Oh, god," I said under my breath. That woman always reminded me of lit dynamite that never quite explodes.

By instinct, the rest of us backed off the court to watch. Carson shot a bullet pass at Thalia's middle. "You go first," she said. Thalia caught the pass as gracefully as if it had been lobbed. Even before Montgomery blew the whistle Carson's hands were working Thalia, cutting the air in front of her face like blades. Thalia maintained a regal stance, casual and un-interested. The whistle blew. Thalia faked a jump shot, then moved left. Carson stayed on her, grinning and chattering like a monkey. "Go ahead, go ahead," she threatened. "Try and get around me. Try."

Thalia tried, her blond ponytail swinging back and forth on her back. When she couldn't get past Carson she stopped, fig-uring she could easily put up a jump shot over Carson's head. Shouting a loud war cry, Carson stuffed the attempted shot. She wiped her hands on her shorts, chased down the ball, and stood at the top of the key waiting for Montgomery's whistle. That's when I first noticed how much Thalia liked to win. She was *mad*. She wore her anger like a queen, chin up and eyes smoldering like rubies. Even so, Carson drove by her three times in a row. After each goal she hooted her triumph in hyena-like howls as she trotted back up to the top of the key.

The fourth time she missed the lay-up and Thalia rebounded. It was her game after that. She'd miscalculated Carson's talents, but now that she knew them, she could meet them. Thalia faked left, drove right, stopped short, and popped a jump shot. Next she sunk a rimless goal from the top of the key, right over Carson's hands. To prove she could drive, Thalia pushed to the left, lost Carson as she cut under the basket, and hooked the ball in. At that point Coach sent Carson to the locker room for cursing out loud and Thalia toweled the back of her neck, easy and casual.

After that day we knew Carson hated Thalia, and some of us wondered if she'd quit the team if Thalia got her starting position. The other starters were Kathy Jones at center, Susan Thurmond and Jackie Sanchez (who I was beginning to fall deeply in something with) as guards, and Stella Stellason at forward. Everyone knew that Stella was sleeping with our coach, Hilary Montgomery, and nobody saw any need to do much more than raise an eyebrow. It would be one thing if Stella were no good and Montgomery were playing her all the time, something like that, but Stella was key to our team— tall, smooth, consistent, just what hotheaded Carson needed out there to shine. No way did Thalia threaten Stella's position.

Well, sure enough, the season started and Thalia wound up bumping Carson mostly. No one blamed Montgomery, except Carson. Carson had been a star all right, but she was too short and needed too much setting up. Thalia could set herself up. Besides, without Carson out there turning cartwheels to the basket, Stella was freer to show off her stuff, and she did. With Thalia on the team we stood a chance of going to the playoffs. What made me mad though was the tiny glint of triumph way back in those cryptic eyes of Thalia's. That wasn't necessary and I just knew it made Carson's blood boil.

Teams always have a lot of tension on them. Sometimes the tension is the main thing holding them together, but Thalia's presence brought a new kind of tension that we couldn't handle in our usual way. She seemed to almost control us. The locker room after practice lost its towel-slapping good-time feeling. A lot of people think jocks are immature, but I think there's something hotly primal about being naked and sweaty in a locker room, the place all steamed up from hot showers, after having sprinted for three hours. I'm never happier than I am then. But with Thalia there everything changed. I got the feeling she didn't like to undress in front of us. Yet, out of pride, she paraded around, displaying her body parts as if to make clear that no lesbians were gonna cow her. We all averted our eyes. Not that I wanted to look. I didn't. A heterosexual energy, the dangerous kind, wafted off her like strong perfume.

Most of us cooled down after practice, pulled on our pants, joked about dinner. Basketball practice launched me into the rest of my life, as if it was the source and everything else flowed from there. But for Thalia, the locker room was a place of transition. She had a routine as amazing as a Dr. Jekyll and Mr. Hyde act. As she applied make-up and pulled on nylon stockings, she transformed from basketball animal to Phi Beta Pi lady. She often shaved her legs in the locker room, slowly and carefully, as if to show how much others of us needed to do the same. By the time she left the locker room, this basketball powerhouse had become a graceful swan. The woman was smooth.

So the locker room was a lot quieter that year. We just showered and went off to dinner. Team jokes from last year fell flat and no new ones arose. Something about Thalia made me feel young and inadequate. Only Stella seemed to be at ease with her, making small conversation as if she didn't notice Thalia's cool response. Thalia was too southern polite not to speak when spoken to, but she didn't want to talk, that was clear. We all saw that and didn't try. Except Stella.

I admired Stella more than anyone on the team. She was so

solid. Jackie told me that Stella went to church every Sunday morning. She struck you as beautiful when you first saw her because of her carriage, but on closer inspection her face was rather plain. At first I didn't get why she, a poised and cultured black woman from L.A., was with Coach Montgomery, a thirty-five-year-old white woman from the Midwest. Coach had broad even features and a jaunty smile—*when* she smiled, which wasn't often. In a way, though black and white, Stella and Montgomery looked a bit alike. The big difference besides color was Stella's elegance and Montgomery's jock walk. The two of them were pretty discreet because much as I tried, I never saw anything pass between them during practices. They must have been scared at times. I sure was, and I didn't have a job to protect. I privately drew from Stella's sure confidence and from Montgomery's courage to live and love as she pleased. Without speaking an intimate word with either of these two women, I considered them my lesbian mentors. As something nameless thickened between Jackie and myself, I kept my eyes trained on Montgomery and Stella, looking for a signal, the go-ahead, something in their plain, forward moving faces that would tell me what my next move should be.


On the night of our third home game I jogged out onto the court with my team, so happy I thought I could die right then and be satisfied with my life. Jackie and I had finally started up our love affair. A sweetness coursed through my limbs, making me feel like an Olympic hurdler flying over life's obstacles with perfect elegance. On top of that our team was winning. Our record was a tremendous 7–0. Thalia's family had donated brand-new uniforms to the team (she had been complaining about how ghastly ugly the old ones were), so we looked pretty sharp too. When we lined up for lay-ups the school band blasted into action. Even the cheerleading squad pranced onto center court and whipped their pompons around. Understand that the band and cheerleaders did not attend women's games until we were on a winning streak, until there was glory to be reaped. I wasn't bitter though. I loved it. I even loved the hordes of fraternity boys that packed the gym. The night was fine.

We were playing North Carolina State, and we held a decent lead during most of the first half. I sat back on the bench and watched Jackie speed up and down the court. The movement of each muscle was a precious sight to me.

Shortly before halftime Montgomery benched Thalia to give her a breather and put in Carson. Suddenly the game turned around. North Carolina State broke our lead and then, in a quick ten minutes, proceeded to fast-break to an eight-point lead. Seconds before halftime, North Carolina State got the ball again, and went for the fast break. The buzzer sounded and the guard tipped the ball in for a lay-up. The official called the basket good. Montgomery lunged onto the court toward the ref, screaming that the basket sunk after the buzzer.

The ref slapped his hand to the back of his head, pointed at Montgomery, and called a technical foul on her. The crowd went crazy because Montgomery was right. That girl wasn't anywhere near the basket when the buzzer sounded. Someone pulled Montgomery back to the bench, and we lined up at half court while the player toed the line for her free throw. Carson was kicking the floor like a mad bull because she knew everyone would interpret our sudden slide to be a result of Montgomery putting her in and taking Thalia out. The North Carolina State player made her shot.

After a good talking-to at halftime we trotted back out onto the court and warmed up. Then Montgomery did something that surprised us all—she started Carson instead of Thalia. I figured she thought Carson was losing her confidence and put her in to let her know she wasn't to blame for the score. Montgomery always emphasized that we were a team, that one woman couldn't make or break anything. A nervous silence fell on the gym as the ten players took positions for the tip-off. A cold sweat saturated the air. I could see Carson's mouth working and would have thought she was praying if I didn't know better. Jackie wiped her hands on her hips and glanced at me. I felt instant warmth again. The ref held the ball up and glanced around the circle. He hesitated as two players suddenly traded places. Then, just as he bent his knees to make the toss, a male voice in the bleachers erupted out of the perfect silence. "Bench the dyke! Play Thalia Peterson."

For a split second everyone in the gym was stunned. The air felt yellow and still. Even the ref, who stood between the two centers with the ball balanced on his fingertips, stepped back and squinted at the stands. Then a gurgling of fraternity laughter eased some people's discomfort and the ref tossed the ball.

Something turned sour for me in that moment at halftime against North Carolina State. Everyone knew the fraternity boy meant Carson, but I knew that he also meant Stella and Montgomery, Jackie and myself. The raw hatred in his voice felt like a boot stomping on a tender green shoot.

We lost that game and the next one too. Every time I stepped into the big, silent gym for practice, I heard an echo of that boy's voice. Sometimes, for a flashing second, I could even see the group of fraternity boys in the stands, jeering, knowing. Montgomery and Stella were no help anymore; they were as indicted as I was. Jackie and I had our first fight that week.

Looking back, I think it's a miracle we ever won any games. So many of us were in some stage of coming out, no one really comfortable, none of us able to say "lesbian" without cringing. We were scared, we were in love, we were all little bundles of explosive passion. Sometimes this energy drove us to victory on the court, other times we crumbled under it.

By midseason Jackie and I were solid. We were crazy for each other, but love isn't everything and we fought a lot. She didn't know what she was doing messing with a white girl and I didn't know what I was doing messing with any girl at all. Our common ground lay in the realm of ideals and primal loves and fears, but our earthbound experiences were different enough to make us both crazy. We carried on just the same.

After the North Carolina State game, Montgomery began switching around the starting line-up. It's not like she substituted one starter for another (say, Carson for Thalia), but out of the top six players she tried different combinations and often Carson was in there. Sometimes Thalia was not.

Mixing up the starting line-up too much might not be smart basketball (though in this case it might have been), but it sure made me like Montgomery. I don't really know why she did it, but I suspect she saw it as a morale issue. She probably noticed how that boy's remark registered on some of our young faces. Maybe she knew she had some power to erase the imprint of that boot. With me she was right, I secretly drew from her strength, but the morale of the rest of the team sagged. When Thalia didn't start she lounged on the bench as if it were a settee, as if she was entertaining in a drawing room and hadn't the faintest interest in the game, and when Montgomery put her in she gave only seventy-five percent. If Montgomery started her, however, Thalia gave her all. The insult to Montgomery, the idea that she could be manipulated by Thalia's insolence, infuriated me. I was glad when Montgomery started her less and less often. A rumor circulated that Thalia's parents offered a large donation to the Women's Intercollegiate Fund on the behind-closed-doors stipulation that Thalia be reinstated as a permanent first stringer. I don't know if this was true, but people swore it was. Someone knew someone who knew someone who worked in Dean Roper's office. She'd heard the offer. I believed the story more than I disbelieved it.

Carson saw the changing line-up as an opportunity to re-establish her position on the team. Her attitude improved. She kept her mouth shut and played ball like it was a matter of life and death. At the same time Carson became more and more out about her lesbianism. She thought everyone else should come out as well. "A bunch of fucking closet dykes," she semi-joked at me and Jackie one night in the library. She took that boy's word like it was a piece of clay and fashioned her own meaning out of it. I cringed and quickly looked over my shoulder to see if anyone was within earshot. Jackie just shrugged. "With Montgomery and Stella we're talking about a job," she said. Yeah, I thought, and with me we're talking about fear. Jackie didn't want to come out and I happily hid behind her wishes. So for lesbians on the team that just left the jealousy-à-trois, as we called them, three women who had not yet managed to come out even to themselves but were involved in a triangle of jealousy complicated, in my opinion, by a lack of sex. Of course there were the four definitely straight women on the team: Susan Thurmond, Amanda Severson, Kathy Jones, and Thalia Peterson. Somehow we were more and more aware of who was who. Somehow that individual clarity seemed to dissolve our team clarity.

One day, near the end of the season, Montgomery came into practice a half hour late. Her face was tight and pasty looking. "Put on sweats," she ordered. "Dean Roper is coming to talk with you. Meet back here." She disappeared into her office.

When we returned to the gym, we sat on the bleachers. Roper came in with a Father-Knows-Best smile on his face. "Carson," he said, forcing a twinkle to his eye, "why don't you come on in first."

"What?" Thalia kept saying, her voice pitched high. "I don't get it."

Thalia was not a good actress. It was obvious that she was the only one who *did* get it.

Five minutes later, Carson came out glaring. "It's the Inquisition," she mumbled, throwing herself on a bench.

"Go on and get dressed, Carson," Roper ordered, knowing an agitator when he saw one.

I expected Carson to challenge Roper, at least by hesitating before obeying, but perhaps she realized the safety of the rest of us hinged on not exciting him further. Carson left and Roper called in Stella, who strode before the dean like a gazelle leading a turtle.

One by one Roper called us into Montgomery's office. Except for Carson, each came back out and sat on the bench with the rest of us. No one spoke a word. Finally, second from last, my turn came. I was surprised to see Coach sitting next to the big oak desk in her own office. I couldn't believe that she had had to sit through each of the interviews. Roper sat at Montgomery's desk. He leaned forward, no longer smiling. "We've had some problems on the team, I understand." He spoke slowly. I could tell that despite some discomfort he was savoring every moment of this scandal. "Many of the women I've spoken to have felt unsafe because of the lesbianism on the team. What about you?"

"I feel safe."

"Are you a lesbian?" Roper looked as if he had tasted the word. I glanced involuntarily at Montgomery, expecting her to protect me, but her eyes were blank. I stared at her folded hands realizing she had been forced to sit through even the interrogation of Stella. My eyes moved from her hands to her chest. She wasn't breathing. Suddenly I wanted to protect her. My mind raced, frantically searching for the right response. I thought of Jackie, of Stella and Montgomery. I looked Roper squarely in the face and remained utterly silent.

He sighed, "I can't force you to speak, young lady. We'll get to the bottom of this one way or another. Whichever side you're on, you may be sure it will be straightened out."

When I went back into the gym the whole team looked at me and I knew they were trying to read my face, to guess what I had said. No one moved, waiting for Roper to call in the last of us—Thalia Peterson. Roper was not a shrewd man. In fact, after this slip I knew he was downright stupid. He never did call Thalia. He left by a back door and Montgomery came to tell us to shower and go to dinner.

"Okay, no one is leaving the locker room," Kathy Jones said after practice two days later.

"What's going on?" Carson stood, pants unzipped and one shoe in hand, ready to fight.

"Be mellow, McDuffy," Amanda Severson warned.

Susan Thurmond was suddenly at Amanda's and Kathy's side. Three of the four straight women stood in a block. Thalia had her back turned and was shoveling her brush, clothes, and blow dryer into her gym bag, fast. She grabbed the bag and headed for the door without even brushing her hair.

"Where're you going, Peterson?" Kathy said. Since when was Thalia called Peterson?

Thalia tossed her blond hair, ran fingers through the top. "This has nothing to do with me."

"Oh, I think it may have everything to do with you."

A First Lady smile. "I'm real busy. Gotta go."

"I bet you could spare five minutes." This from Amanda walking toward Thalia. Thalia sat on the bench, a good distance away from the rest of us.

"What's the deal?" Carson struck her butchest stance, facing off with the straight girls.

"Mellow, McDuffy."

"Don't tell me what to be, Severson." Carson stepped forward, slitting her eyes.

"So what's going on?" Jackie finally said, the only sensible tone of voice so far.

"We thought we should all talk," Amanda said. I understood the first "we" to mean the straight women. "Look, we still have a chance to make it to the playoffs. And this . . . this bullshit about lesbians on the team, well . . ."

"Fuck yourself!" Carson screamed. "You all can just go fuck yourselves."

Kathy Jones lunged for Carson, then stopped half an inch from her face. "Shut up, McDuffy. You ain't got a chip on your shoulder, you got a block of wood so big you can't see your own ugly face in the mirror."

Carson went for her throat. A split second later Jackie was there, wrangling Carson's hands off Kathy. I tried to arrest her kicking legs. At the same time Amanda subdued Kathy.

"For goodness' sakes, *listen*," Amanda screamed.

We all turned when we heard Thalia say, in a near-growl, "Let me out of here." But Susan Thurmond blocked the door.

Shit, what was this? The straight girls getting ready to pound the shit out of us? Threaten or blackmail us? I started to sweat all over again.

"Go ahead, Amanda," Kathy said, her eyes impaling Carson.

"Kathy, Susan, and I wanted to tell you, well, we wanted to talk. None of us three gave any names, okay? None of us told Roper anything. We didn't say whether we were straight or whatever." Amanda sat on the bench and tears flowed into her eyes. "Geez, we used to be a *team*. We've got to pull together. Look, we *are* pulling together. See, that's why we haven't heard anything more from Roper. Don't you get it? He got no information. *None*."

"You mean none of you all said you were straight?" This was me, slow as always, taking it in.

"No. None of us said anything to that sleaze bag. What about the rest of you?"

"I didn't give him a clue."

"Nope."

"I just told him I didn't know and didn't give a shit either."

"I told him I was a lesbian," Carson said slowly, looking at her feet. "I said I had no idea if anyone else was."

"You take the hard road every time," Kathy Jones almost whispered.

"I just tell the truth." Carson tried to harden, but looked soft for once in her life.

"That's everyone but you, Thalia." We all turned to the end of the bench where Thalia sat, her face hot and red. We watched her muster all the aristocratic poise she could, but it wasn't much. For the first time in the year I'd known her, I saw the woman lose it. Her hands were shaking, with anger, I thought. Thalia had assumed her power in this situation. The past few days she had been looking more serene than usual, beauteous, as if a struggle had finally been resolved. It had never occurred to her that she would be sacrificed for the triumph of sisterhood.

"Thalia," pressed Amanda, "what did *you* tell Dean Roper?"

"He didn't call me in."

"Right. Then obviously you had already spoken to him."

Thalia stood and managed to say, "I have no idea what any of you are talking about." Those narrow eyes nearly crossed.

We sat and stared in silence at her straight posture, her composed face with the high cheekbones, her long graceful arms. Suddenly I saw a long line of stern, puritan women, severely beautiful and rich women, stacking up behind her as if she were in a house of mirrors. Mothers, grandmothers and great-grandmothers, all of them echoing, "I have no idea what any of you are talking about . . . I have no idea what any of you are talking about . . . I have no idea . . ."

We partied that night. Me, Jackie, Susan, Amanda, Kathy, Carson, even the jealousy-à-trois. Everyone except for Stella, Coach, and, of course, Thalia, gathered in Jackie's room and hashed over everything we'd missed this year during Thalia Peterson's reign of terror. We died laughing at every story, rocking in our relief at being safe. We raked Thalia over the coals, tearing her apart hair by hair, gesture by gesture. We were cruel.

But we softened as the night wore on and eventually crossed over that magic line into the dark blue waters of early morning. We left Thalia behind like a wrecked ship. Useless. History. Slowly and carefully we began telling stories from last year, only now elaborating on the jock, punch-line versions to fill in nuances, shades of meaning, our feelings. Some of us told our coming-out stories, our fears of others on the team finding out. We spoke, our voices tentative, about how much the team meant to us, how each woman was an experience in our lives we could never replace. Outside the single window of Jackie's dorm room daylight permeated the sky. I switched off the desk lamp. Even Carson, slumped on the corner of Jackie's bed, said in her husky voice, "Yeah, I guess I blew it in the locker room. We're all pulling together. Yeah, we're all pulling our share, aren't we?"

"Yeah," I said. I felt as if I finally understood the source of brilliance in a perfectly executed defense, in a flawless three-on-two fast break, in a full-court press when every team member was exactly where she was supposed to be.

We did not make it to the playoffs, Carson did not make the Eastern Division All-Star team (though Thalia did), and Jackie and I didn't make it through to the end of the year. She began seeing another woman on the team, finally bringing out one corner of the jealous triangle (which allowed the remaining two to collapse together in yet another torrid basketball romance). Naturally I was devastated and mushed through my final exams like a rain-soaked puppy, stupid, sloppy, miserable, and eager for the tiniest show of kindness. On the night before my last exam the phone rang. When I answered, Jackie's voice filled the receiver. I hadn't talked to her in three weeks and was so overwhelmed by her presence in my ear that I didn't even listen to what she said.

"You okay?" she repeated. "I just wanted to say hello."

"I miss you," I blurted.

"I know, babe," she sighed. I could feel her sorrow too, and that helped. "But we had a good year anyway, didn't we?"

"Yeah," I said, crying and then sobbing. In spite of everything it had been the best year of my life.

# FROM ''FIRST PEACE''

1975

### barbara lamblin

i was the all american girl, the winner, the champion,
the swell kid, good gal, national swimmer,
model of the prize daughter bringing it home for dad
i even got the father's trophy

i was also a jock, dyke, stupid dumb blond
frigid, castrating, domineering bitch,
called all these names in silence,
the double standard wearing me down
inside

on the victory stand winning my medals
for father and coach
and perhaps a me deep down somewhere
who couldn't fail because of all the hours
and training and tears
wrapped into an identity of muscle and power
and physical strength
a champion,

not softness and grace

now at 31, still suffering from the overheard
locker room talk, from the bragging and swaggering

the stares past my tank suit
insults about my muscles
the fears, the nameless fears
about my undiscovered womanhood
disturbing unknown femininity,
femaleness

feminine power

# SWEAT

1995

lucy jane bledsoe

**S**haron kisses the three state championship trophies as she always does before leaving her locker room office. She doesn't have to walk through the gymnasium to get to her car, but she always does that too. This evening particularly she needs to breathe in its musky smell of sweat-soaked wood and listen to her sneakers squeak across the varnished floor. When the lights are up and she's running a practice, she thinks only of how well her players execute their skills. But in the evenings, alone in the dark gymnasium, she thinks of past seasons. She's had a fine career, so fine she's been offered a college position.

Sharon stops in the middle of the gymnasium floor, not wanting to go home. "You're forty-three already," Ann, her lover of fifteen years, had shouted this morning. "Shit or get off the pot." Ann wants her to take the college job. It'd be more money.

Money and sex, it's all they ever fight about. Not enough of either for Ann. An accountant, she'd recently pushed her salary into six figures. They bought a luxury house which Sharon can't afford. Ann said don't sweat it, she'd cover it, but now, a year later, Ann would like more help with the mortgage. Sharon misses their former home, small and snug.

Sharon eyes the basket then trots up the key, gently tossing her briefcase toward the hoop. As she catches it, someone says, "Ms. Barnaby?"

Sharon whirls around. Her star point guard sits on the bottom bleacher with a basketball at her hip, still in practice shorts and jersey. Monica is short and chunky with long, curly, light brown hair. Her eyes are the color of cocoa.

"What are you doing here, Monica? It's five o'clock. Didn't you shower?"

"I've been practicing my free throw."

She's lying. From her office in the locker room Sharon can hear every ball bounce. Monica is trying to win her favor. Sharon has been asking her to work on her free throw all season. She's an expert at drawing fouls but she doesn't follow through at the goal. She bets Monica has been napping on the bleachers. She's noticed before that the girl avoids home.

"Help me with my free throw?" she asks.

"You have to leave now. Tomorrow in practice I will."

"Just ten minutes. Please?"

"Mr. Sorenson stays every evening until six o'clock," Sharon tells her and immediately regrets it. Why had she mentioned the principal? What did he have to do with anything? She'd spoken as if she were Monica's peer and Mr. Sorenson the authority, limiting what they both want. Sharon doesn't want to stay here and work on Monica's free throw. She doesn't want to go home and face Ann either. Trying to explain herself, she adds, "All students are supposed to be out of the building by five."

The custodian shoves open the gymnasium door. He doesn't notice the woman and girl standing in the dark under a basketball hoop. He checks something in a circuit panel and then leaves again. Sharon notices she has held her breath. She is grateful that Monica remained silent, then wonders why she cares. Sharon often feels that she is hiding, even when she isn't.

Monica stretches and repeats her request. "Ten minutes, Ms. Barnaby. Then I'll leave."

The custodian comes in again. This time he flips on the lights. "You still here, Coach?" he calls out cheerfully.

"Yeah," Sharon says quickly. She looks at her watch. Five fifteen. "We were doing a little free-throw practice."

Monica's face is impassive. Sharon is mortified that she lied in front of the girl. And why?

"Then you'll need the lights," the custodian suggests.

"No," Sharon says firmly. "Thank you. We're done."

"Good night then, Coach." The custodian salutes and leaves.

Monica moves to the foul line at the top of the key. She stands with her fingers spread around the ball. Sharon puts down her briefcase and kicks it gently away from the key. It slides easily on the polished floor.

Instead of shooting a free throw Monica motions as if she is going to drive to the basket.

The challenge stirs Sharon. She steps in front of Monica and says, "Just try it."

Monica fakes left, goes right. As she leaps for the shot, Sharon pops the ball out of her hands without touching her. "Try again," Sharon says, retrieving the ball and passing it forcefully to Monica. The girl's eyes shine with amazement. Sharon guesses Monica thought she could get by her old coach.

This time Monica drives straight forward, then drops back for a quick turn-around jump shot. Sharon stuffs that one.

"Wow, Ms. Barnaby."

Sharon feels a rich power in her belly. She never plays with the girls. It's a rule. She has nothing to prove, and yet this evening the competition feels like a drug. Monica is the best point guard she's ever had. After ten minutes of play she hasn't scored once, not once, on Sharon.

Not bad for a forty-three-year-old has-been, she says in her mind to Ann, who she knows could care less about how well Sharon plays defense. Sharon wishes she hadn't thought of Ann. She'd tried to call her all day but never got past the secretary. Which means Ann told her secretary to tell Sharon she was unavailable. Increasingly, Ann runs all aspects of her life like a set of books, keeping track of every single interaction.

With a double fake, Monica finally gets past Sharon and stops short for a bank shot. She misses and Sharon beats her to the board. Sharon tosses the ball to Monica.

"You go," Monica says, firing the ball back and breaking a silence that has carried them through several plays. She adds, "I need to practice my D."

Sharon takes the ball to the top of the key. Monica plays her close, resting one hand lightly on Sharon's hip. The girl's curls are dark with sweat and plastered around her ears and neck. She's breathing harder than Sharon.

"0–0," Sharon says, and Monica's eyes widen with surprise that Sharon is keeping track of the score. Monica steels herself, the competition cinching a tension between them. Sharon drives left, hooks right, and gets her own board, popping in a lay-up. She'd left Monica under the left side of the basket, awed.

"1–0." This time Monica plays even tighter defense, insisting with her whole body that her coach will not get by her. She stays at Sharon's side all the way to the hoop, fouling with her full-body press as Sharon goes up for the point. Sharon doesn't call the foul.

"2–0." On the next play, Sharon misses the shot and Monica gets the rebound. The play gets rougher. Monica drives directly into Sharon, then rolls off her as if a pick had been set, and takes the ball to the hoop. She makes the shot.

Sharon swats her behind, congratulating her even though she's angry she gave away a point. That would be the last one.

The desire to win, by the biggest possible margin, thickens in her blood.

At the top of the key, Monica dribbles once and Sharon steals the ball. They trade places and Monica sets herself up for defense. She presses so close that Sharon can feel the sweat from Monica's thigh seep into her own warm-ups. Sharon pauses a minute, waiting for her to back off, but she doesn't. They have silently agreed to a no-fouls rule, but playing this close is bad defense. Sharon rolls past her, feeling Monica's hands brush her behind, and lays in a simple goal.

Soon, exultant, Sharon says, "10–2, I win."

"Let's play full-court," Monica dares.

The girl won't quit. She figures she can win on endurance alone.

They start at mid-court. Sharon lets Monica go first. Monica is fast and the scoring is even as they race up and down the length of the court. The fouls get much rougher. Monica grabs Sharon's shooting arm while she goes up for a lay-up. Sharon seizes the waistband of Monica's shorts when she drives past her. They don't lose contact even while dribbling down court to the opposite goal. When Sharon goes up for game point, Monica wraps both arms around her middle and pulls her away from the basket.

"Hey!" Sharon cries the first protest as the ball falls through the hoop anyway. She drops back down to her feet, still in the circle of Monica's arms, as if she were a ball and Monica the hoop.

"You win," Monica says.

Sharon feels as if she's been tuned. Every atom in her body is radiating in sync. "Yep, I win," she says.

Monica's cocoa eyes are big and needy. Sharon can see that the game has affected her differently. It hasn't satisfied, it has whetted. Losing can be like that. Though Monica drops her arms, they stand so close that Sharon feels the girl's breasts heave with exhausted panting. Monica, a foot shorter than Sharon, drops her forehead onto her coach's chest for a moment, then looks up. Sharon leans down and lightly kisses her lips. Monica's eyes change. Fear mixes in with the neediness. Even so, she places her hands around Sharon's neck and returns the kiss, hard, hungrily. Then she wrenches free, as if Sharon had been holding her there.

Monica backs away from her coach. Her mouth begins to twist into an ugly shape. "Mr. Sorenson," she whispers.

A deep, enormous silence opens up in Sharon's chest. She says, "Don't, Monica. Don't do it."

"Mr. Sorenson," Monica screams. "Mr. Sorenson!"

Sharon watches the girl turn and sprint toward the gymnasium door. The door swings shut behind Monica with a loud clang. Sharon stands sweating, alone in the dark gymnasium.

# DIAMONDS, DYKES, AND DOUBLE PLAYS

## pat griffin

I've known I was queer since I was about twelve years old. I'm twenty-eight now. I've had my share of relationships in that time and I read somewhere that they were "serial monogamous" relationships. Whatever you call them, some were good and some were pretty horrible. Right now I'm coming off of one of the latter: a real tantrum-throwing, kick and screamer of a thing that left me exhausted and looking for a fresh start. So, I left Maryland, my job as a high school gym teacher, my sparring partner, and moved north.

I'd heard that Northampton, Massachusetts, was a great place to be queer, so I packed up my Toyota and took off. Despite all the good things I'd heard about being queer in Northampton, I was one lonely dyke for a long time after I got here in late August. I did get a job right away. I was a long-term sub teaching high school PE and coaching a girls' basketball team, but I could not seem to break into this great lesbian community everyone talked about. I went to the women's bookstore, women's music concerts, college field hockey games, the bars, but I couldn't seem to find a way in.

I was surrounded by dykes, but I felt like a stranger in a strange land, a real alien from outer space. You don't have to

| 197

go out of the country to experience culture shock. What I mean is, the women and the "women's community" in Northampton are nothing like what I was used to in Maryland. Basically, back there we had our crowd who played softball in the summer, basketball in the winter, drank beer all year round, and tried to keep track of who was with who, or not speaking, or putting the moves on who. It may have been crazy, but at least I had some sense of the rules, and I had friends who I could count on in a pinch (most of the time). I felt like a beggar at a banquet in Northampton. All these women and, somehow, I didn't speak their language.

I spent the fall and winter reading about (but not attending) potlucks advertised in *The Labrys*, a local lesbian monthly. You wouldn't believe the options: potlucks for left-handed working-class lesbians who won the state lottery; lesbian children of adults who pick their noses; lesbians who occasionally sleep with men; lesbians against nuclear war, famine, and plastic shrink wrap; you name it, there's a potluck for you. Somehow, I knew that these were not the kind of women who wanted to talk about the Washington Redskins or the New England Patriots. What I needed was to find the jocks. Where were the beer-drinking, sports-minded dykes who were into competition, not contemplation, who were into personal relationships, not political action? I thought about submitting my own potluck notice for lesbians who like to play sports, drink beer, and have serial monogamy with teammates, but I was too shy.

When Susan, the woman I was sharing an apartment with, asked if I wanted to play on her softball team I jumped at the chance. At last, the long drought would be over. I circled April 15, the date of the first team meeting, on my calendar and started oiling up my softball glove in February. I couldn't wait to meet women who slid into second with spikes high, who knew how to stand in at the plate against a fast pitcher, who turned double plays with cool assurance: my kind of dyke. The softball team's first meeting was, you guessed it, a potluck. This was my first clue that even softball in Northampton was to be a new cultural experience.

I found out quickly (and the hard way) that there is an ironclad etiquette surrounding these potluck gatherings. Here's a tip: never (and I mean never) bring, as your contribution to the meal, anything that used to breathe. I found out about this faux pas when my dish of hamburger casserole sat untouched by lesbian hands for the entire evening. Women circled that sucker as if they thought a hoof was going to shoot out of the bowl and beat them senseless next to the table. I learned from overhearing a conversation that lesbians here do not eat "land-walking animals." Being the adaptable dyke that I am (and lonely), I made a mental note never to eat land-walking animal meals in public. In my own home, under the cover of night, well, I figure that's another story.

Anyway, I filled my plate with shit called "tempay" and "toe foo," which I had never seen before. I bypassed my own dish, wrinkling my nose in proper disgust, as if the thought of a big juicy land-walking animal burger was repellent to my politically pure palate. I realized that if I wanted to make friends here, it was going to cost me one casserole dish. I knew I'd have to leave it. I could never admit I had brought that, that abomination, to the potluck. I tried to remember who had seen me come in with it. What would I say if someone asked which dish was mine? What if I claimed one that belonged to the asker? Bullshit! This was getting too complicated. I backtracked and, with a grand, politically incorrect flourish, dug deep into my ground beef casserole. I heaped it on my plate and grabbed a beer out of the cooler. Hey, this is who I am: a burger-eating, beer-drinking kind of dyke. Take it or leave it.

The rest of the evening, introducing new players (there were three of us rookies) and reviewing the league rules, was too bizarre for words. I sat in shocked silence as I learned that in this league (1) we basically play fast-pitch rules, but if the batter thinks the pitcher is too fast, she has to slow it down; (2) it is totally unacceptable to ride the other team. We are to treat them as sisters (hell, I yell at my sister all the time); (3) everyone will play equal amounts of time regardless of skill; (4) we will take turns being coach; (5) no men are allowed to umpire games; and, the one I was most intrigued by, (6) we all must wear clothes to play. Not to worry, the thought of sliding into home bare-assed held no allure for me.

I also learned that after games we will sit in a circle and do something everyone called "processing the experience" where we'd give each other "feedback" and "share our feelings" about how we "interacted" with each other and the other team. Now, this is something I knew about, only in Maryland we just called it "going out for a beer" after the game.

The name of our team is, get this, "Amazon Vision." In fact, I learned that all the teams in this league have names like "The Vegetarians," "Womynpower," "Circle of Peace," "The Raging Hormones," "Revolting Hags," and "I Am Womon." When I asked who won the championship last summer, everyone acted like I'd farted. Uh-oh, another mistake.

A woman wearing a lavender T-shirt with female genitals printed on it finally broke the silence and said:

"This is a noncompetitive league. We don't keep track of our wins and losses. The obsession with winning is a vestige of the patriarchy."

I nodded my head like this was not new information for me. What could I do? I love competition, and the best part of it is winning. I knew to admit this, however, would make me a "male-identified tool of the patriarchy," not a good way to start the season with my strange new teammates.

Little did I know that this was only the beginning of my education about what they kept calling "noncompetitive feminist softball." I left the potluck with lots of doubts about all this, but I was lonely and I wanted to play softball. Maybe it wouldn't be as weird as it sounded once we got out on the field and started whipping that baby around the infield.

Our first practice demolished that illusion. Now, I don't want to sound elitist in any way. I mean, as a gym teacher, coach, and former college athlete, I guess you could think that of me for saying this, but this was one sorry collection of dyke jocks. Since we don't have a coach, like in the traditional sense, we decided what to do by consensus. After tossing the ball around in pairs to warm up, it took us twenty minutes to decide to do infield practice and even at that two women, Moonwolf and Morningdew, had to go off and "process" something before they could "join our energy" on the field.

Finally, I trotted out to third base, my regular position, and spent some time checking the area for little rocks and stuff. Joan, the woman playing first base, sidearmed a ground ball to me, I scooped it up, stepped, and threw it back to her. The ball thwacked deliciously into her glove. At last, we were playing softball. At last something felt familiar. Joan aimed the next grounder at Micki, the shortstop. She fielded the ball with her left boob, retrieved it, and threw it over the fence behind first base. Joan was prepared for this: she had a whole pile of balls beside her in foul territory. This did not look good.

Apparently the woman playing second base, Marie, took her responsibility literally: she was standing on top of the bag waiting for her grounder from Joan. I couldn't stand it, so I said as gently as I could:

"Marie, the second baseman usually plays off the bag about five to ten steps toward first."

Well, by the way she looked at me I knew I had blundered

into another social miscue. I just couldn't figure out what it was. Did they have a rule that whoever played second was supposed to stand on the base? Finally, Micki said:

"In this league, we call it second basewoman."

I could tell there was no "man" in this word by the way she emphasized the "mon."

"Great idea," I said, and then to Marie: "The second basewoman"—I smiled at Micki—"plays off the bag, Marie."

With this translation, Marie moved toward first and looked at me questioningly. "Here?"

"That's great." I smiled back.

Things actually went OK for a while. Janice, our leftfielder, was pretty good at hitting infield practice and we spent about thirty minutes fielding grounders and pop-ups and throwing them to different bases. This was more like it. Then we took a water break. After that, we decided to do outfield practice. Moonwolf asked if anyone could "throw up and hit the ball" to the outfield this year. I had this image of someone alternately retching beside home plate and then hitting fungoes. Apparently, no one else thought this particular image was odd. Moonwolf filled the new players in.

"Last year no one could throw up and hit the ball to the outfield, so we never got to practice outfield."

"I can throw up and hit," I volunteered, blending in with the native culture.

"Great." Moonwolf smiled, and all the outfielders turned to jog out to their positions.

I've always loved hitting fungoes. The challenge of hitting to every field, putting the flies just within the range of the fielders, and occasionally, just for fun, going for the fence. I found myself just naturally kicking into my coach mode.

"Nice try, Morningdew," I wanted to call her Dewey or something, anything but Morningdew, but I knew she wouldn't appreciate a nickname and we'd probably have to process the experience if I tried to give her one without her permission.

"Call it, Janice, that was yours." "Throw it to the cut-off, Gerry." "Call it, Moonwolf," I yelled.

They were a silent bunch, working independently. I started hitting the ball randomly to each fielder so they had to decide whose it was. I hit a high fly to right center. Moonwolf and Morningdew both ran toward it, gloves up. At the last minute, they both stepped aside, parting like the Red Sea, and the ball thudded to the grass and rolled behind them.

"Call it, you have to call it," I yelled for the millionth time.

I started to hit another ball, but caught it instead. I walked out to second base waving all the outfielders in to meet me. They trotted in.

"Look, you have to call the ball. If you're going to catch it, yell 'mine' or 'I have it' or something so other fielders know to back off, OK?"

This information was greeted with silence. "Do you understand what I mean?" I checked.

Morningdew looked troubled. "That's such a commitment. I've always had trouble with commitments. I mean, to yell out 'I have it,' what if I drop it, what if I don't have it?"

Could this really be happening to me? I wondered. I looked at the rest of the outfield for confirmation that this was nutty. They were all looking intently at Morningdew and nodding in agreement.

"I feel the same way," Moonwolf solemnly confessed. "Plus, for me, it seems so, so territorial, so capitalistic, so male."

Gerry and Janice moved over to put their arms around Morningdew, who looked like she was going to cry.

"Look," I said, trying to make the commitment seem more manageable, "it's not like you're promising to catch it every time you call it. You're really just saying that you're going to try to catch it, see?" I didn't have a clue how to deal with the capitalistic shit Moonwolf had brought up.

I could see that they were thinking this over. Finally, Morningdew smiled and said:

"That really helps me. In fact, you could say, that even if you miss it, it helps another womon since we are all sisters on both teams."

I just knew I could hear that music from the "Twilight Zone"—do, do, do, do. This was so weird, but I knew by now not to laugh.

"Well, yes, I guess that's true, but it's OK to want to help our team first, isn't it?" I asked gently. "Then, of course, if you drop the ball it helps the women from the other team." This seemed to make sense to everyone. I exhaled a sigh of relief.

"Water break," Micki, who had been doing tai chi along the first-base line, called. Everyone walked over to the benches on the third-base line.

The rest of practice went pretty well. We did some batting practice and talked about our first game the next week with "I Am Womon." I was given my team T-shirt: lavender with a picture of a fierce-looking womon in full armor on the front of it. Behind her was a rainbow or sunrise, I couldn't tell which. Across the back in big letters was "Amazon Vision." For a dyke used to more traditional uniforms and sponsors like "The Hideaway Lounge" or the "Tick Tock Club," this was quite a change.

On game night everyone on our team arrived early. Moonwolf was coach for this game, so she was hard at work trying to identify a starting lineup and batting order. Janice and Sandy were gathered around second base trying to hammer the base spike in with a large rock. The rest of the "Amazon Visions" were spread out around the infield in pairs throwing balls back and forth and chatting about the fate of the local women's center since the coordinator came out as a bisexual in last month's newsletter. The requisite woman umpire was pacing off the distance between homeplate and the pitcher's rubber, only we didn't have a rubber, so she dragged her toe through the dirt to make a line.

"I Am Womon" had dropped their equipment on the third-base side with our team's stuff. The benches along first base were deserted. This seemed odd to me. I was used to the two teams in a softball game sitting on opposite sides of the infield. As I stretched out my hamstrings, I asked Micki about this.

"Some teams feel that sitting on separate sides presents a false division between teams and leads to objectifying the women on the other team. This way we are reminded that we are all one united sisterhood," Micki explained in her solemn way.

"But don't each team's bats and balls and stuff get mixed up too? Is there room for everyone to sit down?" I asked. This sitting together with the other team felt wrong to me. I'd been able to roll with a lot of strange stuff to play softball here, but this was too much.

"Well, new players sometimes take a while to root out the ways male-identified sports have conditioned us to view the other team as an enemy. This is a more collaborative way," Micki replied.

I shook my head. I'd have to think this one over. I put on my glove and trotted out to take infield practice.

Finally, we were about to begin the game. Since we were the home team, we took the field and Joan, with her pile of balls beside her, threw grounders to the infield. Then the first batter for "I Am Womon" came to the plate. Our pitcher, Tina, was accurate, consistent, and really slow. On a humid night when the air is heavy, I didn't think the ball would make it to the plate. As it was, her pitches spun toward the catcher's glove barely reaching home plate before dropping in the dirt like they had rolled off a table. No worries here about being asked to slow down. The result was pretty interesting. The batter, the catcher, and the umpire all seemed to lean toward the incoming ball on each pitch willing it to stay in the air long enough to be hittable.

As it turned out, Tina's pitching was pretty difficult for "I Am Womon" to hit . . . for most of the game. We were ahead 2–0 going into the seventh. Now, this game wasn't anything pretty, but we were having fun and, though I knew they wouldn't admit it, our team of "noncompetitive" players wanted to win . . . badly. Apparently they hadn't won many games in seasons past, so the experience of being ahead was new and a little dizzying. They could smell a victory.

When "I Am Womon" scored two runs in the top of the seventh to tie it up, Moonwolf gathered us together as we got ready to go to bat for the final time. We all stood huddled in our lavender T-shirts looking expectantly at our coach.

She said, "Come on, Amazons, let's get some hits!"

I looked around the circle. Everyone looked flushed, eyes blazing. I smiled. This was starting to feel like the kind of softball I was familiar with. We all put our hands in the center in a pile and shouted, "Hits and runs" three times.

Micki was up first. She hit the first pitch, a short chopper to the shortstop who snagged it and threw the ball to first. One out. Micki looked back at our team with an apology on her face. We all shouted stuff like, "Nice try, Mick," and "No problem, team."

Morningdew was up next. I don't mean to be unsisterly, but, take my word, Morningdew was not the woman you wanted to see at the plate in this situation. She walked to the plate and took her position in the box. Then she reached down with her bat and tapped home plate three times. She waited for the pitch in an awkward-looking crouch, the bat resting on her shoulder. Well, here comes the second out, I predicted to myself. Morningdew watched the first pitch.

"Strike one!" called the ump.

Morningdew took two practice swings and settled in at the plate again. Both teams were yelling appropriately supportive cheers to teammates. The ump and catcher crouched for the pitch. Morningdew spun in a circle as she aimed her bat at the ball. Unfortunately, there was a foot of air between the ball and bat. "Strike two!" called the ump.

The catcher threw the ball back to the pitcher and everyone regrouped for the next pitch. It came toward Morningdew— she swung and made partial contact. The ball skittered lazily down the third-base line. The third basewoman, the pitcher, and the catcher converged on the ball, hovering over it as they willed it to roll foul. At first, Morningdew stood rooted in the batter's box, looking at her bat in surprise.

"Amazon Vision" erupted from the bench, "Run, run, Morningdew!" She jumped toward first as if we'd goosed her.

Meanwhile the catcher, realizing that the ball was going to die in fair territory, snatched it up and threw it toward the first basewoman's outstretched glove. Sensing the approaching ball, Morningdew ran the last few feet to the bag bent over with her arms wrapped over her head for protection. She reached for the bag with her foot and, forgetting that she could overrun first, fought the momentum of her body to maintain her position. The first basewoman caught the ball. Morning-dew was safe. We yelled and cheered. Morningdew looked somewhat dazed as she realized that she was actually a base runner. We had the winning run on first and Gerry coming to the plate.

Gerry was a pretty good hitter, so things were looking good. The evening air was thick with tension. Both teams shouted encouragement to themselves. Anything was possible here.

Gerry worked the pitcher to a full count, then hit a fly ball to short leftfield. The leftfielder moved under the ball and made the catch. Two outs. Suddenly our whole team realized with horror that Morningdew was standing on second base looking very pleased with herself.

"Go back, go back to first!" we yelled.

Our whole team was on our feet, pointing at first base. Morningdew looked puzzled now. She took a step back toward first and looked at us questioningly.

We all nodded and screamed, "Yes, yes, go back!"

Morningdew shrugged and took off toward first. Meanwhile, the leftfielder was so surprised to see the ball in her glove that she had spent these few minutes jumping up and down in celebration until she realized that her team was yelling at her to throw the ball back to first. She hurriedly made the throw.

Morningdew staggered into first and cowered on the bag with her arms wrapped around her head again. The ball whistled over the first basewoman's outstretched glove. There was a beat of silence and then we began jumping up and down screaming at Morningdew.

"Run, run, go back to second!" We all pointed at second and waved our arms.

Morningdew, looking thoroughly confused, covered her head, and ran back toward second. Morningdew reached the bag and looked to the bench as if to ask, "Is this right?" We nodded and cheered. She smiled and pumped her fist in the air like Arsenio Hall.

OK, two out, bottom of the seventh, score tied, and Tina coming up. Tina can pound the ball, if she can make contact. She strikes out a lot, though. Both teams were quiet. Everyone was concentrating. We all had butterflies. I thought to myself:

it doesn't matter what you call it or even how well everyone can play, softball doesn't get much better than this. Two teams down to the final out with the game on the line.

With the count 2–1, Tina unloaded on the next pitch. It was a long fly to left center. Morningdew took off toward third. We all were jumping up and down, winding our arms in circles to signal that she should go home.

"Go home, run, Morningdew!"

The leftfielder took the ball on the hop and fired it immediately toward the plate. The ball and Morningdew were on two different trajectories heading for the same point. I covered my eyes: this was going to be close.

The catcher stood over the plate reaching for the ball. The umpire stood to the side, her eyes glued on the catcher. The shouting of both teams echoed around the field. Then an amazing thing happened. Morningdew slid into homeplate. It wasn't pretty, but she did it just as the ball arrived and the catcher swept her glove down for the tag. Homeplate was a cloud of dust. The sudden silence of both teams fell over the field like a blanket. Eighteen pairs of eyes looked to the umpire.

She stood motionless blinking into the clearing dust. Morningdew lay on her back looking up, her face hopeful. The catcher, having fallen back on her fanny after the tag, sat with the ball in her glove, her eyes riveted on the umpire's face. Finally, the umpire looked up from the tangle of bodies at her feet and shrugged her shoulders.

"Who knows? I couldn't see with all the dust."

At first, there was a lot of yelling as our team tried to convince the umpire that Morningdew was safe and the other team tried to convince her that Morningdew was out. To be honest, I don't think anyone really knew for sure, even the catcher and Morningdew. Finally, someone suggested that we just leave it a tie and go have a beer together. So we did.

After I got home that night, I realized what a good time I'd had. Everything was still a little odd and I knew there was still a lot I didn't understand about playing softball in Northampton. The rest of the team wanted to pick hand signals, though, and start putting coaches on first and third when we were up at bat. This was hopeful.

Also, I had to hand it to Morningdew—she was tougher than I'd thought to slide into home like that. And Moonwolf turned out to be the biggest surprise of all. We all went to her place later to process the experience. When I went into her kitchen to get another beer, I saw our game schedule stuck to her fridge with a woman symbol magnet. She had filled in the score for our game with "I Am Womon." It read 3–2, us.

# A NIGHT GAME
# IN MENOMONIE PARK

susan firer

A night game in Menomonie Park,
Where the ladies hit the large white balls
like stars through the night they roll
like angelfood cake batter folded through devilsfood.
Again, I want to hear the fans' empty beer cans
being crushed—new ones hissing open.
"You're a gun, Anna."
"She can't hit."
"Lay it on."
Oh, run, swift softball women
under the lights the Kiwanis put in.
Be the wonderful sliding night
animals I remember. Remind me constantly
of human error and redemption.
Hit
ball after ball to the lip of the field
while the lake flies fall like confetti
under the park's night lights.
Sunlight Dairy Team, remember me
as you lift your bats,
pump energy into

them bats, whirling circular as helicopter
blades above your heads.
Was it the ball Julie on the "Honey B" Tavern Team
hit toward my head that made me so soft-
ball crazy that right in the middle of a tune
by Gentleman Jim's Orchestra, here in Bingo/Polka
Heaven at Saint Mary of Czestochowa's annual Kielbasa
Festival, I go homesick for Oshkosh women's softball?
I order another kielbasa and wonder
if Donna will stay on third next game or
again run head down wild into Menomonie homeplate.
Play louder, Gentleman Jim,
Saint Mary of Czestochowa throws a swell festival, but
Oshkosh women's softball—that's a whole other ballgame.

# FROM *IN THE YEAR OF THE BOAR AND JACKIE ROBINSON*

1984

### bette bao lord

**S**hirley had reached the top of the stairs when suddenly from nowhere Mabel appeared. "Hey, you wanna play stickball?"

Shirley turned to see whom the girl was asking. No one else was around. "Me?"

"Yeah, you. How about it?"

Shaking her head, Shirley smiled and started down the steps. Mabel, riding on the handrail, whizzed by and blocked her progress on the first landing. "Why not?"

"Dumb hands. No can catch." Shirley slipped past and continued on, only to find the way blocked again on the second landing.

"Nothing to it. I'll show ya."

Shirley shook her head again.

"Come on, it's fun."

"Yes, fun. But nobody take me on team."

"Leave that to me."

Shirley still hesitated. But Mabel was hardly the patient sort and pulled her by the sleeves into the school yard. When the others saw her coming, they groaned.

"What ya want to bring the midget for?"

"Oh no, ya don't. Not on my team."

"Are you kidding me?"

"Yeah. She'd bow first and then ask permission to cop a fly."

"Send her back to the laundry."

"The only way she can get in this game is to lie down and be the plate."

Shirley was ready to leave quietly, but Mabel hissed through her teeth, "Who says my friend Shirley here can't play?"

Advancing with mighty shoves, she pushed each objector aside.

"You, Spaghetti Snot?

"You, Kosher Creep?

"You, Damp Drawers?

"You, Brown Blubber?

"You, Dog Breath?

"You, Puerto Rican Coconut?"

Mabel was most persuasive, for everyone named now twitched a shoulder to signal okay. "That's what I thought. And as captain, I get first pick and Shirley's it."

When the sides were chosen, Mabel pointed to a spot by the iron fence. "Shirley, you play right field. If a ball comes your way, catch it and throw it to me. I'll take care of the rest."

"Where you be?"

"I'm the pitcher."

"Picture?"

"Ah, forget it. Look for me, I'll be around."

Resisting the temptation to bow, Shirley headed for her spot.

Mabel's picture was something to see. First, hiding the ball, she gave the stick the evil eye. Then, twisting her torso and jiggling a leg, she whirled her arm around in a most impressive fashion, probably a ritual to shoo away any unfriendly spirits, before speeding the ball furiously into the hands of squatting Joseph.

Once in a great while, the stick got a lucky hit, but the Goddess Kwan Yin was again merciful and sent the ball nowhere near the fence.

After the change of sides, Mabel stood Shirley in place and told her she would be first to hit. Shirley would have preferred to study the problem some more, but was afraid to protest and lose face for her captain. Standing tall, with her feet together, stick on her shoulder, she waited bravely. Dog Breath had a ritual of his own to perform, but then, suddenly, the ball was coming her way. Her eyes squeezed shut.

"Ball one!" shouted the umpire.

"Good eye!" shouted Mabel.

Shirley sighed and started to leave, but was told to stay put.

Again the ball came. Again her eyes shut.

"Ball two!"

"Good eye!" shouted the team. "Two more of those and you're on."

Shirley grinned. How easy it was!

Sure enough, every time she shut her eyes, the ball went astray.

"Take your base," said the umpire.

Mabel came running over. "Stand on that red bookbag until someone hits the ball, then run like mad to touch the blue one. Got it?"

"I got."

Mabel then picked up the stick and with one try sent the ball flying. In no time, Shirley, despite her pigeon toes, had dashed to the blue bookbag. But something was wrong. Mabel was chasing her. "Go. Get going. Run."

Shirley, puzzled over which bookbag to run to next, took a

chance and sped off. But Mabel was still chasing her. "Go home! Go home!"

Oh no! She had done the wrong thing. Now even her new friend was angry. "Go home," her teammates shouted. "Go home."

She was starting off the field when she saw Joseph waving. "Here! Over here!" And off she went for the green one. Just before she reached it, she stumbled, knocking over the opponent who stood in her way. He dropped the ball, and Shirley fell on top of the bag like a piece of ripe bean curd.

Her teammates shouted with happiness. Some helped her up. Others patted her back. Then they took up Mabel's chant.

*"Hey, hey, you're just great*
*Jackie Robinson crossed the plate.*
*Hey, hey, you're a dream*
*Jackie Robinson's on our team."*

Mabel's team won. The score was 10 to 2, and though the Chinese rookie never got on base again or caught even one ball, Shirley was confident that the next time . . . next time, she could. And yes, of course, naturally, stickball was now her favorite game.

On Saturday, Mabel taught her how to throw—overhand. How to catch—with her fingers. How to stand—feet two shoes apart. How to bat—on the level.

On Sunday, Mabel showed her how to propel herself on one skate at a time, then pulled her about on both until Shirley had learned how to go up and down the street without a fall . . .

. . .

"Who is dodgers?" Shirley asked.

That question, like a wayward torch in a roomful of fire-crackers, sparked answers from everyone.

"De Bums!"

"The best in the history of baseball!"

"Kings of Ebbets Field!"

"They'll kill the Giants!"

"They'll murder the Yankees!"

"The swellest guys in the world!"

"America's favorites!"

"Winners!"

Mrs. Rappaport clapped her hands for order. The girls quieted down first, followed reluctantly by the boys. "That's better. Participation is welcome, but one at a time. Let's do talk about baseball!"

"Yay!" shouted the class.

"And let's combine it with civics too!"

The class did not welcome this proposal as eagerly, but Mrs. Rappaport went ahead anyway.

"Mabel, tell us why baseball is America's favorite pastime."

Pursing her lips in disgust at so ridiculous a question, Mabel answered. " 'Cause it's a great game. Everybody plays it, loves it and follows the games on the radio and nabs every chance to go and see it."

"True," said Mrs. Rappaport, nodding. "But what is it about baseball that is ideally suited to Americans?"

Mabel turned around, looking for an answer from someone else, but to no avail. There was nothing to do but throw the question back. "Whatta ya mean by 'suits'?"

"I mean, is there something special about baseball that fits the special kind of people we are and the special kind of country America is?" Mrs. Rappaport tilted her head to one side, inviting a response. When none came, she sighed a sigh so fraught with disappointment that it sounded as if her heart were breaking.

No one wished to be a party to such a sad event, so everybody found some urgent business to attend to like scratching, slumping, sniffing, scribbling, squinting, sucking teeth or removing dirt from underneath a fingernail. Joseph cracked his knuckles.

The ticking of the big clock became so loud that President Washington and President Lincoln, who occupied the wall space to either side of it, exchanged a look of shared displeasure.

But within the frail, birdlike body of Mrs. Rappaport was the spirit of a dragon capable of tackling the heavens and earth. With a quick toss of her red hair, she proceeded to answer her own question with such feeling that no one who heard could be so unkind as to ever forget. Least of all Shirley.

"Baseball is not just another sport. America is not just another country . . ."

If Shirley did not understand every word, she took its meaning to heart. Unlike Grandfather's stories which quieted the warring spirits within her with the softness of moonlight or the lyric timbre of a lone flute, Mrs. Rappaport's speech thrilled her like sunlight and trumpets.

"In our national pastime, each player is a member of a team, but when he comes to bat, he stands alone. One man. Many opportunities. For no matter how far behind, how late in the game, he, by himself, can make a difference. He can change what has been. He can make it a new ball game.

"In the life of our nation, each man is a citizen of the United States, but he has the right to pursue his own happiness. For no matter what his race, religion or creed, be he pauper or president, he has the right to speak his mind, to live as he wishes within the law, to elect our officials and stand for office, to excel. To make a difference. To change what has been. To make a better America.

"And so can you! And so must you!"

Shirley felt as if the walls of the classroom had vanished. In their stead was a frontier of doors to which she held the keys.

"This year, Jackie Robinson is at bat. He stands for himself, for Americans of every hue, for an America that honors fair play.

"Jackie Robinson is the grandson of a slave, the son of a sharecropper, raised in poverty by a lone mother who took in ironing and washing. But a woman determined to achieve a better life for her son. And she did. For despite hostility and injustice, Jackie Robinson went to college, excelled in all sports, served his country in war. And now, Jackie Robinson is at bat in the big leagues. Jackie Robinson is making a difference. Jackie Robinson has changed what has been. And Jackie Robinson is making a better America.

"And so can you! And so must you!"

Suddenly Shirley understood why her father had brought her ten thousand miles to live among strangers. Here, she did not have to wait for gray hairs to be considered wise. Here, she could speak up, question even the conduct of the President. Here, Shirley Temple Wong was somebody. She felt as if she had the power of ten tigers, as if she had grown as tall as the Statue of Liberty . . .


Before long, Shirley was infected by a most severe case of Dodger fever. Not even strawberry ice cream could lure her away from the radio when Red Barber was broadcasting the latest adventure of de Bums. Truly nothing else mattered. Not the heat that glued her skin to the plastic chair, not an outing to the beach, not even a movie followed by a beef pot pie at the Automat. Every time Number 42 came to bat, she imagined herself in Jackie Robinson's shoes. Every time the pigeon-toed runner got on base, she was ready to help him steal home. And when Jackie's sixteen-game hitting streak ended, Shirley blamed herself. On that day, she had had to accompany her parents to greet Mr. Lee from Chungking. Obviously, it was her absence from the radio that had made all the difference.

Neither Mother nor Father shared her enthusiasm. In fact, they welcomed the mayhem that emanated from the talking box as if it were a plague of locusts at harvest time. But none of their usual parental tricks succeeded in undoing the spell. What could possibly compete with the goose bumps Shirley sprouted each time Gladys Gooding and her organ led the crowd at Ebbets Field in the singing of "The Star-Spangled Banner"?

# LINDY LOWE AT BAT

1995

rebecca rule

Lindy Lowe, at the plate, is mad.

One strike has been called on her—unfairly. Low and outside, it was not a strike. Either the umpire has bad eyesight or he's cheating.

She shivers. The anemic sun that had warmed them at the start of the game has disappeared in clouds. She hears thunder in the distance. She adjusts her safety goggles, raises her bat high over her shoulder, points her toe, sticks her butt out, and glares at that boob of a Beaumont pitcher looming on the mound like big-time, big-league, I'll strike you out or knock you down, take your choice, little girl.

But Lindy knows she has the power to drive Brian Millitello around the bases. If that Beaumont pitcher gets the ball anywhere near the plate, she'll give it a good ride. She'll follow it all the way in, *all* the way in. And she'll smack it *all* the way out.

Coach, meanwhile, in the dugout tries to ignore his ex-girlfriend, Tina, posing beside the Beaumont cheering section —cheering for Beaumont she'll *say* because her weaselly nephews play. Her cheeks are red from a rouge overdose. Her new perm frizzes in the cool humidity of rain on the way. Her purple scarf, knotted at the neck, makes an inverted V over her right breast.

She hates baseball. She loathes her sassy nephews. Coach knows she is here for one reason only: to torment him.

Hard-eyed Marcia is solemn on the dugout steps; straight, waist-length hair fans over her shoulders and down her back. She folds her arms tight over the scorebook and takes in the whole sorry situation: a glance across the way at Tina, a glance sidelong at Coach, a jut of her chin in Tina's direction as if to say, "What's *she* doing here?" Marcia is hot for Coach, but he doesn't know it and she won't admit it.

Chilled, Coach reaches behind the bench for his crumpled sweatshirt. Tina screams, "Go Beaumont." When she claps, she undulates. Coach focuses on Lindy Lowe, who has the power to advance Brian Millitello and place herself in scoring position: she's thin as a stick, but strong as an alder. She wants to play good ball; Coach wants to teach her. Simple—the way relationships should be. He calls to her and she hears his voice rising over the others: "Settle down, Lindy. Choke up."

Lindy thinks he is the best coach in the world. He hardly ever yells except when they do something really stupid like forget to tag up on a fly ball. But he doesn't lie to them either. Sometimes he says: "You looked good out there. You lost, but you looked good." Sometimes he says, "*That* was a pathetic display. If you can't do better than that we might as well pack up and go home right now."

Early in the season Lindy was hitting well and Coach was pleased. Her specialty was the low power-slug that found the hole in the infield, dropped in for an easy single, an occasional sliding double. Marcia, also known as Little Clay's Mom, said Lindy had the third-highest batting average and if Jason and Brian didn't watch out, she was going to zoom right by them.

After that, though, she came up against some bad pitching,

got smacked a couple of times, backed off the base, started anticipating too much, trying too hard. When her average began to slide, her confidence went with it.

Her dad maintains it was just her eyesight that went and the new glasses will make all the difference. "Helps if you can see the ball," he told Coach. "Poor kid's been swinging at ghosts all summer."

Tina reaches for the soda somebody holds out to her from the top of the Beaumont bleachers. Her T-shirt rides up. She puts the red can to her red lips. "If you *really* loved me," she used to tell Coach, "you wouldn't be so crazy jealous." Which made no sense at all to Coach when she parked on his cousin Nate's lap and twined herself around Nate's neck, tickling his pits. Some jerk takes a Polaroid picture, the chair falls over, and the two of them are in a tangle on the floor, laughing like drunks. In the end, what drove Coach away was her if-you-really-loved-me song, and the way she used Nate, but mostly the way she changed the rules as they went along so he couldn't possibly win.

Coach likes to win.

Marcia says Tina's a loser and always has been.

The Beaumont pitcher—a long-bodied, short-legged boy, with the tight-muscled arms of a wrestler—is trying to stare Lindy down, but she stares back the way Coach taught her, the way she might stare at a mosquito sucking blood from her forearm—just before she smacks it.

Brian Millitello takes a healthy lead off first base. He's fast, unpredictable, cocky. He's bouncing on the balls of his feet. Coach signals: Don't take chances; wait for a break. Brian, wild-eyed, stops bouncing for three beats as he absorbs the message. "Hey, Pitch," he taunts. "Hey, hey, Pitch." He flaps his arms and smiles like a demon.

"Come on, Lindy," Coach says. "You can do it." The team

takes its cue: WHACK IT, LINDY, WHACK IT OVER THE FENCE
JUST LIKE ENFIELD—OUTTA THE PARK, LINDY—JUST LIKE YOU
ALWAYS DO.

She appreciates the beautiful lie. She has never whacked one
over the fence—not in Enfield, not in Avery, not anywhere.
She hasn't even connected with the ball, except to foul, in the
last three games. But her new glasses make the ball look big—
big as a cantaloupe hurtling toward her, big enough to hit with
a broom handle. She's not afraid of the burly pitcher with the
wicked fast ball that, in previous at-bats, blew her away from
the plate, heart pounding because she knows what it feels like
to be hit with a wicked fast ball in the side or the hip or the
thigh. The ball-sized black and blue on her rear end is a souvenir of batting practice opposite James Schlitz—their own
wild fast-ball pitcher. "James has the arm," Coach says, "if he
could just control it." Lindy's butt agrees.

The pitcher winds up. Lindy stiffens. Her grip is firm and
steady. The pitcher fires. Her eye is on the ball *all* the way in.
She twitches, but does not reach. The ball slides by, nose-high
and outside.

"Steeeee-rike," yells the umpire.

Lindy whirls to face him: "Strike?"

The umpire tries to shrink her with a watery stare. His jaw
is set and the color high in his pockmarked cheeks. But Lindy
is unshrinkable. She stares back. The catcher smirks under his
mask. "Strike," he hisses, just loud enough for Lindy to hear.

She turns to the dugout for support. Coach emerges into
the mist along the foul line, scowling, hands deep in the pouch
of his sweatshirt. He blows, like a whale, a gust of frustration.

Lindy pantomimes "Strike?"—all teeth—afraid to say it
aloud again; she's been warned to hold back around umpires.
They're touchy.

Her dad says he got thrown out of a game when he was a

kid—for spitting on the umpire's shoe. She understands the impulse, and she knows how dramatic Old Dad gets when his temper kicks in.

"That's all right, honey," she hears him boom from the bleachers—on the verge of dramatics. "Good eye!"

"That's all right, Lindy," Marcia yells, "it just takes one." Little Clay is on deck, so Marcia is excited. She gets that way when her boy comes up to bat. Sometimes it's so bad she forgets to mark the score in the book. They'll say: "What's the score, what's the score, Marcia?" She'll say: "Don't worry about the score. You just play ball and I'll worry about the score."

Lindy thinks the reason Marcia helps out (besides wanting to be around Coach) is so she can watch after Little Clay, make sure he doesn't get hurt, make sure he doesn't get his feelings hurt when he messes up—which he usually does. Earlier in the game Little Clay's dad—Big Clay—showed up. Drunk. Lindy knows drunk when she sees it. He walked light and unsteady as though he didn't quite know where his feet were. He and Coach almost got into a fight when Coach signaled for a steal with two outs and Jason got picked off at third. Big Clay said that was a stupid move.

Coach said: "If you want to run this team, Mister, you come over here and run it. Otherwise, shut your mouth."

"This is a public park," Big Clay said. "I'll say what I want to say to who I . . . who I want to say it to if I want to. I got as much right to be here as anybody else."

But Marcia said he had to stay away from them (because of the restraining order). She said she'd call the police if he didn't get out. Now. He backed off. "I got an appointment anyway. Things to do. I can't stand to watch this figgin' . . . friggin' . . . farce," he said. On the way out, he slipped on the grass and rolled down the bank onto the tar of the parking lot. His friend picked him up and maneuvered him into the passenger side of the truck. Little Clay put his head down and studied the webbing on his glove. To make him feel better, all the kids pretended they hadn't noticed his dad at all. The game went on. Pretty soon Clay lifted his head. Pretty soon he was chattering along with the rest of them. Lindy looked closely at his eyes. They were red.

Clay is the second-worst player on the team. In the field he's slow, he often misjudges grounders, and he inevitably hesitates before the throw. At bat, he goes for sucker balls—high and too far outside or, sometimes, bouncing off the plate. When he does connect though . . . pow! This is what makes him better than the worst player, who's littler, scared of the ball, and only nine: Clay's ability to, on occasion, hit a home run. A plump boy with a soft freckled face, Little Clay brags sometimes, but nobody minds: "Did you see that? Did you see me hit that good one? That was a wicked good hit, wasn't it?"

If Lindy gets on base, it'll be up to him to hit her in. On deck, he taps his favorite aluminum bat against the sides of his cleats to knock the dirt out.

"Settle down, Lindy," Coach says. "This is your ball. You own this ball. Take your time." He offers a small, cool smile that means: pay those cheaters back the only way it really counts—with a hit. The smile curls the wisp of mustache on his lip. Lindy thinks he's almost as handsome as her dad. She nods back, determined: *I understand, Coach; I will not let you down.*

But she has run short of choices. Unless she gets smacked by the pitch and takes a base that way, her only option is to swing at whatever comes down the pike. This umpire sees nothing but strikes, so a walk is out of the question. If she has to reach, she'll reach. If she has to leap over the base or into the air or scrunch like a squirrel to connect, she is prepared to do so.

A third called strike in a game this important and this close is a humiliation Lindy Lowe is unwilling to bear. If she has to go down, she'll go down swinging. She will spit in the face of injustice. She will, at the very least, spit in her palm when it's time to line up and shake hands with the other team. She will spit fresh when she sees that smirking catcher coming her way. She scrapes her feet vigorously on the damp earth, hoping to splat him with a clod as he squats behind her.

She is worried though. A glance at the bleachers reveals her dad's death grip on the seat; he's leaning forward, his chest just about touching his knees. He looks like a spring about to be sprung and he hasn't been feeling good—the sweat breaks out and his face gets tight and pale. It's not good for him to lose his temper and get dramatic anymore. Doctor said so.

She shakes her hair out of her eyes, sniffs and blinks hard to focus. A hit at this point could avert any number of disasters.

She hears her dad call: "Choke up. Choke up, Lindy. Nice level swing." He's about two turns short of hurtling off the bleachers, telling that strike-happy umpire what he thinks of his attitude and eyesight. God knows what will happen if the umpire makes the mistake of trying to defend himself. Her dad, once his temper's lit, is apt to spark like Fourth of July.

The team yells: KILL IT, LINDY, KILL IT. OUT OF THE PARK, LINDY. JUST LIKE LAST TIME.

Right. Just like last time. Listening to them, she can almost believe there was a last time. The pitcher believes she can hit the ball. Something in her stance, in the tilt of her chin, in the lift of the bat tells him so.

The voices fade. Lindy feels the smooth, curved wood in her hands, the mist on her face. She and the burly Beaumont pitcher are alone, transfixed in a naked staredown. Everything fades except the dark holes that are her opponent's eyes.

*Come on, Pitcher. Fire it in here. I am ready.*

She takes a deep, steadying breath.

*Ready.*

But Brian Millitello—the speed demon on first base—sees his chance and takes it. He breaks for second, a full-speed torpedo in cleats, out of the chute and no turning back. Coach screams a long hoarse "Go!"

The pitcher twists, throws.

Lindy steps away from the plate.

Brian slides, belly down, fingers reaching. He touches the bag. The ball slaps the second baseman's glove.

The team screams, "yes."

"out," yells the base umpire.

"out?" yell the parents in the bleachers. "out?" Old Dad wails, leaping to his feet. She hopes he's got his pills with him. Mr. Schlitz, on the bleachers behind, grabs him by the shoulders, holds him back. They hold each other back. Marcia presses her lips together and pushes at her hair. Coach's head drops to his chest. His eyes close. Slowly, he opens them—but the nightmare persists. Brian is still out. Lindy stands quiet, stunned.

Coach and the plate umpire stalk to second base. Coach points at the bag. He points at Brian, who is brushing himself off, wild-eyed. He'd waited for his moment, just like Coach said. He'd run hard. He'd slid perfectly. He was safe!

"I was safe," Brian says, keeping one foot on the bag, just in case the umpire comes to his senses and reverses his decision. "Shut up," Coach says. "I'll handle this." Brian shuts up. He's going nowhere until Coach tells him to. They'll have to pry him off this base like a bloodsucker from a swimmer's calf. They'll have to burn him off with giant matches. They'll have to sprinkle ten pounds of salt on his head.

From the dugout the team protests, agonized. "Shut up," Marcia says. The protest diminishes to a collective sob, a quiet moan. Marcia blocks the exit with her body, a plug in the zing hole of a hornet's nest: they are subdued now, but for how long? Her mission, a mother's mission: keep the kids out of the fray. She watches Coach and the umpires in their nose-to-nose exchange. She can't hear a word of it, but she is transfixed by the passion shimmering in the air around them. Or is it the beginning of the rain—the drops almost too fine to detect.

Tina's face, suddenly, fills Marcia's field of vision. Tina is bigger than life and stinking of drug-store cologne. Marcia steps to the side to see around her. Tina steps that way too. They are dancing the two-step. Marcia catches at the dugout post to hold her position on the edge of the stairs.

Tina says: "If I want him back, I'll get him back."

Marcia says: "What *is* your problem?"

Tina says: "You're going to be the one with the problem if you keep it up. I'm embarrassed for you. You're at least five years older than him for one thing."

Marcia says: "Do you want to eat this scorebook?"

Meanwhile, the confrontation at second base escalates. The arrogant Beaumont coach, his belly girdled by the tight polyester uniform, thrusts himself into the huddle. Coach—slight and intense, his hands fisted at his sides—talks fast, face flushing.

It starts to rain. Marcia, in the shelter of the dugout overhang, stays dry. Tina gets hit with both the rain and the runoff. Her perm flattens like tissue paper. Water catches on her lashes, pools there momentarily, then her mascara starts to run in hideous black rivulets down her face. Her chin drips black. Her purple scarf will soon be bleeding into her T-shirt.

Lindy worries that the rain will ruin her baseball hat: there's a waterfall flowing over the bill. Should she run for shelter or stay put between the on-deck box and the plate? She and Little Clay look at each other and shrug; they move closer together. They stay put, side by side, hats dripping.

The deluge breaks up the huddle at second base. Coach puts

his hand on Brian Millitello's head and they stalk together off the field—Brian stalking twice as fast as Coach, just to keep up. The thunder comes again. Closer now. Close enough to startle people.

"Are they going to call it?" Lindy's dad yells from the bleachers, a newspaper tented over his head. The others have run for their cars but Old Dad doesn't budge. His girl is still at bat.

"No way!" Coach says. "Lindy—get ready. We're going to finish our ups if we have to swim the bases."

Old Dad says, "Ya, but . . ."

Coach says, "I told them we're going to finish our ups. That's it."

Lindy believes him.

Marcia has draped herself in a plastic poncho—just the bill of her cap and the tip of her nose exposed. She stands beside Coach at the baseline. "There's three kids crying in the dug-out," she says.

"We're not going home," he says, "until we turn this thing around."

She says, "They're pretty discouraged—they think we're getting knocked out of the playoffs because of cheating."

Coach says, "No way!" And as he says it, the downpour lets up a little—it's a drizzle, it's a shower, it's nothing to be concerned about, certainly nothing to call a game on account of. Marcia pictures Tina, drowned ratty, huddling in her car, waiting for Coach to come to her so she can hurt him again. But she won't. Marcia will make sure of that.

Coach says, "TEAM! Talk it up—talk it up! All it takes is one."

Lindy steps into the batter's box.

GO LINDY—SHOW 'EM WHAT YOU CAN DO—OUTTA THE PARK, LIN-DY.

Little Clay, in the on-deck box, takes warm-up swings so vigorous there appears to be some danger he'll hit himself in the head on the follow-through. "Good cut, Clay," Coach says over a rumble of thunder, a thin, distant flash of lightning, "but don't use the aluminum bat," tossing him a wooden one.

Marcia whispers in Coach's ear: "Did you see Tina over here, causing trouble?"

"I didn't notice," he says.

Marcia smiles.

Coach claps his hands three times. The team picks up the rhythm, increases its chatter—the hive is humming.

Lindy adjusts her safety goggles, raises her good old wooden bat high over her shoulder, points her toe, sticks her butt out. The tip of the bat makes small menacing circles in the air.

"One good pitch," the Beaumont coach yells. "Strike her out, Don-Don. Strike her out and we're out of here."

Lindy's dad disentangles himself from the wet newspaper. He yells: "HIT IT." The crack of the bat making solid contact with a not-so-wicked fast ball punctuates the sentiment and Lindy, always light on her feet, is hydroplaning toward first base.

Don-Don, having lost his balance on the wet mound, is down, trying to find his feet when the ball whizzes over his head. He reaches—but too late.

Old Dad says, reverently: "Line drive."

Lindy rounds first, heads for second. The center fielder, who underestimated her power, has to run back for the ball which is rolling away from him toward the fence but stops just short. He gets a glove on it, grips it with his throwing hand, hesitates: Where's the play?

Someone screams second.

Lindy runs full speed, focused on the base ahead, conscious only of the power of her muscles, the strength of her bones.

She pumps as hard as she can. She doesn't look for where the ball has gone, or who has it, or where it is going. She doesn't look at Coach for a green light or a red light. She doesn't look at anybody—she just goes.

No one knows it yet (except possibly Old Dad, from whom she inherited a good deal of her spirit and bull-headedness), but the moment bat connected with ball, Lindy Lowe made up her mind to run the bases. All of them. Full out. Non-stop. Whatever the consequences.

The center fielder, a logical boy, throws to second. But Lindy blows by the second baseman long before the lobbed ball arrives. And the second baseman, watching Lindy run, is forced to hop out of her way or be barreled over. He throws his glove up too late—the ball rolls out of it, onto the ground.

He can't see. The ball is muddy, there's water in his eyes— he feels around, knocking the ball a few feet down the baseline. He dives, throws from his knees to some phantom player standing halfway between the third baseman and the shortstop.

By then Lindy has already whizzed by third and is on her way home.

As the ball slides into foul territory, with three humiliated Beaumont players hot on its trail, Lindy slides home. She is jumping up and down on the puddle that used to be home plate and the team is rushing out to greet her. Little Clay gets there first. They high-five and he says, "I'm gonna hit a good one. You're gonna see me hit a home run now. Everybody's gonna see."

And Little Clay is right. The rally has begun.

# DOUBLE PLAY

1985

eloise  klein  healy

If Gertrude Stein had played second base
she would have said "there's only there there"
and putting thoughts in order.

The outfield is the place to dream,
where slow moons fall out of the sky
and rise clean over a green horizon.

The infield is tense as blank paper
and changeable as the cuneiform
of cleats along the path.

Stein would have loved the arc of arm
from short to second
and the spill of one white star
out of a hand.

# FROM *IN SHELLY'S LEG*

1981

sara vogan

**S**ummer light lasted until almost ten o'clock. On evenings when Margaret didn't have a game or a practice she and Woody would play ball with the children in the backyard. At the heart of the season Margaret felt her arm and shoulder tightening into a perpetual ache located somewhere beneath her muscles. She felt good and loose only when pitching and for a few hours right after. She wondered about professional pitchers; they must hurt all the time, their muscles bound in tight knots until the arm was being used.

Woody caught and called the imaginary hits. If the whiffle bat connected with one of Margaret's pitches, the ball dropped like a shot pigeon. The kids always swung past the pitch. Woody invented the plays for them, giving them a lot of triples and home runs.

Adam had been talking about trying out for Little League next summer and he started concentrating on hitting Margaret's curves, slowballs, and sliders. Sometimes he would just stand holding the bat and watch the arc of the ball as it left Margaret's hand and sailed toward him, across the car mat they used for home plate, and into Woody's glove.

Margaret pitched a riser. Adam swung. The bat whistled

through the air. "A double!" Woody yelled, expecting Adam to run to the maple tree, first base, and pull up at the garage corner, second base.

Adam stood with the bat resting in his arms. "Don't do that," he said. "Do that for Allison, not for me."

Woody looked at him quizzically. "Don't you want to run?"

"No. I mean yes. But I only want to run if I hit the ball. Then you can tell me if it's a double or something."

"I get all the home runs!" Allison yelled.

"Okay," Woody said. "You sure? It'll be easier to hit a Little League pitcher than one of Maggie's."

"I know," Adam said. "But I want to really hit them. Not just pretend."

Woody studied the boy. He seemed to be measuring Adam's height with his eyes. "There's more to it than that," Woody said. "You got to lob them into holes in the outfield."

"Woody." Margaret didn't like Woody trying to dampen Adam's enthusiasm. In some way Adam's seriousness about pretend ballgames seemed to her an indication he was growing up.

"We don't have an outfield," Allison said.

"I'll tell you what," Margaret said. "I'll give you seven pitches."

"Seven?"

"Sure. Four balls, three strikes." Margaret smiled. "It will give you a chance to practice."

Adam grinned. "Okay!"

Allison pouted. "I'll never get to bat."

Woody touched her hair. "But you'll get all the home runs."

Margaret's first pitch was a nice, slow ball, directly across the plate.

Adam did not swing and stood to the side and watched the

ball sail by. "That's a little kid's pitch, Mom. Do your regular stuff."

"You sure?" Woody asked. "It might take a while to get a hit."

Adam glared at Woody. "I'm not going to be a little kid forever."

Margaret pitched Adam three slowballs and four risers. He missed them all. As he handed the bat to his sister, Adam looked at Woody, over to Margaret, then back to Woody. "It's just kid's stuff the other way," he said.

Allison stood next to Woody, the whifflebat held high in the air. She wiggled her butt the way she had seen the women on the Shelly's Leg team shift when they settled their feet into the box. "I'm ready," she said. Woody, crouched behind the car mat, looked to be exactly her height.

"This will be a double home run," Allison said. "I've got Billie Jean King on second."

Margaret practiced another slider. Allison swung after the ball landed in Woody's mitt. "A home run!" Allison yelled.

Woody played the announcer. "Look at that, folks! That ball's gone right out of the park! A cute little girl in the second bleachers is going to catch that ball and take it home as a souvenir."

Allison slapped her hand against the tree trunk. "We've got the second-base runner coming in," Woody called.

"Billie Jean King!" Allison screamed as she tagged the corner of the garage.

Woody tossed the ball back to Margaret. "Look at that girl run, ladies and gentlemen. In case you folks in the stands didn't know, Allison is also an Olympic short-sprinter."

Allison ran past the piece of cardboard at third.

"She's coming down the home stretch now." Woody held his hands up like a megaphone. "And here she comes! A home run for Allison and a run batted in!" Woody caught her up in his arms as she crossed the car mat and swung her as easily as an infant in a circle through the air. He kissed her loudly on the top of the head when he set her back on the ground.

Allison giggled and squirmed in his hands. "Too bad," she panted, "you can't kiss Billie Jean King too. She doesn't like boys."

Margaret worked on her knuckleball for the next seven pitches to Adam. She watched his small body standing by the plate, studying the first pitch as if he were concentrating for a test. He swung at the next five pitches, missing them all. As he watched the last pitch, he seemed to be memorizing its pattern through the air. Then he handed the bat to his sister.

"I'm going to beat you," Allison said. "I'm going to cream you." She told Woody she had Phyllis Schlafly and Gloria Steinem on bases this time.

"Christ!" Woody laughed. "You sure have one hell of a team."

"We're all famous," Allison said. "Even me. That's what makes us so good."

Woody gave Allison only a single, but allowed Gloria Steinem to score another run. "Just to keep things interesting," he told her when she looked disappointed. "You can't get a home run every time."

Adam varied his attack on the slowballs Margaret pitched. He lunged at the first two, studied the third, walked lazily through the fourth, and on the fifth slowball he tipped it. The ball dropped and rolled off toward Margaret in the center of the yard.

"Okay!" Woody said. "Mightyfine!"

Adam stopped running halfway to the maple tree. "What is it? What'd I hit?"

"A triple for sure," Woody shouted. "Maybe you can steal into home. There's a muff-up in the outfield."

Adam ran hard past the maple.

"Hurry!" Allison shouted. "They're gaining on you!"

Adam slapped past second at the garage and ran, head down, toward the piece of cardboard at third. Sticking his arms straight ahead of him, he dove to the ground five feet in front of the car mat and scrambled in on his hands and knees.

"An in-the-park homer, folks!" Woody called as he stood Adam up, dusted him off, and patted him professionally on the shoulder. "That was all right. Mightyfine!"

Adam beamed at him. "See? I can do it. Someday me and Mom will have a real game."

# HOTSHOT

1992

nancy boutilier

**A** five-foot-eight-inch fifth grader is probably going to be one of the best basketball players in her school no matter if she's girl or boy. But I happen to be a girl, and pretty good at sticking the "J" too, so don't go challenging me to one-on-one, unless, of course, you don't mind losing. And I'm not gonna play you easy on account of what Mom calls "ego"— especially no "male ego" that some boys got. I don't play easy for any reason or anyone. It's that simple.

Most of life is simple. Too many people want to make stuff way more difficult than it is. Like the time school pictures came back and I was holding a pencil behind Tony Kramer's head so it looked like the pencil grew right out of his ear. Well, Mrs. Kramer goes and calls my teacher and then my Mom and we all have to sit down and discuss it. They all try to tell me what a horrible thing I did, messing up the picture and all. And I kept trying to tell them how funny it was—and even Tony thought so too—but no one else was laughing. So I end up feeling bad about something I thought was fun—and I would never have done it to someone like Laurie Strandy or Darius Silvers because I know it would have made them feel bad. But Tony—I knew he could take it.

Oh, well, I guess I'm supposed to be learning the when's and where's of having fun. And what I like most is fun on the basketball court. Shooting, dribbling, rebounding—I can out-run and out-jump anyone in the fifth or sixth grade—anyone!

Most of the teachers gave up on trying to make me stay on the girls' side of the hardtop. But old Miss Monzelli, who I call Miss Von Smelly when she can't hear me, sometimes still screeches from behind those pointy glasses with the fake little diamonds for me to get onto the hopscotch side of the black-top. She says I can't play with the boys because it ain't ladylike. She says I might get hurt. She also says that saying *ain't* ain't ladylike neither, so I do it just to remind her who's boss. We'll see who's going to get hurt.

Truth is, no boy ever hurt me more than I hurt him. Besides, I've had stitches four different times, and not once have I even cried at the blood or the needles. Broke a bundle of bones, too—three fingers, my wrist, both collarbones, and my left ankle—seven all together.

That's how I learned that basketball is in me—it's in my bones. Every time I've been sidelined, I don't mind missing out on a football game, or the roller coaster at the carnival, but not being able to play hoops sets my skin crawling. I know it's in my blood too because my Dad is six-foot-four and played in college. He still plays at the Y, and I get to shoot around at half-time of his games. All the referees there like me. Sure, they have to show off, spinning the ball on their fingers or throwing it to me behind the back, but they all like me. I figure they are jealous of the guys like Dad who get to strut their stuff while they only get to run up and down the court blowing whistles and ticking everyone off.

But at halftime, the refs rebound for me and call me Hotshot.

I'm telling you all this so you can see how some things are

born in a girl even though most people seem to think they're reserved only for boys. And don't go calling me Tomboy unless you can give account of what it means. I'm a girl who can throw a football further and with a better spiral than anyone at Maple Street School, except for Greg Merrit, who is my best friend, and Mr. Leon, the gym teacher. I don't mind that Greg can throw further than me because he's real good and that's just that. I can respect that. Besides, I'm a better free-throw shooter than he is, so really, we're even. But don't go saying that I throw like a boy any quicker than you'd say that Greg throws like a girl, which he does, because he throws like me, and I'm a girl. There's nothing Tomboy about it. I'm a girl and I can play a wizard game of Horse, I'm unbeatable at 'Round the World, I hold my own in "21," and you'll want me on your side if we're playing five-on-a-side pickup. I told you, it's that simple.

And I'm not good just because I'm tall. My Dad told me not to be worried about being a six-foot girl because he says if any girl is going to dunk in high school it's going to be me. Mom says I slouch too much. I don't think I slouch at all. I just lean kind of forward when I walk and bounce on my toes so I can feel my hightops hugging my ankles. Air Hotshot! I hit the ground and my treads spring me right back up on my toes. I can see that it scares the boys a bit when I stride out onto the court bouncing like I'm the best thing since the hook shot in my black leather Cons. I'll take hightops over high heels any day!

Anyhow, what I'm trying to tell you about is my problem with Miss Monzelli. She's my Social Studies teacher who seems to think she got hired by the school solely to mess with my life. She tries to make me play only with the other girls at recess, and I told her I don't have anything against girls, but I like playing basketball, and it's the boys who play basketball.

She says I'm not learning to be a lady if I don't play with girls and held me after school to point out that if I dress like the boys and talk like the boys, I'll find myself in trouble. It seemed to me that the only trouble I was in was with her, but I didn't think I'd score points by telling her so. Instead, I asked her if it was bad for me to be like the boys, why wasn't it bad for the boys to be like boys. After all, I didn't see her making no fuss about what they were wearing or playing.

Miss Monzelli got all red in the face so that her cheeks and neck matched the fire-engine-red lipstick she wears. She chewed me out for being fresh, and then insisted that the boys are supposed to act like boys because they are boys. It didn't make sense to me, so I didn't listen to most of what she was saying until I caught on that she had phoned my Mom to say that I was supposed to wear dresses to school unless we were scheduled for gym class. Well, we only have gym twice a week, so Miss Von Smelly was saying that I had to wear a dress every Monday, Wednesday, and Friday! Now, I don't even like wearing dresses when I go to see my grandmother in the city, but that's the deal. And even then I don't like it, but my grandmother does. Gram is worth pleasing for the way she lets me climb on through the attic to the roof. Gram keeps a treasure chest for me in the closet and takes me to the zoo. Her oatmeal cookies are the best on this planet, and I get to lick the batter from the bowl. She even sewed me a pair of pajamas with tiger stripes and a long tail stuffed with nylon stockings. For Gram I will wear a dress.

Mom gave up with me and dresses when I was in the third grade. That's when we agreed that I wouldn't fight over wearing a dress for Sunday Mass or for visits to Gram. If I didn't put up a stink on those occasions, I wouldn't have to wear dresses the rest of the whole year. At Gram's house and God's house, it makes Mom happy if I wear a dress, but no way am I wearing no dress for no old Miss Von Smelly—not even if she could bake oatmeal cookies like Gram's. Mom's only other rule was "No hightop sneakers when wearing a dress!" I don't much mind that rule, because hightops just don't look right when you got a skirt flapping around your thighs.

Mom lets me wear low-cut sneakers with my knee socks, so I can still run around, because I wear shorts underneath. I just don't like the idea that when I sprint, jump, fall, or wrestle the whole world has a front-row seat to my underwear. And if I wear a dress to school, I have to put up with all Miss Von Smelly's stupid comments to us girls to sit with our knees locked together so our legs get all sore and cramped from trying to keep ourselves all shut up tight under our desks, as if it isn't easier to just tell the boys they got no business looking up our skirts in the first place.

I've never seen Miss Von Smelly in pants, and I feel like telling her how much happier she'd be if she didn't have to pay so much worrytime making sure her underwear ain't on display when she bends over, or reaches up high, or just stands in the wind. She wears all these silly shoes that make her look like a Barbie doll when she walks—stiff-kneed and pointy-toed, scuttering along.

I don't understand Miss Monzelli any better than she understands me, but I don't go telling her that she should be wearing hightop sneakers and jeans, so where does she get off calling my Mom to say that I have to dress like her? That's all I want to know.

So anyway, I go home, and at dinner, Mom tells Dad about Miss Monzelli's phone call, and I just about choke on a tomato when Dad says, "If that's what the teacher says, I suppose Angela will just have to put up with the rule."

"But Dad, Miss Monzelli is such a witch. She's just making me wear dresses because she knows how much I hate it! She's out to get me!"

"Now, Tiger." Dad calls me "Tiger" when we horse around

or when he wants me to think that he's on my side, but he's really not. "I'm sure Miss Monzelli is not out to get you. She is your teacher, and she knows what is best for you and for the school."

"I'm not wearing dresses three times a week!"

"Honey." Mom calls me that when I start getting stubborn, and I can tell it's going to be two against one, three against one if you count Miss Monzelli. "I've let you take responsibility for your wardrobe this year, but maybe it's time that we take another look at what is appropriate attire for a young lady in your school. What do the other girls wear?"

"Mom"—I could hear the whine in my voice, which meant that I knew reasoning wouldn't really work—"the other girls in my school play hopscotch at recess, and go to the corner store for Doritos and Coke after school. They don't play basketball or football or even climb on the jungle gym."

"Well, you could come home and change into your play clothes after school if you wanted to . . ."

"Aww, come on, Mom, I'd never get in the game if I came home while the kids were choosing up teams. Dad . . ." I looked hopefully to my father for support, but he was staying out of this argument for as long as possible.

"Angela," my father said with a mix of sympathy and hesitation in his voice, "your teacher seems to think . . ."

"Dad, my teacher is a witch who waddles around in high heels and can't even hold a football in one hand. She picks it up at arm's length with two hands, like it's a piece of corn on the cob, too hot to bring within three feet of her body."

"Now, that's no way to talk about your teacher."

"Then there's no way she should talk about me as if I have no right to dress as I please."

Both my parents seemed to be defending Miss Monzelli only because she was my teacher, but I could tell that words were not going to convince them of what a jerk Miss Monzelli was being. So I sat quiet, hoping they would just forget about it, and life would go on as usual as I trotted off to school in my hightops and jeans the next morning. Besides, I didn't even own enough dresses to get through a week without repeating, unless I wore the satin dress I had from being the flower girl at my cousin's wedding. That dress puffed out so that I looked like a piece of Double Bubble Chewing Gum wrapped up and twisted in bows at both ends. No way was I stepping out of the house in that thing!

My other two dresses had both been made by Gram. My favorite was yellow with purple and white stripes down the side and a big number 32 on the front. Gram made it special to look like Magic Johnson's Lakers uniform. For a dress, it's pretty neat; but it's still a dress. None of the other dresses I own fit me because I've been growing too fast for my clothes to keep up with me. The only reason the gum-wrapper dress fits is because an older cousin was supposed to be the flower girl, but she got some mono-disease right before the wedding, and I had to take her place. The dress was too big in the first place.

So Mom and Dad go on as if this conversation is over. I dig into my fish stick as if there's something special about fish sticks, which there definitely is not. I hear my fork scratching my plate, Mom's bracelets knocking against each other, and Dad's jaw cracking the way that it does when he chews. In our family, that's a silent dinner table.

When Mom gets up to clear the table, I leap up to help because I don't want anyone pointing out how much I hate all this housework stuff as if it's because I don't wear dresses often enough. Besides, it helps change the tone of everything for dessert, and we have forgotten the whole conversation enough so that Dad pulls out the weekend football pool that he gets at work. It's the first round of the playoffs, and I'm still hopeful enough to believe that I can bet on the Patriots to make it to the Super Bowl. Dad says that his football sense overrules his loyalty to the hometeam, so he plays his card differently than I play mine. We argue a bit about whether or not the Patriots can get their ground game going, and then we turn attention to the chocolate pudding Mom puts in front of us. The silence is broken, and when I go to bed I feel sure no one will notice what I wear to school in the morning.

"Do you have Phys Ed today?" Mom asks as I throw my backpack full of books on the kitchen floor by the backdoor.

"Umm, no. Why?" I pretend innocence and ignorance of Miss Monzelli's mandate.

"Well, because, we agreed that you'd save your jeans for gym days." Mom's trying to be as forgetful of the argument as I am.

"We agreed that I could wear whatever I wanted except for church and for Gram. We never agreed to anything about wearing dresses to school. Miss Von Smelly just poked her nose into something that is not her business." Since this was not one of those times when giving in for the sake of keeping Mom happy was worth it, I made sure not to say *ain't*. I didn't want her to have any dirt on me in any way. Otherwise, I'd be stuck for good. I hoped she'd see this as one of those times when giving in for the sake of keeping ME happy would be worth HER while.

It wasn't.

"Angie, the school has its expectations and standards, and you have to—"

"Mom it's not the school. It's Miss Monzelli! And she's an old witch anyway. Why listen to her?"

Dad walked in and silence returned.

I grew impatient and started pleading. "Mom, watch. No one will say anything's wrong if you just let me keep doing what I'm doing."

"Oh-oh, dresses again, huh? Tiger, why don't you just put on a dress, go to school, and do whatever it is you always do?" offered Dad, trying to be helpful and healing to the conversation.

"Daaadddd," I whined, hoping the tone said more than the word itself.

"Tiger, no one is asking you to change yourself. Nobody is going to stop you from being who you are. It's only your clothes we're asking you to change."

"Well, if it's only clothes, then why is everyone else making such a gigantic deal about what I wear?"

For a moment I grew hopeful when my Dad had no answer for me, but then Mom filled the pause. "Because your teacher thinks you ought to dress up a bit more—like the other girls."

"Exactly," seconded Dad. "So why don't you run back into your room, slip those clothes into your backpack for after school, and put on a dress for classes?"

It was more of a commandment than a question, and I knew I wasn't going to get out of the house in my jeans. So I just glared at Dad a bit, then glared even harder at Mom, and stormed back to my room.

I had tried to be honest with my parents, but my honest opinions had gotten me nowhere. I didn't really want to cut school, although that option did come to mind. I figured I could change my clothes as soon as I got around the corner from the house. So, I put on the dress I hated most, the candy-wrapper one from Rico's wedding. It looked really stupid with my sneakers, and I felt like irking my folks because they were siding with Miss Von Smelly. I wore one tube sock with black and orange stripes and one with green and blue stripes, all of which completely clashed with the yellow and red of the dress.

I stomped my way back into the kitchen, no longer hungry for breakfast. I stood in the doorway as defiantly as possible with legs spread wide and arms folded across my chest. Mom and Dad looked at each other, unimpressed by me, and pleased as punch they'd won the argument. I stuffed my jeans and a T-shirt into my backpack as Dad had suggested, but I guess he must of been onto my plan to change before I reached the schoolyard because he offered to drive me to school.

Next thing I know, Dad's dropping me off in the school parking lot, and I'm facing a blacktop filled with my friends who have never even seen me in a dress, let alone in a flower girl gown, and I can't believe it. I'm angry as can be at Mom, Dad, Miss Monzelli, and any kid who dares to look at me. I turn to get back into the car, and when Dad innocently waves "So long, Tiger. See you tonight," I can't believe he's humiliating me this way. I see a few kids pointing toward me, laughing, and I want to punch them all. I don't know where to begin swinging, so I run inside to the girls' room, leap into the second stall, lock the door, and stand up on the seat so that no one can find me.

As I'm catching my breath, I discover that I left my backpack in the car.

Everybody has already seen me and I'm weighing my options while perched atop of the toilet. Then I hear the bathroom squeak open. By the clicking of tiny footsteps echoing across the tile, I know Miss Monzelli has stalked me down.

"Hello? Is anyone in here? Hello? Angela? Angela?"

I say nothing, but I think of how stupid I'll feel if she finds me hiding in the stall. I know she knows I'm in here. I quickly and quietly slide my feet down so that it looks like I'm sitting on the toilet, and I drop my underpants down around my ankles. "Yes, Miss Monzelli," in the sweetest voice I can put together. "I'm just, well, ya know, doing what I have to do."

"Oh, Angela, it's you," she says, as if she's surprised I'm here. "I saw someone sneak in, and you know you shouldn't leave the playground without permission. Unless of course it's an emergency. I suppose it's all right this one time if Nature caught you by surprise." She's trying to make me feel better, but it sure as cinnamon ain't working.

"By the way, I thought you looked very pretty when I saw your father drop you off."

That was the final straw. I wanted to scream, punch or puke at her. She sounded so smug in her triumph, like those TV preachers who have saved some stupid sinner from the clutches of the devil. But fighting Miss Von Smelly would be no solution. It would only help prove to her that I behaved unladylike. So I said nothing, and she filled the silence by explaining that she was going back out before the bell rang to line everyone up for homeroom. Again, the bathroom door squeaked and the echoing heel clicks out the door and down the hallway.

I hated the thought of being made a fool by Miss Monzelli's dumb rules. I needed a way to make her own rules work for me rather than against me. So I sat for a bit, realizing I might as well pee while I was on the toilet seat. After finishing my piss, I stood and reached to pull my underwear back up. As I turned to flush, a comic vision flashed through my head. I quickly dropped my underwear back to my ankles and stepped out of one leg hole. With my other leg, I kicked it up into the air, then with one arm I reached out to first catch and then slam dunk my underwear into the toilet bowl. A quick kick to the metal bar flushed it all away. No more underwear!

Miss Monzelli could gloat all she wanted over her little victory because I knew I'd have the last laugh. I wasn't thrilled about the razzing I'd have to put up with in the meantime, but it would all be worthwhile.

I returned to the blacktop where everyone was lining up

silent and military. Eyes flashed my way, and an occasional head turned, but always at the risk of Miss Monzelli taking away recess period for headturners to practice standing at attention. I always wondered what it was we were supposed to pay attention to.

I held my head high and looked at no one. I had a secret that would teach Miss Monzelli not to mess with my life or my wardrobe, so I figured I didn't have to deal with any kid's questions or stares. I just strutted to my place in the back of the line, glad that my last name was Vickery so I was at the end of the alphabetical order that Miss Monzelli organizes her life by. I glared down at Eric Tydings, who stood in front of me every time we lined up for anything. He turned with a giggle held under his breath, and I answered his jeering. "If you don't turn around and get rid of that jackass grin, I'm gonna make your teeth permanent fixtures in your stomach."

Eric quickly turned back to the front, and it was a good thing for him, because the line was filing into the school, and Miss Monzelli for sure would have slapped him with some detention time for not paying attention. And no way was she going to blame me for his mischief today. After all, I was wearing a dress, and in Miss Monzelli's book, girls in dresses act ladylike and stay out of trouble.

I spoke to no one all morning except to answer questions with "yes" or "no," because I had nothing much I wanted to say to anyone. We had lots of stuff to do, including a worksheet of word problems, some reading about astronauts, and a spelling test. I pretended not to notice all the attention I was getting—the muffled laughter, stolen glances and flat-out stares—but inside I wasn't missing a single sidelook or whisper. All the while I sat real careful not to let on that I wore nothing beneath my dress. I wanted to be sure that Miss Monzelli could not get word that I had no underwear on. I was determined that the whole school should see for themselves all at the same time, so I waited patiently for morning recess.

The recess bell finally rang at 10:30 just as I was completing an essay about my favorite animal. I had written all that I could think of writing about kangaroos about five minutes earlier, but I added one final sentence to my essay before putting up my pencil and folding my hands together on my desk top the way Miss Monzelli insists we all sit before she will consider allowing us to line up for recess. I wrote, "Kangaroos prove God has a sense of humor, because the only reason kangaroos exist is to jump around and have fun."

I signed my essay the way I always do at the end. Miss Monzelli hates it because she wants my name squished up at the top right corner of the page, neatly printed with her name and the date. She insists we use the "proper heading" on our work, so I do that, but I also let loose in big script letters at the end "by Angela Vickery" like a painter signing a master-piece.

"All right, children. You may line up quietly in alphabetical order if you would like to go outside for recess." Of course everyone wanted to go out for recess, but Miss Monzelli always made it sound like an option and an invitation all at the same time that it was really, deep down, just another Von Smelly command.

We lined up, with me in the back again, and filed silently down the corridor to the double doors that led to the play-ground. Once outside we were allowed to break file, and we scattered ourselves across the blacktop. Kevin Marino was close on my heels asking, "Hey, Angela. What's with the dress?" and I was answering only with an all-out sprint to the basketball court. Tyrone Freeman had the ball, and he was starting a game of "21" rather than choosing up sides for full court. Recess was too short for a game, and "21" gave everyone a chance to play because it's one big half-court game that leaves everyone against everyone scrapping to make a basket. You just have to keep track of your own score, and it's you against everyone any time you get the ball.

So I threw out my elbows the way I always did and made space for myself in the middle of the crowd huddled below the basket. The boys knew me well enough to tell from the scowl on my face that questions or jokes were completely out of order, so we all just settled in to play basketball. When Tyrone missed an outside shot, the rebound went off my fingers, and Stu Jackster came up with the ball. He cleared the ball out past the foul line, and I went out with him to play defense. He drove to my left, but his leg caught my knee, and we both went to the pavement. I landed sitting flat on my fanny with Stu sprawling across my legs. My dress was all in place, and Stu spit at the pavement beside me as he extended a hand to help me up. Meanwhile, the ball had gotten loose, and Greg Merrit had scored on a jump shot.

Greg got to take the ball up top because it's "make it–take it" where you get the ball back after you score a hoop. As Greg went to take a shot from the top of the key, I went back under to rebound. Sure enough, I came up with the ball, and put it straight up for a point of my own. It was my ball, at the top, and I took the ball left, spun around back to the right, and after two dribbles, I put the ball up and off the backboard for another basket.

My ball again. This time Tyrone decides to play me close, and as I move to spin past him, he gets help on the double team from Greg Merrit. BANG! Greg and I collide, and this time I'm on my back with my hightop sneakers looking down at me. Tyrone screams, "She's got no underwear on!" and they're all laughing hysterically. I clench my teeth almost as tightly as my fists and hiss out at them with squinted eyes,

"Miss Monzelli says I gotta wear a dress. Man, I'm wearing a dress, aren't I? You laugh at her, not at me, Tyrone Freeman. If any of you wanna laugh at me, you gonna have all your faces rearranged!"

Tyrone backed down on account we're friends, but Doug McDermott wasn't so smart. He starts chanting, "I see London. I see France. Angela got no underpants." Once Doug gets going, everyone joins him, and I go right for his throat. He lands a half-punch the side of my head, and I throw one he ducks away from. Next thing I know, we're rolling around on the court, neither one of us landing any punches, but my dress is caught up high and my naked butt must be mooning the whole world just as Miss Monzelli arrives at the fight. Her voice is an extra two octaves higher than usual when I hear her scream, "Angela Vickery, stop it! Stop this instant. Stop!"

Of course, I'm not stopping. I'm barely listening, but she tells one of the kids to run and get Mr. Stoller, the school principal.

Well, lots of fussing went on about this whole scene. The kids loved it. It was a scandal that had teachers and the principal unsure about what to do. After all, they had brought it on themselves. As Greg Merrit said, "You ask Angie to wear a dress and you gotta expect something crazy!"

Mr. Stoller lectured me a long while about fighting, but he never said anything directly about my lack of underwear. The school nurse gave me a whole lot of nurse-like advice about being clean and wearing the proper undergarments. My Mom and Dad had a conference that afternoon with Miss Monzelli, but didn't say much to me about it.

The next day, when I arrived at breakfast in jeans and a Lakers sweatshirt, Mom asked if I wanted Wheaties or Grape-Nuts and that was that. Even after all the dust settled, Miss Monzelli never brought up the subject of dresses or underwear.

When the weekend arrived, Mom announced that Gram had invited us to the city for the day. I ran back upstairs to my room and happily put on my Magic Johnson dress. When I returned to the kitchen for breakfast, Mom and Dad looked at me, and then at each other, relieved.

I answered their unasked question by quickly turning, bending, and lifting my skirt to show them my underwear.

"Looking good, Tiger!" cheered Dad as I turned around to face my smiling parents.

"What are you waiting for? Go on, get dressed. I want to sink my teeth into Gram's oatmeal cookies while they're still warm."

# MOST VALUABLE PLAYER

1988

sarah  van  arsdale

If I had a trophy
I'd put it on the middle shelf
of my bookcase. I'd dust
it every day
and polish it once a week.

It would have a statue of a woman
holding a bat, her golden arm
cocked up a little
waiting for the pitch.
When my friends came over
I'd stand next to the bookcase casual-like
till they said, "Is that a trophy?"
I'd read the inscription every morning.
I'd ask someone to take my picture
with my trophy.

My trophy would say
"Softball Player" on the bottom,
and everyone would know
that in summer I tie on my cleats,

run onto the field,
slapping high fives.
They'd know I take third base,
put my glove to the dry dirt,
scatter dust in the air.
They'd hear the fans shout,

"Hey, some catch!"
when that white ball comes slamming
into my glove,
and, "Watch out, she'll steal home,"
as my cleats dig and dig.
They'd feel the weight of the little statue
and think, "I bet she's going out
with her team tonight,"
"I bet she could teach me how to throw,"
"I bet she plays softball,"
and I do,

I do.

# A GOLF LULLABY

1900

margaret barbour

O hush-a-by Baby and shut thy blue eyes,
Thy father's a-golfing and hears not thy cries—
Thy father's a-golfing and mother must go,
So shut thine eyes, Heart's Love, and be not so slow.

O hush-a-by, Sweetling, and weep thou no more,
Thy mother must hasten to bring up her score;
Her putting and teeing and driving, Dear Eyes,
Must surely this day win the beautiful prize.

So hush-a-by Baby and dry thy tears up,
   And thou shalt drink milk
From thy mother's gold cup—
   So hush-a-by, hush-a-by, hush-a-by—low—
At last little Heart-Link,
   Thy mother may go.

# TWO CHAMPIONS
# IN THE FAMILY

elizabeth corbett

Since I've been in high school I've always thought Friday afternoon was the pleasantest time of the week. Not that I object at all to school; I'm different from my sister Beth, who lives in the hope that some morning she'll get to school and find the building has burned down, which will give her the whole day free for her tennis.

But Friday afternoon when we bang up our seats in the Assembly Room, I know there are two clear days ahead. The spring after Beth got the Graper family into the newspapers by being runner-up in the State Junior Tennis Match, we got in the habit of celebrating every Friday. Bob Hammond and Tom Cummings always waited at the school door for Beth and me; they took us to the movies, and then came home to dinner with us.

After dinner we played cards in the dining-room and tried the stunts we'd seen in the movies. Dad and Mother had to take to the library, because Friday and Saturday evenings Marian is always at the piano in the drawing-room, with suitors around her three or four deep. They all sing "Little Grey Home in the West," and "Forgotten," and "Slumber On, My Little Gipsy Sweetheart," and I don't suppose they feel as bad as they sound, or they wouldn't keep it up the way they do. Ralph Stevens even had one spell of bringing along his ukulele, but Dad put a stop to that. He said grown people still had some rights . . .

Because of Beth's showing the summer before, everybody took for granted that she had the junior State championship this year sewed up. There isn't any junior match in golf, but from sixteen on you can play regularly in the women's matches. Somebody always has to win, and though I'd never played much golf, I'd always been a fair all-round athlete. Wouldn't it be great, I thought, with a glow at my heart (only it was more like a warmth in the pit of my stomach), if we had two champions in the family? . . .

I had several things planned for that Saturday morning. But at the breakfast-table Dad announced: "I've just telephoned to the pro at the country club, Ernie. He's going to give you a lesson this morning; then you can do a few holes and put into practice what he tells you."

I opened my eyes wide. A word from an expert certainly makes a lot of difference. But I said modestly, "I'm not sure my golf is worth serious attention, Dad."

"I think it is," said Dad; and Mother struck in, "Very likely golf is really your game, as tennis is Beth's."

I felt pretty important to be hauled off that way for special instruction. Old Professor Perkins came to the house to give us music-lessons, and Mother used to take us up to Miss Blakeslee's for dancing-class. But that was always three-in-a-bunch. Now that I had developed a specialty, Mother drove me out alone to the club, in the big car.

She talked to the pro, and he said it was just as important for me to practise regularly as to have lessons, so she arranged to bring me out certain days after school . . .

For the first three or four weeks my golf improved. Then it

seemed to stand still; and then I had a perfectly rotten day. When I had fanned the air all around the course, I marched up to the club-house to tell Mother I was quitting.

She was on the veranda, but instead of knitting she was watching a party of women who were just leaving the first tee. "I suppose it's silly for me to think of taking up golf again," she said sort of wistfully.

"Again?" I echoed.

"I played a pretty good game before I was married. But I haven't touched a club in years," she explained.

I was surprised to hear that she'd ever played, but I said politely, "I don't see why you don't play. Lots of the girls' mothers do. Mrs. Mallinson, and Mrs. Rigby, and—"

"Would it help you any if I played around with you?" she asked. "I could practise up mornings, so that I wouldn't be too much of a drag."

"You couldn't possibly be a drag on the way I played to-day," I said disgustedly.

She went around the links with me the very next day, and she was a lot better than I'd expected. She took lessons two mornings a week, too, and improved right along. Once I suggested that if she kept at it she'd be beating me one of these days.

"Oh, no! My athletic days are over," she answered. "I have you girls to attend to things like that for me now. I get more pleasure from your success than I would from my own."

I thought no more about it at the time. My mother's awfully sweet and darling, and so pretty that my early life was blighted because I don't look like her, the way Marian does. But she's always there, and always telling us things: we must eat our hot breakfast food, and not wear that pair of stockings with that dress, and she wants to see our light out in five minutes. So I've always sort of taken Mother for granted.

When I hinted to Dad that I thought golf should be a game, not a business, he gave me a little lecture on sticking to what I'd begun. Luckily I came out of my slump after that, and it was more fun, now that Mother played around with me. I couldn't get her to keep her own score, but she took a great interest in mine . . .

But on Labor Day our country club has a special match for women players, and this year Ralph Stevens' father had offered a special cup. I don't say I had my eye on that cup, exactly, and I don't believe in signs. But the first week in August, Beth won the Junior State Tennis Match, and Dad had a special shelf put up in the hall for her cup. The shelf was about four feet long, and the cup hit company in the eye as soon as they came into the hall. Most people remarked on how splendid it was for Beth to win such an important cup. But Tom Cummings, who was Beth's particular pal, grinned when he saw it, and said, "My, but that cup looks lonesome!"

Mother and I were going around the course every day, and some days we did thirty-six holes. I was fascinated with the game by that time; I ate golf and dreamed golf, and I moved Bobby Jones' picture where it would be the first thing my eyes lighted on in the morning. I planned to do thirty-six holes every day until Labor Day, and things which had amused me once, such as hiking out to the woods on Sundays, or taking a chance on driving the small car when Dad's back was turned, now struck me simply as childish folly . . .

I came through victorious in the morning match, and so, a little to my surprise, did Mother. It added to the excitement when people found out that she and I were included in the four who were to play off that afternoon. A photographer took our picture together for the "Mount Airy Beacon," and Dad and Beth and Marian were all running in circles in their excitement.

At the last moment Mother drew me aside.

"Ernestine," she said, "you know I wish you luck. It was the dream of my own girlhood to be a golf champion. Now that I have you to do it for me, it means even more to me."

"That's a funny way to talk," I said, "when you're playing against me."

"But I don't go in with any hopes of winning," she said. "I'm just going to do the best I can to give you girls a game."

I suppose I was excited, or I never would have spoken as I did, but it came over me all at once that she sounded just like Dear Old Mother in the movies. "I'm sorry you feel that way about it," I said, "because I'd think a lot more of you if you went out like anybody else, and played to win."

Mother flushed and bit her lip; then all at once, instead of looking like Marian, the way she usually does, she looked like Beth taking a hard volley at tennis. Usually Beth's face is so round and good-natured that all she needs is the whiskers to be a perfect picture of Santa Claus: but her fighting face would scare a burglar away. Mother's face set just that way. She started to say, "Sorry," and sort of choked on it. Instead she said, "Very well," and turned on her heel.

Phyllis Greene and Mrs. Mallinson, who were in the match with us, are two of the best players in the club. That afternoon I led up to the ninth hole. Then I got in the rough, and after that I made two bad putts. Mrs. Mallinson was in the lead then, but from the eleventh hole on, it was Mother and Phyllis.

I got so excited watching them I almost forgot about my own play. But Mother never looked at me, and never glanced around at the crowd. She was playing for all she was worth, and at the eighteenth hole she made a wonderful putt, winning the match by one stroke. It was the prettiest thing I ever saw in golf.

But when the crowd burst into applause, she looked around in a startled way, and said in an imploring tone, "Ernie!"

I rushed up and threw my arms around her. "You're great!" I said . . .

Mother's cup stands on the special shelf in the hall with Beth's. The Grapers have two champions in the family, if not just the two we expected. I'm not trying to sound noble when I say I'm glad Mother won that match instead of me. I'm not exactly fonder of her than I was before, but I don't take her for granted any more, the way I used to. It's different even being told to eat your hot breakfast food, when you're told so by a golf champion.

# THE PREGNANT LADY PLAYING TENNIS

1992

karen volkman

The pregnant lady playing tennis
bobs on her toes at the court's left side,
raises the green ball high, and sets it

spinning. Then moving in circles
of deliberate size, she returns the lob
with the same giddy grace. In the quiet glide

of the lady playing tennis,
there's a knowledge of speeds and angles,
arcs and aims. From the other courts,

the players watch, dismayed, half-fearing
for the safety of the lady playing tennis,
half-wishing this odd distraction shut away.

Tennis, they notice, is a dangerous game.
But the ovals close
on the lady playing tennis, as if

the tight-knit mesh of her racket
were a magnet, with the ball
a perfect pole veering home. Watching

each hard-shot lob clear the net,
the pregnant lady playing tennis
braces in the pure sensation of her game,

in her body's stretch and haul, and plants
a crazy slam past the net: past the lines,
past the out zone, past the court's steel network wall.

# SCOTTI SCORES

1923

**jane gilliland**

**H**ockey-sticks had fallen from listless hands. Scotti, black-eyed forward, dug a vicious heel into the ground and rendered her verdict.

"It's plain enough to me," she said to the group of bloomered girls sprawled disconsolately around the goal-posts of the Huntley High athletic-field; "we can't get any more games because they're all afraid to play us."

Hoots greeted the remark.

"A modest little violet lived upon a little hill—" singsonged a derisive voice; but the jingle was cut short by the appearance of a figure which waved jauntily from the other end of the field.

"It's Coach Mackenzie!" cried Winifred, captain and center-forward. "She's a peach!" She paused reflectively. "If only we could do something for her—something really helpful. We can't just simply offer money."

"But some one will have to offer money soon," spoke up the irrepressible Scotti, "or I don't know what will happen. I learned yesterday that her mother is worse, and Miss Mackenzie hasn't enough to send her away to the only place where she can get well. It's awful that such a wonderful coach can't get a better-paying position."

"I know," added Captain Winifred; "Mrs. Mackenzie has been in bed for months and is seriously ill. What would Miss Mackenzie do if anything happened to her mother? They have no friends or relatives in this part of the country."

"Sh-h! here she is."

Smiling down at her frankly adoring team, the subject of this discussion showed none of the trouble which was supposed to weigh heavily on her slim young shoulders. Her vivacious face expressed many things, but there was no hint of sorrow.

"Well," she asked gaily, "have you managed to get any more games?"

"Any more?" echoed a tragic chorus. "Why, Grayling has canceled their date!"

"And that," pouted the dark-skinned Scotti, "leaves us with exactly no game with which to finish the season."

The coach laughed. "Well, don't look as though you'd lost your very last hope. I have a suggestion." She hesitated. "I don't know if you'll like it, though." Some humorous thought twisted the corners of her mouth.

The girls caught a note in the coach's tones which brought them quickly to their knees. "What is it? What is it?" they begged.

Miss Mackenzie went on. "I've just been talking to a friend of mine who plays on the Livingston eleven, the club that holds the championship of the east coast. They have a big game coming, but haven't been able to get a scrub team together for practice. I mentioned that you wanted games and suggested they use you to practise on. They'd like very much to have you go out for a game some afternoon, they said. The club isn't far. Would you play them?"

"Oh, Miss Mackenzie!" gasped the girls, delighted, but awed by the thought of a game with the champions. "Do you want to see us thoroughly beaten?"

"It wouldn't be a question of who would win," answered

the coach. "They're much older than you, most of them college graduates, and the club has held the title four years. I just thought it would be fun, if only to try to score against them. It would be wonderful practice, too. How about it, Winifred?"

The entire team accepted the offer clamorously.

Greatly thrilled, they were afraid they weren't good enough; they had instant visions of calamitous defeat, of the other schools laughing at them if the news got out. But, one and all, they were willing to take a beating, provided it was on a hockey-field.

"Fine!" laughed the coach, affectionate approval shining in her eyes. "They gave a tentative date—a week from next Saturday. I'll let Livingston know."

"Come on!" whooped Scotti. "Let's practise. Maybe we'll get a few goals from them when they're not looking."

In the week that followed, the hockey-field was worn to a threadbare brown by the eager feet that raced back and forth, back and forth, in tremulous preparation for the game.

And on the eventful Saturday a hilarious group of youthful players boarded the train for Livingston. There was spirited discussion as to the score they could hold the champions to, and whether or not Huntley would shoot a single goal. Christine, the goal-keeper, a girl of generous weight, brought shouts of laughter when she announced she would lie down between the goal-posts before she'd let the champions score.

But the imposing Livingston club-house and luxurious locker-rooms decidedly dampened Huntley's high spirits. In the impressive and businesslike atmosphere of the place, this did not feel like an informal practice.

"I'm so nervous!" fidgeted Scotti, lacing her shoe. "My fingers are all thumbs."

Coach Mackenzie rushed in. "Ready to go up to the field?" she asked.

"Anywhere for a breath of cool air," answered Scotti.

Miss Mackenzie laughed. "I have a surprise for you," she said, unable to suppress her own agitation. "The National Hockey Association happened to hold a luncheon at the club to-day, and most of the guests have decided to stay for the game. Several N.H.A. officials were speakers, and have offered to referee." She paused. "That makes it more of a game than I had expected."

The girls were speechless. Even Scotti was overcome. Decidedly, this was not the practice they had anticipated.

The coach glanced quickly from one sober face to the other, reading their thoughts.

"Pshaw!" she chided; "don't take it so seriously. Go out and give them a good fight. That's all that's necessary. Get your passes working the way they were last week, and no team will walk over you." She smiled reassuringly. "Come on; all ready?"

Keyed to top pitch, the team followed its coach upstairs, and in the thrill of walking out on the great playing-field Scotti began talking to herself. It was a habit she had when unduly excited. "Going to show that team something!" she muttered.

And in the short warming-up before the game, Huntley did show the stands something. Their shots went clean and true, and the girls ran with all the ease and grace of their youth.

Then Livingston appeared, amid hand-clapping. Dressed in dark bloomers and middies embroidered with the flaming L, heavy shin-guards, head-protectors, and gauntlets, the champions presented a formidable, almost sinister, appearance. As they trotted, tall and confident, to their positions, the high-school team seemed suddenly pathetically youthful and ill equipped for the contest.

There were other disadvantages, too. Not only was the field very much larger than the one to which Huntley was accustomed, but the halves were to be thirty minutes instead of the usual twenty.

Coach Mackenzie, sitting on the side-lines, grew apprehensive. In the crowded stands were many prominent coaches and hockey enthusiasts, and she feared that the conditions under which the game was being played would not show her girls to their best advantage. It seemed unfair that her team should, so unexpectedly, have to parade its inexperience before such a gathering.

She need not have worried.

To the hushed stands, the referee announced the line-up. Then a whistle blew, the sticks of the center-forwards cracked in the bully-off, and the game was on.

In the first flash of play, Livingston rooters were dumfounded. Huntley's forward line, running like the wind, took possession of the ball and swept down the field, the champions in futile pursuit. To the dismay of all, this fleet-footed group reached the goal circle without opposition. Then a Livingston full-back tore through and sent the white sphere cannonading back down the field again.

Huntley had not scored. But it had shown one tremendous asset—it could run infinitely faster than its opponents.

However, Livingston soon exhibited its justly famed teamwork. Again and again the title-holders dribbled relentlessly past Huntley's half-backs, and only reckless blocking by arms and legs, as well as sticks, kept them from breaking through the grimly determined defense. Yet each time, when it seemed beyond all hope that the ball would not bore in on one of those crashing drives, it would miraculously shoot out from the players bunched within the goal-circle. A Huntley forward would swoop down upon it, and again the speeding line would carry it to the very brink of Livingston's goal.

As Miss Mackenzie stared, amazed to see this repeated time after time, her apprehension turned into an uncontrollable excitement. Her girls were not only holding Livingston, but they were threatening the champion's goal! It was unbelievable.

Those slim, unassuming, clear-eyed school-girls were showing a grit and coolness far beyond their years.

When it seemed that the first half must end with neither team scoring, suddenly Livingston smashed down the field, ripped through the opposing full-backs, and shot a goal. A minute later the whistle blew.

As Huntley ran off the field, the girls caught exclamations from the stands, hurried questions. They heard their names being spelled out, saw people writing things. Dazed and panting, they hardly knew what they saw or heard.

When Miss Mackenzie reached them, down in the locker-rooms, the team was lying breathless, apparently engrossed in sucking lemons. But at the coach's enthusiastic entrance, the girls could not conceal pleased and bashful grins. They knew they had done well, and they waited delightedly for the coach's praise.

Her first words were more startling than anything that had yet happened on this thoroughly exciting day.

"Do you realize what you're doing?" gasped Miss Mackenzie. "You're contending for the championship of the east coast."

"But it's only practice," put in the flushed Captain Winifred.

Miss Mackenzie shook her head. Then the thunderbolt fell. "According to N.H.A. rules, it is only necessary that a game be played on the Livingston field and be refereed by N.H.A. officials to make it a contest for the title."

There was a single startled exclamation in that large locker-room. The girls were stunned.

"There are only two goals between you and the Eastern championship," said the coach.

The girls looked at each other open-mouthed. The championship! Then all began talking at once.

In a voice which she tried to keep from trembling, Miss Mackenzie quieted them and helped them plan the attack for the next half. She praised, she criticized, and at last sent them out to the field, the most determined team Livingston had encountered in four successful years.

As the teams took their positions and the whistle blew, the buzz of voices sank to a deadly silence.

It was impossible to restrain Scotti in her anxiety to get started, and when, at the bully-off, Winifred shot the ball directly down to this black-haired young dynamo, she set upon it with the greedy snatch of a young terrier. According to instructions, she should have carried it a few yards and then passed to the wing. But Scotti was keyed beyond such tactics. Straight at the Livingston half-back she charged; and when it seemed the two must meet in thundering collision, she deftly swerved and continued down the field. Livingston pounded after her.

She reached the goal-circle well ahead of her other forwards, and, by a lightning manoeuvre, passed the full-backs. Only the goal-keeper remained. And when the stands rose, expecting to see Scotti take a tremendous swing and count on main force to carry the ball between the posts, the astonishing forward surprised the onlookers and outguessed the goal-keeper. Scotti continued to dribble the ball and, as she and the Livingston girl collided, slipped it diagonally over the line. Huntley's first goal! Tossed sticks flashed the news to the other end of the field.

Again, up and down, up and down, thundered the teams, attacking furiously, eluding, Huntley with dazzling speed, Livingston with cruel precision. Each girl was giving every ounce of strength she had. The champions began to show the strain, and it was only nervous excitement that kept the younger girls going. It seemed that the score would stay 1–1 forever.

Again Huntley's line was passing down the field. It was a beautiful exhibition, and the stands rose to follow each play more closely. From right-wing to right-forward shot the ball, to center, was carried a few yards, shot off to the left-forward and then to left-wing. Now it was within the circle. Would the Livingston full-backs be able to break the attack again?

Just as one threatened to, the wing shot the ball to Winifred. The captain caught it on her stick, twisted, and with one blow sent it flying—for another goal. There was tremendous applause. The play had been absolutely perfect. The score was 2–1, in favor of Huntley.

Again the clash of stick against stick. Then a long drive by Livingston, their forwards charging after the ball. But a Huntley half-back was on it first. She swung, and the sphere flew into the air. A Livingston half-back flung herself at it, and ball and player went to the ground. Quick as a flash, the Livingston line was passing triumphantly down the field.

Huntley's defense was ready. As a full-back advanced, the ball was swung behind her. In the scrimmage that followed it was impossible to follow the play. Only splintering crashes told the story of a frantic defense.

Then Livingston sticks flashed in the air. The champions had scored—2–2.

To Coach Mackenzie it seemed the game would never end. Time must be almost up, and Livingston again was threatening Huntley's goal, driving the ball with deadly accuracy. Suddenly it shot out of bounds.

Winifred ran to throw it into play again, and, without waiting for signals, Scotti started a mad flight down the field.

The captain was not slow to complete the play. She threw straight and true, and Scotti picked the ball up at the fifty-yard line—with a clear field before her.

Black head low, she sped along, Livingston's half-backs close at her heels.

The full-backs dropped back to guard goal. This time the surprising Scotti changed her tactics. Stopping just inside the circle, she swung with all her might, and a white streak glanced off the shin of a Livingston full-back. It crashed into the goal-post, bounded back, and, as the goal-keeper lunged desperately, took a reeling hop—and skidded over the line!

Just in time. The final whistle blew, and a championship had passed to the team from Huntley High.

Excited groups swarmed on the field, congratulating the young team, wringing hands. Confused, and only knowing they were more tired than they ever had been before, the Huntley girls gave their cheer and, as quickly as the crowd would allow them, wormed their way off the field.

In the locker-rooms they threw themselves down, fighting to keep back tears of exhaustion. Knuckles were skinned, shins bruised, and bodies and minds too tired to take in the real glory of their victory.

The door opened, and in burst Miss Mackenzie. There were tears in her eyes, but a smile on her lips.

"Do you know what you've done?" she gulped.

"Yes," sniffled Scotti, "we've won the championship of the east coast."

"Yes, and I'm terribly, terribly proud of you. But you've won something wonderful for me, too."

The girls jumped to their feet.

Coach Mackenzie choked a little. "The head coach of Harleigh Hall was at the game, and she was so impressed with your splendid spirit and the way you played that she has asked me to coach hockey at Harleigh. The position pays better and carries more prestige than any other school in the East."

"Oh, Miss Mackenzie," cried Captain Winifred, "I'm so

glad! Now your mother can have the proper care. To think we've really helped after all! I'm *so* happy."

"There's one thing I can't bear to think of, though," gulped Miss Mackenzie; "it means I'll lose you all."

"Oh no, you won't," asserted Scotti, vehemently. "When we graduate from Huntley, we'll go right straight to Harleigh!"

# SKATING AFTER SCHOOL

1985

barbara    crooker

In the space between school & supper,
light flat as a china plate,
sky and ice a single seam
stitched by the black trees,
we raced over the railroad tracks
down the embankment
to the frozen pond,
mufflers trailing,
snow embroidering our flannel jeans.
Then out, onto the ice, blades dividing
the surface into geometry,
ice writing from an old language,
the calligraphy of snow . . .
And then, as the baggage of school disappeared,
became ephemeral as smoke from the bonfire
where we charred hot dogs, made dark cocoa
that burned our tongues,
we went back out onto the ice again,
feeling the slap and chock of the hockey puck,
the body contact muffled in layers of wool,
the ache of air inside our lungs . . .

And as the dark came down like a coffee cup,
we saw the yellow lights come on
up over the tracks.
But we kept on playing, icing the puck,
shooting straight for the goal,
legs aching beyond endurance . . .
Home, where the yellow lights are growing,
is filling with the smell of macaroni & cheese
and muffins, but we stay out, still checking & hitting
wood against wood, our steel blades marking the ice
until it's a blackboard in need of erasing . . .
And, when we knew we could not stand it
any longer out in the cold,
we clambered up the banks,
always falling on the cinders,
woodsmoke and winter clinging to our clothes,
climbing, climbing, toward the steady yellow lights of home.

# REVENGE

### abbe carter goodloe

**M**iss Atterbury put the paper she was reading carefully and slowly down upon the table. It was the *Boston* ———, and there was a long article upon the first page marked ostentatiously around with a blue lead-pencil, and headed in glaring letters, "Athletics in Girls' Colleges."

There was a dangerous gleam in Miss Atterbury's dark-gray eyes, and she seemed a trifle more than her ordinary five feet eight inches as she drew herself up and turned, with that careful repression of irritation which always denotes the extreme limit of self-control, upon an inoffensive freshman, comfortably installed in the window-seat, playing a mandolin.

"I was in Antwerp two weeks last summer," she remarked, with careful emphasis, "and I heard the cathedral chimes play 'La Mandolinata' twice every five minutes, I think. I would be obliged if you would play something else, or even stop altogether for a while—I have something important to talk about just now."

The freshman stuck her pick guiltily in the strings, and shifted her position upon the cushions into one of extreme and flattering attention, while the four girls who had been playing whist over in a corner turned hastily around toward Miss Atterbury.

"What is it now, Katharine?" inquired Miss Yale, reproachfully, laying down her cards. "She always takes things so terribly *au grand sérieux*," she explained plaintively to the rest. Miss Yale had her rooms with Miss Atterbury, and stood rather in awe of that young woman, and was very proud of her athletic prowess, and could always be relied upon to tell her friends "that Katharine Atterbury was the captain of the senior crew, and could pull an oar as well as a 'Varsity stroke, and that the champion tennis-player of a certain year had said that she was an antagonist to be feared and respected."

"*This* is what is the matter," said Miss Atterbury, in a tragic voice, picking up the paper. "I don't know who it is that writes such absurd, such wilfully misleading articles about us, but I do know that if I could get at him I would—"

What Miss Atterbury would do was apparently too awful to speak of just then.

One of the girls got up and went over to her.

"But what is it?—what have they said about us now?" she inquired, impatiently.

"What they are always doing—poking fun at us," replied Miss Atterbury, hotly, and with a fine disregard of grammar. "To read this article one would imagine that we were imbecile babies. One would think that a girl was as weak as a kitten, and didn't know a boat from an elevator, or a five-lap running track from an ice-wagon, or a golf club from a sewing-machine. He—whoever the man is who wrote this ridiculous article— seems to think that all our training and physical development is a huge joke. He don't even know how stupid he is. That's the worst of it—he isn't even aware of his unutterable, his colossal ignorance!"

"Wouldn't it be fun to have him drawn and quartered, as an awful example, a sort of warning to the other newspaper men not to write about what they are totally ignorant of, and to leave us alone," suggested the inoffensive little freshman, with a base but entirely successful attempt to get back into Miss Atterbury's good graces.

The senior gave her a brief but cordial glance, and then ran on:

"Something must be done about it. I'm tired of reading this sort of trash about women's colleges. It is time the public was learning the true state of things—that girls can and do swim, and row and play golf and tennis, and run and walk about, just as their brothers do, and that we have courage and muscle enough to go in for football even, except that we have some *little* regard for our personal appearance!"

"And it's so degrading and irritating to go home in the vacations, and have one's brother tease one to death about it all, and try to be funny, and ask one if the color of one's gymnasium suit is becoming, and if the golf captain knows the caddie from a cleek," interposed Miss Thayer, a pretty blond girl who got up slowly and sauntered over to Miss Atterbury, putting her face over that young lady's shoulder to get a look at the unfortunate paper. As she did so she gave a little cry of surprise.

"Why, I know the man who wrote that," she gasped. "There! J. E. N.—see those initials at the end?—they mean Jack Newbold. I remember now he is writing for that paper. He told me this summer at the sea-shore that he was going in for newspaper work. His grandfather owns this paper, you know, and has promised him half a million when he is twenty-five if he will go through the whole thing—learn everything a newspaper man must know. He didn't want to do it much, but, of course, he would go in for almost anything sooner than lose all that pile of money."

Miss Atterbury looked thoughtfully and intently at Miss Thayer.

"You say he is a friend of yours?" she demanded, slowly.

"Oh, yes; we got to be very good friends this summer. He taught me how to play fifteen-ball pool—that's about all he knows," went on the girl, scornfully. "He's an awful duffer about everything else. You ought to see him play tennis! It's not very edifying, but it's awfully funny."

Miss Atterbury gave a little gasp of delight.

"That's too good to be true," she said, enthusiastically.

Miss Thayer rather stared. "Why?" she demanded, and then, without waiting for a reply, she swept on. "You wouldn't think so if you had to play doubles with him! And he simply can't walk—gets awfully tired, he says. *I* think it's his clothes. Gets 'em in London, and they are terribly swell and uncomfortable. And he is always afraid his collar is going to melt; it's quite painful to be with him on a warm day. And I couldn't induce him to come out in my cat-boat with me. Said he didn't think a girl could learn to handle one with any degree of safety. Did you ever hear of anything so unjust? I think he was *afraid*."

Miss Atterbury was leaning on the table now, and her countenance had assumed such a cheerful look that the freshman felt quite relieved and ventured to pick up her mandolin again.

"Go on!" demanded the senior, delightedly.

"Well, I don't know anything more," declared Miss Thayer, impatiently. "Isn't that enough for you? He's no good at outdoor sports, and what he is doing writing us up or down is more than I can imagine. He oughtn't to be allowed to do so. He don't know anything about it at all, and I should think he would be ashamed of himself. I suppose his editor told him to do it, and he simply 'made up' and put down everything he had ever heard about us, and worked in all the old jokes about girls' colleges."

Miss Atterbury got up slowly.

"Well!" she said, impressively, to Miss Thayer. "I'm sorry if that young man is much of a friend of yours, for we have got to make an example of him. I suppose you know him well enough to invite him out here Monday afternoon?—for you've got to do it," she added, with calm decision.

Miss Thayer said she thought she might venture on that simple act of courtesy, though she could not quite understand why Miss Atterbury was so anxious to see him since she disapproved of him so entirely; to which that young woman replied that she wished to see him once, so that she might never see him again, and that the next day she would explain her plans, in which she expected their hearty co-operation.

Mr. Jack Newbold had just comfortably installed himself in the 1.50 B. and A. train, when it occurred to him that he might possibly have made a mistake as to the time Miss Thayer expected him. He pulled out the note which he had received from her, and read it again.

"MY DEAR MR. NEWBOLD: I have been *so* interested in what you have written about athletics in girls' colleges! I saw the article in your paper and knew immediately by the initials that it was your work. Ever since seeing it I have been wishing to redeem my promise to have you come out here and see our college.

"All the girls are anxious to see you. I hope you won't mind receiving a great deal of attention! You know how enthusiastic and unconventional college girls are, and you are of the greatest interest to us just now. Miss Atterbury, a charming girl, is especially eager to meet you. Don't be *too* flattered! But we shall all be delighted to see the man who has so ably written up girls' colleges, and unless I hear from you to the contrary, shall look for you out Monday afternoon by the 1.50 train.

"Of course I shall expect you to take dinner and go to the concert in the evening. I tell you this now, so you can wear just the right 'dress'—men are so ridiculously particular about their clothes!

"Very cordially yours,

"ELEANOR THAYER."


Mr. Jack Newbold was not a particularly vain youth, but he had a slight feeling of satisfaction on perusing that note which made him settle himself even more comfortably in his seat and resign himself cheerfully to the short journey.

"Had no idea that article would make such a sensation," he was saying to himself, "and I'm glad she expects me by this train. Of course she will bring her trap to the station for me. I believe the college is quite a little distance from the town. Nice little trap—she drives well for a girl, I remember." And then he fell to wondering whether he had selected just the right things to wear. "Girls are so deucedly critical," he soliloquized, and it had been rather hard to decide on just what would be in good taste for an afternoon call and would still do without change for the concert in the evening, and he rather complimented himself on his judicious selection, and was assuring himself that the particular shade of his gloves had not been a mistake, when he found that he was at the station.

Miss Thayer welcomed him effusively.

"I knew you wouldn't have the vaguest idea of how to get up to the college," she was saying, "and so I came down for you myself. No, I didn't bring my trap. I knew you would enjoy the walk up, and I wanted to show you it myself. I remember how fond you were of walking, last summer," she added, with a bright smile at him.

Newbold stared a little.

"I don't think," he began doubtfully; but Miss Thayer interrupted him quickly—

"You cannot imagine how anxious the girls are to see you. Each one wants to show you what she is particularly interested in. Really you are quite a martyr—I mean a hero—in our eyes! We will go up this way," she ran on. "It's a little longer and there is a pretty bad hill, but of course a man doesn't mind a little extra exertion, and it's even more beautiful than the other way."

Newbold said he would be charmed to go any way that Miss Thayer might choose, but that he didn't want to lose any of his visit at the college, and that perhaps it would be wiser to take the short cut. But Miss Thayer said that if they walked a little faster they would get there just as soon, and he would see the finer view, too. So they started off briskly, and Newbold wished that he had worn the other pair of patent leathers, and finally, when he felt ready to drop, and thought they must have walked about five miles, and she told him they had only two more to go, he blamed himself most severely for not having firmly refused anything but the short cut and a cab. One of Miss Thayer's friends who met her told her the next day that she was glad to see that she had joined the Pedestrian Club, and that she had often wondered why she had not done so before.

"I hardly think it is worth while to go into the drawing-room now," remarked Miss Thayer, argumentatively, as they strolled up the broad drive to the college. "I see Miss Atterbury down there on the campus playing tennis, and I promised to bring you to her immediately," she went on. Newbold felt a horrible inclination to say that he didn't care if he never met Miss Atterbury, and that personally he would very much prefer going into the drawing-room and stopping there for the rest of the afternoon, in the most comfortable chair to be found;

but he managed to murmur a weary assent to Miss Thayer's proposition, and together they started down the steep hill at the bottom of which stretched the campus. But he could not seem to keep up with Miss Thayer, and by the time he had reached the tennis grounds and had decided that in all probability his heart would never beat normally again, he was conscious that he was bowing, and that Miss Atterbury, flushed from playing, was standing before him and was laughing and saying—"I don't often give acquaintances such a warm welcome!" The next thing he knew was that someone had thrust a racket into his hand, and he heard, as in a dream, Miss Thayer telling her friend that Mr. Newbold was a splendid tennis-player, and that she would have to do her best to beat him, but that she hoped she would for the honor of the college. And then he found himself, somehow, walking over to the court, and, before he could protest, Miss Atterbury was on the other side, and was asking him kindly but briskly if he were ready to play. He thought he was as near ready as he ever would be, so he said "Play!" and waited resignedly for her serve.

It was just after Miss Atterbury had piled up an appalling number of games against him, and he had come to the conclusion that he knew what it would be like to stand fire from a Krupp gun, and had decided that tight patent leathers and a long coat were not just what he would have chosen to play tennis in, that he saw Miss Atterbury, to his intense relief, throw down her racket and run up the hill a little way. She was back in an instant with Miss Thayer and a tall, handsome girl, carrying a lot of golf clubs. When young Newbold saw the golf clubs he felt so tired that he thought he would sit down on the cold ground, although he knew how dangerous such a proceeding was, especially when he was so painfully aware of how hot his head was and how clammy his linen felt.

"Mr. Newbold!" he heard Miss Atterbury say, "I want to

present you to Miss Yale. She is the captain of the Golf Club, and I knew you would want to meet her. Anyone who is such an authority on the subject as you proved yourself to be in that article would, of course, want to see the links out here."

"Ah! thank you!" murmured Newbold; "but I play very little, you know, and I wouldn't interrupt your game for the world!"

But Miss Yale told him how interested she had been in his article, and that she wouldn't feel that she had done her duty by the college unless she showed him the links, and that he really must come with them and tell them whether the meadow-land was too stiff a bit of ground to be gone over. And so Newbold found himself trudging wearily along again between Miss Atterbury and Miss Yale, who seemed as fresh as though they hadn't moved that day. The links seemed distressingly far off, and the holes absurdly distant from each other. His arms ached so from tennis that he could scarcely hold the driver Miss Yale gave him.

"I wish you would drive off this tee once—men do that sort of thing so much better than girls," she was saying, admiringly. "They don't seem to need any practice at all—just comes natural to them." Newbold had a very distinct impression that it hadn't come at all natural to him, and he would greatly have preferred not trying before Miss Yale and the knot of young women who had drawn together at some little distance, and were very obviously watching him under the shallowest pretence of hunting for a lost ball. He felt desperately nervous, and his nervousness did not tend to disappear when he made a frantic try at the ball, digging a hole in the ground about a foot in front of the tee, and almost hitting Miss Atterbury, who jumped back with a little cry very unlike her ordinary calm self.

"I—I beg your pardon," he began, desperately; but Miss Atterbury assured him that she was all right, and urged him to try again. He did so, and although he balanced himself cautiously on one foot and then on the other, and snapped at the ball several times before trying to hit it, and wobbled his driver after the most approved methods, he topped his ball miserably, and had the mortification of seeing it land in a most difficult hazard. And then he watched Miss Yale drive off with a good backward swing of her club, which hit the ball "sweet and clean," and sent it a good ninety yards.

"Of course, as you said in your article," remarked that young woman, picking up her clubs and starting off energetically after the ball, "this is no game for women. It is pre-eminently a man's game, and a woman's short collar-bone is never such an obvious mistake as in golf. A man can do so much with a driver or a cleek or a lofter, and the walking is so easy for him, and he is so entirely independent of the weather." Newbold murmured inarticulate assents as he walked wearily by her. He wondered if she could keep up that pace all around the course, and he especially wondered how far around it was. He had a great deal of difficulty in getting his ball out of the hazard and lofting it up a steep hill, and he savagely wished that he had joined that golf club all his friends were urging him to join, and decided firmly to do so before he slept that night, and to engage the professional's services for himself, and to practise till he could drive a ball off without utterly destroying all the turf in the vicinity.

They were on the second round, and Newbold was roughly calculating that his erratic plays had made him walk about three miles, and was wondering if he could live to get up the hill in front of him, when he saw Miss Thayer and Miss Yale, who were three holes ahead of him, coming back toward him.

"You look awfully tired and hot," said Miss Thayer, sympathetically. "What's the matter? Don't you like golf? But what an absurd question! Anyone who could write the article on athletics *you* did must like it. Only, I suppose, girls seem such duffers at it, to you!"

Newbold looked at her sharply. He had an uneasy suspicion that she was laughing at him, but he was too tired to think of any way of finding out whether she was or not, and so he walked on taciturnly and sufferingly.

"I have such a nice surprise for you," ran on Miss Thayer. "But I won't tell you what it is yet." She pulled out her watch. "It is just a quarter to four now, and I think the surprise will not be ready until a quarter after. Can you possibly wait that long?"

Newbold said he thought he might if he could sit down; but Miss Thayer said she disapproved of getting over-heated and then cooling off rapidly, and that she thought they had better keep moving until it was time to see the "surprise." So they strolled across the grounds, and the two girls seemed to meet an astonishing number of friends, all going their way. And while Newbold was vaguely wondering what their destination might be, and what new torture was in store for him, he heard Miss Yale say, in what sounded to him like the voice of an avenging angel:

"I think we had better show Mr. Newbold our new running-track while we are waiting. He is so interested in such things, and he might suggest some improvements." And then Newbold felt himself irresistibly compelled to walk on farther and farther. He wondered sadly why they thought *he* knew anything about running-tracks for girls, and decided that his humorous remarks on the subject in his article had been a great mistake.

"Do you think it's a fair track?" inquired Miss Yale, anxiously, as they came in sight of it. "It is an eight-lap track, you see, and of course a great many girls only go around four times at first—girls get tired so absurdly easy! Now I suppose men think nothing of making two miles at a time—it is just play for them. Men are so strong—that is their greatest fascination, I think," she ran on enthusiastically. "Haven't you seen football players after a hard practice game start off and run two miles around the track, and seem to think absolutely nothing of it?"

"Oh, that's nothing," said Newbold, unwarily and warmly. "Fellows are so different from girls, you know. A girl cries when she's tired, doesn't she? Well, a man just keeps going, you know, and doesn't let it make any difference to him."

"I am so glad to hear that, Mr. Newbold," said Miss Yale, with prompt and suspicious sympathy, and a sudden firmness of tone, "because I wanted dreadfully to ask you to try the track, but hated to do so, for I knew you were tired—at least you look so. But since you just keep going, and it doesn't make any difference to you, why I would be so awfully obliged if you would run around three or four times. I want to see just how you hold your head and arms. I don't believe we do it in the best way, you know."

It was a rare and pleasingly curious sight that Miss Yale and Miss Thayer and a great many other young women assembled near the track, apparently by a strange coincidence, looked upon. It is not often that one has the chance of seeing an immaculately dressed youth, with flushed and desperate countenance, tear madly around an eight-lap track in the presence of a number of flatteringly attentive young women. It occurred to Newbold as he dashed around and around that it would be far preferable to keep going until he fainted away or dropped dead, than to stop and encounter the remarks and glances of those young women. They would at least feel sorry for him in that case, he thought, gloomily. But even that modest and simple desire was not granted him. As he started on the fifth lap he heard Miss Yale call to him to stop. He had a wild inclination to pay no attention to her, but to keep going on and on, but as he got nearer he saw her step out toward him and put up a warning hand.

"Thank you so much," she said, warmly. "I think we have all had a lesson in running which we shall not forget soon. I hope you are not tired?" she went on, anxiously.

Newbold said, "Oh, no!" but he felt very tired indeed. His feet ached horribly and his head felt hot and dizzy, and there were queer, sharp pains shooting through his body which made him think forebodingly of pneumonia.

"The surprise is ready—Miss Atterbury is going to have the crew out for your especial benefit!" went on Miss Yale, triumphantly. "Don't you feel complimented? And you are to pull Miss Thayer and myself about while they go through a little practice for you. Not much, you know, but just enough to show you the stroke and speed we get. The boat is a beauty—but then, of course, you know so much more about it than we do! I imagine from your article that you must pull an oar capitally. Miss Thayer says a cat-boat is your especial hobby, though."

"Did Miss Thayer say that?" began Newbold, hotly. "Beastly things, I think—hate 'em!"

Miss Yale smiled incredulously and brightly at him.

"How modest you are!" she said, admiringly. "Ah! there is Miss Atterbury!"

Newbold saw some one waving frantically at them.

"Come on!" exclaimed Miss Yale; "we want to see them start off—that's the best part."

Newbold never remembered afterward how he got across the

intervening space, or how he got into a boat with the two young women. The first thing he heard was Miss Atterbury asking him anxiously how he liked the new sliding-seats, and what he thought of the proportions of the boat, and about outriggers in general, and where he thought they could be built best and cheapest. Newbold felt about as capable of instructing her on such points as of judging the pictures at a Salon exhibit, and he longed, with a longing born of utter exhaustion and desperation, to get away. As he wearily pulled the heavy, un-wieldy boat about after the light practice-barge, which kept an appalling distance ahead of him, he decided within himself that the physical development of women had been carried to an absurd and alarming extent, and that men simply were not in it with them when it came to endurance and enthusiasm, and that he had made the mistake of his life when he wrote that article on athletics in girls' colleges, and that his chief might talk until he was blue in the face before he would ever consent again to write about anything of which he knew so little.

They were very disappointed when he told them firmly that he could not stay to dinner or to the concert, but that he had a pressing engagement that would take him back to the city. And they said that there were still the Swedish gymnastics and basket-ball and pole-vaulting to see, and that they were afraid he had not enjoyed himself or he would have got rid of that engagement in some way; but he assured them impressively that he had never spent a more instructive or peculiarly inter-esting afternoon in his life.

Miss Thayer took him back to the station in her trap, and remarked on how much shorter the way seemed with a good horse; and when she bade him good-by she told him that she would be looking out for another article in his paper, and that she would be much disappointed if his visit had not inspired him to write something. To which Newbold replied that that was his pressing engagement—he was going back to the city to write another article on athletics in girls' colleges, and that he thought it would be different and better than the former one, but that he would not put his initials to it this time.

# HER MARATHON

jenifer levin

*I wrote this story for Julie DeLaurier.*

*All events herein are fictional, except for the New York City Marathon and the Women's Mini-Marathon (once sponsored by L'Eggs, now sponsored by Advil, under the auspices of the New York City Road Runners Club). I have used these events here solely in a fictional context.*

*All characters herein are fictional, too, with the exception of the great American marathon runner Alberto Salazar. I use him here in an imaginary way, as a dream figment or a sort of divinity—and with all due respect. I have never met Mr. Salazar, and do not know if he is a child of Chango . . .*

I was drunk sick, I was bleeding. Not the kind that comes from somebody smashing your face in, but the bleeding inside when you're hurt, when you're down, and this whole damn city's like a bunch of sharks smelling something wounded, circling you to bite, swimming around. Stare in the mirror and you say to yourself: Baby, you look like shit. Which I did. Hell, it was true. Like some piece of worm shit crawled out from under a log, squirming around all white, all stripped of the natural color God gave her, crawling in the sunlight. I brushed my teeth. I put lipstick on. Said to myself: Girlfriend, you still got about a ounce of pride left, maybe, so get your ass downstairs and over to the Walgreen's and get some of that stomach-settle shit before you puke all over.

The kid was sleeping. So was Needa and her fucking friends from the grocery shift, snoring, burping beer dreams in a chair, on the sofa, I mean every which place. I tiptoed over bodies. Wrapped keys in a hanky, didn't want to wake them. Then I went down the three flights into autumn, cold sunlight, Sunday.

Usually up here on Sundays you could roll an old empty down First Avenue and it wouldn't touch nothing. Only this day was different. Stepping out of the building was like being wrapped in a big screaming people-circus of arms and shouts. They stayed on the sidewalk, jammed in like fish so you couldn't shove through them to cross the street, you could not hardly move, and some guy's got a radio, and around me every once in a while they're saying, really hushed: "He's coming."

"He's coming."

"He's coming."

There was sirens, red and yellow-white flashes, shadows of light on the empty paved street vivisected by a yellow line, by a pale blue line, and this buzz got loud everywhere around and through me and then, like a Band-Aid, stopped the bleeding.

"Who?" I whispered. "Who's coming?"

"The first man."

"Who?"

"The first runner."

Still, a big sick was in my belly, threatening to lurch out, and there was a part of me thinking: I gotta cross the street, get to Walgreen's. So I started to push, try to make it through the crowd. Some dyke turned to me looking nasty and says,

*Mira*, bitch, stay where you are, did your mother raise you in a cave? I mean have some respect! This is the Marathon.

Any other day I would have clawed out her fucking eyeballs. But the sirens, the tires, got closer. Bringing with them the whirling, spattering lights, bright motorcade chrome, October wind, silent feet. And a scream rose up from the whole shark city, from its garbage tins and sidewalk cement, from the sweat and love and hope of human bodies, from my own insides.

Then I saw him.

No, I didn't see him, I caught him with my eyes. But he escaped.

He was tall, and dark, with dark eyebrows and burning black eyes and a fierce young face, and he ran like some great hot flame on the breath of the wind. When he breathed he breathed in the air of the world so that, in that second, there was nothing left for us. His feet were fast, a blur, a howl. He ran like God. Chango, I said silently, here he is, your son. In that second all the air of the world was gone. I choked. I thought I would die. Tears came to my eyes.

"Salazar!" someone yelled.

"It's Salazar!"

"Salazar!"

"Bravo!"

"*Viv!*"

"*Viv*, Salazar!"

He passed, spattering pavement with his sweat.

The sun blew cold, sirens and screams twisted around, wrapped me up into them. Until I fell down into the center of the storm. It blinked up at me, one-eyed, black and fierce.

Woman, it said, you must burn thus. Light a candle. Save your life.

"Help me!" I sobbed. And bit through my lip.

When I opened my eyes the sun had stopped moving. People yelled, cheered, pressed in against me, radios blared, my tears were dry, so I yelled and cheered too, and wind whipped leaves down the street as more runners came by, more and more, thousands, until it seemed that they filled the whole city, and that all of us, all of us, were running.

I stayed there screaming for hours. Until the sun started to fade a little, and I lost my voice. Then I stayed there still, way past the time when this guy with the radio said, Okay oye everybody, he won, Salazar won, didn't nobody come close, plus he set a world record.

But here, on our side of town, were still most of the rest of the runners. Fifteen, twenty thousand, someone said. And they all had plenty more to go, more than ten miles, the radio guy said, before they got to the finish.

There were people skinnier than toothpicks running, and a guy wearing pink rabbit ears. Men and girls, both, wearing those mesh shirts so light you can see right through, and men and girls both wearing T-shirts with their names Magic-Markered on front and back: HELENA, says one; BERNIE'S BOY, says another; and as they went past everyone yells out, "Go, Helena!" and "Attaway, Bernie's Boy!" There were old people running, too, and daughters, and mothers, black and white and every shade in between, from every one of these United States and from plenty of other countries, France and Mexico and Belgium and Trinidad, you had better believe it, so many people, and not all of them real fast, nor all of them skinny— some even looked like me.

I waited screaming with no sound until the crowd began to disappear, lights went on in windows all around, and the sun was going down. There weren't so many runners now but still lots of people walking. Some limping. In the shadows you could see how some had these half-dead, half-crazy expressions. All right, honey, I croaked out about every two minutes to another one, all right, honey, keep going, you're gonna finish. Pretty soon I realized I was shivering and went upstairs.

The kid was watching TV, eating Fritos, most of Needa's scumbag friends were gone, and Needa was pissed. Where you been? she said. You look like something the tide washed in, and how come you didn't get no more beer?

I told her shut up, have some respect, today is the Marathon. The what? she says. The Marathon, I said, the Marathon, and if you didn't spend your weekends being mean and bossing me around like some man, you coulda seen Salazar run. What the fuck, she grumbled. But then she shrugged. We didn't fight after all—even though, truth be told, I was feeling pretty sick of her just then and I wouldn't have minded. I mean, we never even *did* it anymore.

I picked the kid up and danced him around the room a little until he laughed. I thought about how handsome he was—bright smile and big black eyes the girls would all fight and die over some day—and how he was doing okay with the alphabet in kindergarten, too, and the teachers said real nice things about him, and other kids wanted to be his friend. Then I thought, squeezing him close, what a fucking miracle it was, maybe, that such a great kid had come out of a loser like me. Fact of the matter being that neither me nor his father is all that great in the looks department; neither one of us remembered, really, why we ever did that boy-girl shit in the first place—I always did like the ladies better, maybe just got curious. Then first thing I know I'm about to pop, mister father there blows, and, later, there's Needa and me. She came on so sweet to me at first, so butch and pretty. Now life was more or less her working and me working, paying rent, keeping things clean, getting the kid back and forth to school, on weekends some videos, arguments, TV, beer. And neither one of us with a nice word or touch for the other. Nights, I'd get filled with a sudden big darkness when all the lights went out. Filled with a power so black and brown and green, Oggun, Yemaya, iron, water, a big washing-over foaming waving ocean sadness. Then plain exhaustion that pressed my eyelids down. Needa would already be snoring. I'd turn my back, start to dream. In the morning, would not remember.

Stop dancing your son around the room, snapped Needa, you'll turn him into a fucking fairy. Come here, kid. We're gonna get a couple movies.

Fine, I told her, look who's talking. Biggest bull I ever knew. Go on, both of you. Get a couple of Real Man movies. Get a couple of Let's-Kill-Everyone-in-Sight things, why don't you. Fill his head with a bunch of real machitos getting their guts blown out.

When they left, I cleaned up Fritos and beer cans. Got some frozen chicken out. Then halfway through soaking it in a pot of warm water, I wiped my hands with a fresh white cloth, lit a couple candles, offered up a plate of half-thawed gizzards. I stay away from the powers, mostly, but that night felt different. Kneeling in front of the plate for at least a little proper respect, red candles, white candles dripping, watching thin pieces of ice melt off the gizzards and the thawing organs swim in remains of their own dark blood, I thought again about Salazar. I wondered if he ran so hard and so fast that, when he won, his feet were crusted with blood. I remembered things my grandma told me, long ago, when I'd walk out laughing into the sun of a hot sweet summer morning. About the happiness of the air filled with voices and smells, joy of loving, the ferocity of vengeance and of hate, how to heal what you care for, how to ruin an enemy. The holiness of sacrifice.

Not that I even did it right.

When they want live roosters, they don't mean half-thawed chicken gizzards. But it was all for the fire, hungry holy fire that doesn't die, even when the world tries to kill it, that stays alive, eating, eating—I offered it truly in my heart—and God sees everything.

The next morning Needa groaned and stuck her head under a pillow when the alarm clock rang early. I tiptoed around, stuck on a pair of sweatpants, socks, old tennis sneakers, one of her used-up sweatshirts. It was cold out, wind coming off the river. Sun wasn't even up yet. I held keys in the space between fingers and balled up my hand like a fist, like a metal-bristling weapon, and when I started to run could feel the fat bobbling around my stomach and arms and hips and thighs, heavy and disgusting, bringing me a little bit closer to the ground each time the skin folds flopped up and down. After a couple minutes I thought I was gonna die. I had to stop and gasp and walk. Then when I could breathe okay I'd run as fast as I could another half a minute or so, stop and gasp and walk awhile, then run again. I did this about fifteen, twenty minutes. Until snot dripped to my lip, and my face was running wet in the cold, blotching Needa's sweatshirt in chilly clinging puddles. I started to cry. Then I told myself, Shut up you. It worked, the tears stopped. I went back inside, climbed stairs with legs that were already numb and hurting, and made everybody breakfast. Needa growled her way through a shower and padded around with a coffee cup making wet footprints everywhere, watching "Good Morning America."

There he is, she grumbled, there's your *man*, your Salazar.

I ignored her sarcasm.

But I was stuck there in the kitchen, making sure the kid's toast didn't burn. I told Needa tell me what they're saying.

They're saying about how he won yesterday. You know, the race. Guy set a fucking world record or something.

I wanted to run and see, but couldn't.

That's how the weeks went: me getting up early in the dark, going to bash my fat brains out trying to run, getting breakfast for everyone, showering when they were all finished with the bathroom, getting Needa to work and the kid to school and then getting myself to work too. My eyes started hurting bad from being open extra long. My legs were sore, thighs feeling like they were all bruised and bloodied on the inside, calves with pinpricks of pain searing through them. Needa noticed me limping around all the time, and laughed. What's with you, girl? You think you gonna be in the Olympics or something? You think you gonna run that marathon?

Finally, one Saturday, I went to see Madrita.

She took out the cards and beads and shells, there in her little place in the basement, pulled all the curtains closed so everything was cozy and safe like your mother's womb. Outside, it rained. She was trained the old way, did everything absolutely right, took her time. After a while I asked her, Well, how does it look?

"Sweetheart, you gotta lotta obstacles."

Hey, I told her, that ain't exactly news.

She sighed. "You gotta stop worrying about the home. Home's gonna take care of themselves, you be surprised. Lots of rage and pain but lots of love too. See, sweetheart, you can do what you want, only it's difficult. First, purify yourself."

"Purify? Myself?"

"What I said."

She wrote down all the stuff I had to get, white and red roses and violet water and rose water, mint, coconut, a bunch of sunflowers and herbs and things, and made me memorize how to do the bath right. Then she told me go up to the little shop the Jew man has, here's the address, he's one of them from Spain and he knows the right things, even *babalaus* goes there for supplies. And while you're there get a couple pieces of camphor, sweetheart, and some fresh mint leaves. Put them in a little bag, pin it inside your bra, it'll keep you healthier. You got a cold coming on.

Needa wasn't too happy about the bathwater sitting all night, reeking herbs and flower petals, before I got into it—first!—the next morning. Yaaah, she grumped, you and that devil shit. Ever since the Marathon. Makes me feel like I'm living with some fucking boogy. But listen, woman: don't you go casting no spells on me.

I was stripping sweaty sweats and socks to bathe. Caught her staring, out of the corner of my eye, and bared my teeth. Then she rubbed my naked butt, friendly like, and the both of us laughed.

The mornings got darker, closer to winter, but every once in a while I'd wake up easier when the alarm hit, sometimes even with a feel of burning red excitement in my chest and throat, like the running was something pleasurable, good, a gift. Truth is that it did feel good some mornings. I'd breathe splendidly. Thighs move like water, arms pump rhythm. The feet did not want to stop. Those days I'd stay out longer—half an hour or more—with happy buzzing like music in my head.

Celía, one of the girls at work said, just before New Year's, I been meaning to tell you, you are looking really terrific these days.

It was true.

I circled around the file cabinets all afternoon, putting things away, singing.

That night, after picking the kid up and dropping him and his cousin off with his grandma for a couple hours, I skipped grocery shopping and just went home, changed into some sweaty old things, and I went outside into the wind and dark and I ran again, very sweet and happy and like music, the way I had that morning, running off and onto curbs, twisting around cars and garbage cans and people, I didn't care. I hummed and sang going back upstairs. Needa opened the door for me, mad.

"Where the fuck you been? I feel like I ain't got a lover these days."

"Oh you got one, honey. Whether you want one or not."

"What's that supposed to mean?"

"Whatever you want it to, girlfriend."

She moped around the rest of the evening, drank about a six-pack of Ballantine and fell asleep on the sofa. Later I went to pick up the kid. Walking home he said how big he was getting, how he was gonna be in first grade next year and could take gym, and run at the school track meet next spring.

That's good, I told him, it's good to have a plan.

We ordered pizza, watched TV and drank Coca-Cola while Needa snored away on the sofa. I was feeling different, lighter, happy-headed and full of fresh cold air from running again, but at the same time dark and warm inside. I put the kid to bed and left a kitchen light on for Needa, then turned in myself, breathing full and deep, sniffing camphor, mint, letting some calm, clean-burning soft red feeling wash over me, droop my eyelids shut, wrap me up all safe and bright, and soon I dreamed.

In the dream I was running on dirt and grass through trees near the Reservoir in Central Park—quick, effortless, light, my toes and ankles bouncing and strong—and next to me a man was running, and we breathed in perfect rhythm. I looked over. It was Salazar.

Alberto, I said, I want to run the Marathon.

Listen to me, Celía, he said, you're not ready yet. You gotta do some shorter races first.

Okay, I said.

Then we stopped running.

He faced me, hands on hips, fierce dark flame face, slender and serious and young. I noticed he wore a collar of beads, scarlet-wine red and white. Oh, I laughed, I thought so, you really are a child of Chango. So am I.

It's fire, Celía, he said. But everyone has a power. Use it for running. Use it for loving. Use it for God.

I woke up smelling rotten beer breath. Needa was sitting slumped over, head in hands on my side of the bed, crying.

"What is it, honey?"

"Lost," she sobbed, "I got lost."

I put my arms around her. Her cheeks were all soft and smelly, but there was that nice odor to her too, one it seemed like I remembered from long, long ago, woman smell, soap smell, a crumply warm feel of her hair and clothes.

Lost, she sobbed.

No, honey, I told her, holding her, rocking the both of us back and forth. No, honey, no, sweet woman, my Needa, don't you cry. You didn't get lost, you been found.

Help me, Celía, she said. Help me, God. Gotta work harder, keep up with you. I am so ashamed of my life.

I remembered the dream. I pulled her down alongside me on the bed, held her, rocking, whispering true things to the back of her neck. Telling how I was proud of her, and of our child, and our home. How hard we had worked. How far we had come. How, before taking on the whole rest of our lives, we had to do the small, obvious, necessary tasks, one step at a time.

"Like how I'm not gonna just jump in and run the Marathon right off, honey. I gotta do some shorter races first."

"Huh," she sniffed, "get you, the expert. Who you think you been talking to, the angels?"

But she pulled my arms tighter around her when she said that, and I didn't want to fight, or let her go.

It happened like this: no more booze. No more videos. No more shit food.

I shifted the force of the power to purifying myself, for real. And, like magic, once I did that, Needa and the kid came around. Maybe one or both of them would make barf sounds whenever I dished up some brown rice shit for dinner. But Needa's belly flab was littler, and she even started going after work a couple days each week to pump iron with her buddies at some smelly old gym. Those nights she came back fresh from the shower, cold air in her face, smelling of powder with a warm skin glow. Have to keep up with the little lady, she said, but in my own way, love, understand? I mean, running, racing, turning into some skinny fag, that is *not* your Needa's style.

End of May, I was going to run the Women's Mini-Marathon in Central Park, a little more than six miles. I laid down the law at home. No fucking up and no messing up between now and then. Cold weather, warm, and warmer, rains and damp hot sunlight and hazy mist of all the city seasons started floating past, through us, like we were nothing but thin vessels that for a moment could catch a whiff of the breeze and the universe, then lose it, let it go. I kept running, every day. The kid did okay in school. Needa and I started making love again some nights, oh so nice, rubbing back and forth. Oh, so nice, to feel her touch around inside me again. And then, late spring.

How it was, the night before: I'm sitting around, we had some of them buckwheat noodles with vegetables for dinner, everybody's quiet, no TV, thinking about how I'm gonna run the race tomorrow with about nine thousand other women and how they, the family, they have got to cheer us and watch, and I look at Needa and the kid and see how slender they are now, and healthy, how beautiful and handsome and slender, and start thinking how much they are mine—just that, they are mine. And I look down at my own bare feet and see that they are skinny, too. Bumpy with calluses and with veins. Bashed a little bloody around the big-toe edges. The littlest toenail on my left foot is dead and black. All from running through the mornings and the nights. From running in my dreams. We got changed, poof. Just like that. Thought we were gonna change ourselves, maybe even the world. But, poof. The world changed us. Through work, love, sacrifice.

Holy, I thought. This is holy.

I chewed cinnamon sticks for dessert the way Madrita recommended, went to sleep with a hint of fire inside. Morning I got up scared, scared. Too scared to notice how Needa was being so sweet, feeding the kid, making sure I drank water because it was looking to be a hot, hot day, pinning my racing number on my T-shirt straight with safety pins, #6489-F-OPEN. Too scared to notice we were leaving—leaving our home, taking the subway, walking, silent, through the heat and the morning.

There we made it, finally, to the West Side, into the park. To hear music play over loudspeakers. Announcements blaring, half-heard. Reminders about some awards ceremony later. On a lawn. The lawn. Some lawn. To hot bright light crystallized through the trees, sunlight, damp blazing air, water stacked in paper cups on tables, and tables, and the laughing, crying voices like in my childhood, so many people. A banner, a big blinking magic electronic clock, zeroed out, waiting. And runners, waiting—women, all shapes and sizes and ages and colors, thousands of them, of us, just thousands.

Baby, says Needa, I'm proud of you.

The kid'd made friends already. Some other woman's twin sons, about his age. I catch sight of him, out of the corner of an eye, his half-smiling, half-serious little handsome face, glowing under the rim of a baseball cap. Yeah, he's telling them, my mom's fast, too. My mom's gonna run the race. Me and my other mom's gonna watch.

Some things are forever inside us. Some things cannot get said.

That's why, when the gun went off, it was like this piece of me fell deep, deep down inside, into the big dark well of myself—this was the piece of me that recorded, in absolute detail, every moment of the race—and lodged there, safe but never recoverable, at least not in words. I can say that the different-colored crowd of thousands moved in a big shuffle at first, all together; then, little by little, began to unwind into space, like it was some light-stitched vast fabric coming apart at the seams—so that first, we were all the same, then some of us swayed forward, some back, some to one side or another, and the tarred hot surface of the road melted uphill into trees, green, brown, into a hot misty blasting summer air running blue and gray and yellow under sunlight. I can say that my heart popped right into the base of my throat and stayed there for the first mile or so that I staggered along, sweating after the first few yards, gasping to breathe; then something inside me let up—or gave up, yes—and my heart settled down into my chest where it belonged, I was sweating and suffering but could breathe again, and the elbows and bouncing breasts and shoulders and hair and flesh of women was all around me, smells of bodies and of the city and the trees and sun, and I drank water from somebody's paper cup, kept running, tossed it like a leaf to the cup-littered ground. I can say that in the second mile, once in a while, sweating and running, avoiding veering hips and limbs, I saw some girl run by with a Sony Walkman, wearing sunglasses with mirrored lenses, closed off to the world; once in a while, too, conversation filtered into the sponging soaking deep-down fallen-off piece of me, women's voices in English and in Spanish and in other languages, too, trying to laugh, muttering encouragement; but by the third mile, fact is, there was not anyone chatting.

What there was, was the breathing. Hard and uneven, or measured, controlled. I kept the feet moving, slow, steady, like the pace I did each morning, the pace I did some nights—but never as fast and light and easy as my dreams. Still, it moved me forward. Clumsy. Slow. With a little fat bobbling, yet, around hips and belly and thighs. Around me, all shapes. Like crazy soldiers in some war. The sweat gushed down me. It was hotter than I'd thought. At each mile, you heard them, calling out the time. Time? Time? I never thought of it before. How much it took to do one mile, or one block, or twenty—each morning, some evenings, even in my dreams, I ran by the minutes. Thirty-five, thirty-six minutes. Into the fourth mile. Now it was feeling like forever. Now it was feeling like one more hill would be the last. My fat, bouncing thighs and sweating, gushing body would never be things of beauty, like maybe in foolish moments I'd imagined; and maybe in my stupid dreams I talked about marathons—but here, here was a little stupid miniature marathon, and it hurt so bad I could not ever imagine doing this again, much less running anything longer. But more water, more flesh around me, slipping on paper cups in my flopping old tennis shoes with this number safety-pinned right under my tits, over flabbing belly, every slight upgrade of road sending sunlight searing through me, stabbing thighs and ankles, making me gasp and hurt and, without killing myself, I ran as fast as I could. Clumsy. Fat. Slow. But the heart settled back down, pounding with breaths, with mint and cinnamon and camphor. Sunlight shot through the leaves of trees. Hose spray cooled our skin, drenched our socks. More sunlight shot through, blinded me. Fire, I thought. For your husband, your child, your God. To hell with that, Celía. For your own living self. Okay, man, fuck everything. Fuck the whole sunlit sweat-smelling cinnamon-smelling fucking shark-circling world. Whiff of Chango. Fire in the belly. Fuck even your world of dreams. Because this, sweetheart—this, here, is real.

Then, for a mile, I knew what was real. All this, steeped in the miserable sweat and sacrifice. I knew it without knowledge of the mind, only the sure unlying knowledge of the body that can run and love, give birth, sob, suffer. And knowing what was real, and that this, this, was it, now, only this, and it was enough, and that I lived now, really lived, and knew now what it was to breathe—knowing this, blind with pain, sweating and gasping and almost dead, I stared down and saw that there was a little hole in the tip of my right tennis shoe, near the little toe; it had rubbed the toe raw and, around the little hole, the dirty white fabric was soaking through with blood. Then I felt all the dried-up pieces of me come to life and, suffering, I ran on the breath of the wind. Until, after a while, the wind deserted me. Just before six miles. Left me, one faulty woman, in a mob of suffering moving flesh, to finish the last few hundred yards alone. It was all uphill, there were people watching and I was ashamed, people screaming around me, I was running so slow, nearly dead of exhaustion and of shame, stomach in spasms, drenched with sweat, crying. Until I heard someone yell out *Mom* with a voice, among all the other little voices, meant only for me. And I heard Needa, laughing, crying, yelling, and heard that her voice was hoarse, a croak, almost gone: Attagirl, baby! My baby! My lady! You can do it youcandoit-

youcandoityoucandoit! Break an hour breakanhourbreakanhour-breakanhour!

Fifty-nine minutes and fifty-nine seconds. But I was not lost, and I was not last.

Girlfriend, I said, get some pride.

I did.

Then I staggered under the big heartless blinking clock, the yellow sun, dripping water, my shoe spraying blood.


I got a medal. They gave everyone medals. Slipped around your neck, in the finishing chutes crowded with beaten, grinning women, a silvery goldlike medal on a red and blue ribbon, like a necklace, just for finishing. Then they gave you a carton of Gatorade. A free Mars bar. And a plastic egg-shaped container full of mesh tan pantyhose.

Needa hugged me. So did the kid.

They were all over me, screaming, proud and happy.

Runners were still finishing, running, staggering, walking. I moved through the crowds. I lay on the grass. Closed my eyes, with Needa sitting on one side and the kid on the other, each holding a hand, and I fell down into the deepest, blasted-off piece of me that had come apart and wedged down inside with the explosion of the starting gun, that would never, ever be the same. It was so dark, falling deep down there, full of iron and of water, musty brown and wet wet green and the still malignant air; but also, it was red like blood, and bright, and filled with a bubbling, smoldering, surprising color. It was filled with this work and this imperfect love, and with chicken gizzards, sacrifice, camphor oil, rainbow light.

Something blared over a loudspeaker.

"—And now, a special treat for all you ladies! To present the awards, we have with us here—"

I fell into a place of half-dream, half-sleep.

Needa poked my ribs.

There he is, Celía. There.

Who?

Your Salazar.

I turned my head in the grass. Salt was full in my sweat, salt on my lips, I licked it with the air and it tasted real, good, sweet. Opened my eyes to see the young, slender, serious man standing above me, body and clothes of a runner, his eyes in shadow, fierce face gazing down.

He nodded. Saying softly, politely, Good for you, Celía.

Alberto, I said, can I stop now?

No, Celía. He said it gently. Then he smiled. Not until you die. And even then—who knows?

I opened my eyes.

There was an awards podium, in the sun on the grass. Women, slender and beautiful, gifted young magnificent runners, walking up, intermittently, when their names were called over fuzzy loudspeakers, accepting the bright gold and silver statues they gave for awards. And there, with famous men and women athletes and politicians behind the podium on the stage in the sun and the park, there he was, handing out each statue, shaking each woman's hand. Salazar. There was no collar around his neck, no red and white of gods or saints of fire, as in my dream. Not running, he seemed different. Quiet. Humbly human. Pale and young, and far away.

I started to cry.

Needa held me in her arms.

The kid crawled into my lap, laid his soft little cheek against my drenched, floppy chest.

"What is it, sweet?"

"It don't stop, Needa."

"No, my love."

"I gotta do some more of these."

"Okay, baby."

"And then, in a few years I think, I gotta do the Marathon."

*Yes!* Alberto muttered, through a microphone, and shook some woman's hand. I squeezed the hand of Needa, and of our child. The fire poured down. It kissed me. It moved in to stay.

# CONTRIBUTOR NOTES

**Carol Anshaw**'s first novel, *Aquamarine*, won the Carl Sandburg and Society of Midland Authors awards; her second is *Seven Moves* (Houghton Mifflin, 1996). Anshaw was awarded an NEA Creative Writing Fellowship in 1995.

Activist, filmmaker, teacher, and writer **Toni Cade Bambara** is widely recognized as having written valuably and seriously—although with humor—about oppression and African American life. She won a 1981 American Book Award for her novel *The Salt Eaters*. Bambara died in 1995.

**Margaret Barbour**'s poem "A Golf Lullaby" appeared in the May 1900 issue of *Outing*, a popular outdoor recreation magazine of the day.

**Lucy Jane Bledsoe** is the author of *Sweat: Stories and a Novella* (Seal Press, 1995), the novel *Working Parts* (Seal, 1997), and two children's novels, *The Big Bike Race* (Holiday House, 1995) and *Tracks in the Snow* (Holiday House, 1997).

A collection of **Nancy Boutilier**'s short fiction and poetry, *According to Her Contours* (Black Sparrow Press, 1992), was chosen as a Lambda Literary Award finalist in 1993.

Cookbook and fiction writer, journalist and translator **Laurie Colwin** also wrote a column for *Gourmet* magazine and worked for various New York publishers and literary agents before her death in 1992. *A Big Storm Knocked It Over* (HarperCollins, 1994) was her final novel.

**Ellen Cooney**'s short fiction has appeared in *The New Yorker* and many literary journals. She lives in Cambridge, Massachusetts, and teaches in the writing program at MIT and at Harvard in the Extension and Summer School. In addition to *All the Way Home* (G. P. Putnam's Sons, 1984), Cooney is the author of a young adult novel, *Small-Town Girl* (Houghton Mifflin, 1983).

The author of more than fifty popular novels, **Elizabeth Corbett** created the well-known fictional characters of Mrs. Meigs, introduced in *The Young Mrs. Meigs* (Century, 1931), and the Graper sisters, stars of a young adult series begun with *The Graper Girls* (Century, 1931). She died in 1981.

**Barbara Crooker,** the winner of three Pennsylvania Council on the Arts Fellowships in Literature, has published more than 550 poems in magazines and anthologies and six books, including *Obbligato* (Linwood, 1993). She has a crooked little finger, broken playing hockey.

**Rina Ferrarelli**'s latest book of poems is *Home Is a Foreign Country* (Eadmer Press, 1996). Her sport of choice is walking.

**Susan Firer**'s poems can be found in literary magazines, periodicals, and anthologies, including *Best American Poetry, Ms., The Iowa Review, Chicago Review*, and *Prairie Schooner*. She has published three books, including *The Lives of the Saints and Everything* (Cleveland State University Press, 1993).

**Tess Gallagher**'s poetry, essays and short fiction appear in numerous publications, including her more than a dozen books. *At the Owl Woman Saloon: Stories* (Scribner) came out in 1997.

In addition to *Lady Lobo* (New Victoria Publishers, 1993), **Kristen Garrett** authored *You Light the Fire* (Rising Tide Press, 1992).

The author of numerous books of fiction, nonfiction and poetry, Mississippi native **Ellen Gilchrist** has been a journalist and broadcaster on National Public Radio. Her most recent work is a collection of stories, *The Courts of Love* (Little, Brown and Company, 1996).

*St. Nicholas Magazine*, a very popular children's periodical, published **Jane Gilliland**'s story "Scotti Scores" in its April 1923 issue.

**Abbe Carter Goodloe** published numerous articles and short stories in popular magazines around the turn of the century. Her short fiction collection *College Girls* (Charles Scribner's Sons, 1895) included "Revenge," one of the first published pieces of U.S. women's sport fiction.

**Stephanie Grant**'s first novel, *The Passion of Alice* (Houghton Mifflin, 1995), received nominations for a Lammy Award for Best Lesbian Fiction and The Orange Prize, a British award for women writers. She is at work on a new novel, *The Map of Ireland*.

**Pat Griffin** is an associate professor in social justice education at the University of Massachusetts-Amherst. In addition to her writings and research on homophobia in athletics and education, she has published fictional and first person stories about lesbians in sport in *Sportsdykes* (St. Martin's Press, 1994) and *Tomboys* (Alyson, 1995).

**Eloise Klein Healy** chairs the new MFA program in Creative Writing at Antioch University Los Angeles. She is the author of four books of poetry—including *Artemis in Echo Park* (Firebrand Books, 1991), which received a Lambda Book Award nomination—and the Associate Editor/Poetry Editor of *The Lesbian Review of Books*.

Well-known popular writer and social activist **Fannie Hurst**'s published work spanned fifty-four years; some twenty-nine films were made from her thirty novels, of which her own favorite was *Lummox* (Harper and Brothers, 1923), and three hundred short stories. She played tennis and basketball at Central High School in St. Louis at the turn of the century. Hurst died in 1968.

**Carolyn Kremers** writes poetry and creative nonfiction, teaches at Eastern Washington University, and summers in Alaska. Her book *Place of the Pretend People: Gifts from a Yup'ik Eskimo Village* (Alaska Northwest Books) came out in 1996. She seeks to balance her indoor passions—writing, music, and teaching—with her (usually!) outdoor passions—running, biking, backpacking, and all kinds of skiing.

**Maxine Kumin,** winner of the 1973 Pulitzer Prize for her volume of poems *Up Country* (HarperCollins, 1972), has published eighteen books of poetry, fiction, and essays for adults as well as a number of children's stories. She trained for international swimming competition as a teenager.

**Barbara Lamblin** wrote a book of poetry, *my skin barely covers me* (Uncle John Sports Art, 1975). Her work was anthologized in *American Sports Poetry* (Orchard Books, 1988).

Former coach and competitive swimmer **Jenifer Levin** has written two sports novels, *The Sea of Light* (Penguin Books, 1993) and *Water Dancer* (Poseidon Press, 1982), each of which received nomination for a national award. Firebrand Books recently published a collection of Levin's short fiction, *Love and Death, & Other Disasters: Stories 1977–1995*.

**Myra Cohn Livingston**'s unusual career included playing the French horn professionally, and serving as social secretary to Dinah Shore and Jascha Heifetz. She is best remembered as an educator, poet, and anthologist, however; her forty-plus books of children's poetry earned her a national reputation, including a 1980 National Council of Teachers of English award. Livingston died in 1996.

**Bette Bao Lord**'s novels and nonfiction reflect in part her own life as a young immigrant to the United States, and the experiences of her relatives who remained in China. *In the Year of the Boar and Jackie Robinson* (Harper, 1984), loosely based on Lord's first years in this country, won the Jefferson Cup Award from the American Library Association.

Following a career as an opera singer, **Cynthia Macdonald** turned to teaching and writing. She has authored several books of poetry, including *I Can't Remember* (Knopf, 1997), and her poems and prose have appeared in numerous publications, such as *The New Yorker, Ms.,* and the *Tri-Quarterly Review.*

British fiction writer, journalist, and lecturer **Sara Maitland** won the Somerset Maugham Award for her first novel, *Daughters of Jerusalem* (Blond and Briggs, 1978; published as *Languages of Love* by Doubleday in 1981). Her latest work is *A Big Enough God* (Henry Holt, 1995). "The Loveliness of the Long-Distance Runner," one of the first pieces of sport fiction published in the United States to feature openly lesbian characters, appeared here in an anthology edited by Adam Mars-Jones, *Mae West Is Dead* (Faber and Faber, 1987).

Award-winning writer **Mariah Burton Nelson** played basketball for Stanford and professionally. She has published fiction, poetry, a one-act play, and two books, *Are We Winning Yet? How Women Are Changing Sports and Sports Are Changing Women* (Random House, 1991), and *The Stronger Women Get, The More Men Love Football: Sexism and The American Culture of Sports* (Avon, 1995).

**Marge Piercy** has published thirteen books of poetry, most recently *What Are Big Girls Made Of?* (Knopf, 1997). Her latest novel (also her thirteenth) is *City of Darkness, City of Light* (Fawcett Books, 1996), a story of the French Revolution.

As a high-school student, **Jessie Rehder** threw the javelin, played basketball, and won a statewide poetry contest. Her status as a legendary teacher of writing lives on at the University of North Carolina at Chapel Hill, where she worked when she wrote her novel *Remembrance Way* (Putnam, 1956). Rehder died in 1967.

**Adrienne Rich**'s published work includes more than twenty volumes of poetry and prose, among them *Collected Early Poems: 1950–1970*

(W. W. Norton, 1993) and *Dark Fields of the Republic: Poems 1991–1995* (W. W. Norton, 1995). A 1974 National Book Award (for *Diving into the Wreck* [W. W. Norton, 1973]) and a MacArthur Fellowship are among the many awards and honors accorded her.

**Rebecca Rule** overheard someone say, "There's three kids crying in the dugout" (a line that made its way into "Lindy Lowe at Bat"), while watching her daughter, Adi, play in a Little League game. Rule's stories have been collected in *Wood Heat* (Nightshade Press, 1992) and *The Best Revenge* (University Press of New England, 1995).

**Sarah Van Arsdale** lives in San Francisco. *Toward Amnesia*, her first novel, was published by Riverhead Books (1996).

Writer and educator **Sara Vogan**'s work appeared in numerous literary journals, periodicals, and anthologies, including *Best American Short Stories. In Shelly's Leg* (Alfred A. Knopf, Inc., 1981) was the first of her three novels. Vogan died in 1991.

**Karen Volkman**'s first book of poems, *Crash's Law* (W. W. Norton, 1996), was selected for publisher W. W. Norton's National Poetry Series. Her poetry has appeared in *The Paris Review, Partisan Review, Ms.,* and *APR,* and in the 1996 and 1997 editions of *Best American Poetry.* Volkman lives in Brooklyn and teaches writing at New York University.

Prolific Australian author **Judith Wright** has won many honors for her work, which includes both prose and poetry. Raised on a "station," or ranch, Wright is known especially for her feeling for the land. "Sports Field" appeared earlier in the United States in Tom Dodge's anthology *A Literature of Sports* (D. C. Heath and Company, 1980).

# ACKNOWLEDGMENTS

The first piece of women's sport poetry I ever read—Barbara Lamblin's "First Peace"—spoke my own experience so clearly that I spent twenty years collecting poetry and fiction telling the truths of sportswomen's lives. Many thanks, especially, to the women who—in every decade since the 1880s—have written from the heart about sport.

For access to these writers' words, we all owe gratitude to editors, booksellers, and librarians. I'm particularly grateful to the librarians at the Olympia Timberland Library, The Evergreen State College, Seattle Public Library, University of Washington, Portland State University, and University of Oregon.

The following list acknowledges writers whose work in the broad range of sport studies has encouraged and enriched my own: Susan Birrell, Mary A. Boutilier, Susan K. Cahn, Mary Jo Festle, Cindy Himes Gissendanner, Allen Guttmann, M. Ann Hall, Sherrie A. Inness, Helen Jefferson Lenskyj, Elinor Nauen, Mariah Burton Nelson, Michael Oriard, Doris H. Pieroth, and Lucinda SanGiovanni. Many women and men whose names must go unlisted here have contributed significantly to contemporary understandings of sport.

Special thanks to the athletes, students and colleagues with whom I've played and worked, most recently at The Evergreen State College, Olympia, Washington. Thank you, especially, to Lloyd Wilson.

This book would not exist without Sally-Jo Bowman, who planted the seed; the calm professionalism of Elisabeth Kallick Dyssegaard and Denise Oswald at Farrar, Straus and Giroux; Ann Strother Sandoz, whose passion for reading lit my own; and the love and laughter of Joby Winans.